Testimonials for *The Joy of Hiking*

"Nothing simplifies a busy life like a hike. And nothing will prepare a hiker for the outdoors quite like *The Joy of Hiking*."
—*American Hiking Society*

"... highly informative and spiritual, as well as a fun and enjoyable read."
—*Carl Pope, Executive Director Sierra Club*

"Take this book home and find out how to avoid being a 'touron.' *The Joy of Hiking* is fun to read and is good for the soles!"
—*Bryce Stevens, Co-founder Trails.com*

"The ultimate compendium of anything—and everything—hiking-related. Everybody from the novice walker to the accomplished long-distance hiker will learn something new—and fun—from this book."
—*Matt Heid, Senior Editor AMC Outdoors magazine*

"Stacked full of useful advice."
—*Alistair Wearmouth, Editor Gorp.com*

"An excellent primer for the novice hiker and an even better companion for experienced adventurers with boot smarts."
—*Jaime Rodriguez, Editor-In-Chief American Scouting Digest*

"As refreshing as a great hike. *The Joy of Hiking* is inspiring, full of good advice, and motivates you to get out and enjoy the many pleasures of the trail."
—*Alex Chadwick, Host, National Public Radio Day to Day and National Geographic Radio Expeditions*

"Discover the peacefulness of hiking and the health benefits that tag along. This book is loaded with tips. John's The Trailmaster."
—*Kathleen Doheny, columnist for The Healthy Traveler Los Angeles Times*

"Excellent information in an easy to read format... from what to bring to where to go, *The Joy of Hiking* covers it all. I highly recommend this book for every hiker's library."
Liz Bergeron, Executive Director The Pacific Crest Trail Association

"A masterpiece of information... exceptionally well written."
—*The South Coast Beacon*

"This book is a masterpiece... a must read for anyone who has ever thought of putting on a pair of boots and hitting the trail!"
—*Gene and Jo Ann Taylor, Owners The Walking Connection*

"Hiking nourishes the soul, exhilarates the senses, and allows a moment's rest amidst a frenetic day; John McKinney illuminates the pure joy of hiking."
—*Laurel House co-author of The Gurus' Guide to Serenity West Coast Editor, Fit magazine*

The Joy of Hiking

Hiking The Trailmaster Way

JOHN McKINNEY

 **WILDERNESS PRESS** · BERKELEY, CA

The Joy of Hiking: Hiking The Trailmaster Way

1st EDITION April 2005

Copyright © 2005, The Trailmaster, Inc.

Cover design: Lisa Pletka
Cover illustrations: Art Parts
Book design: Jim Cook
Book editor: Cheri Rae
Research assistant: Carla Neufeldt

ISBN 0-89997-385-X
UPC 7-19609-97385

Manufactured in the United States of America

Published by: **Wilderness Press**
1200 5th Street
Berkeley, CA 94710
(800) 443-7227; FAX (510) 558-1696
info@wildernesspress.com
www.wildernesspress.com

Visit our website for a complete listing of our books and for ordering
information.

Portions of this book have appeared previously in *American Way, California, Islands,* and the *National Geographic Adventure* magazines, and the *Los Angeles Times.*

The Trailmaster, Trailmaster Tale, Trailmaster Tip, Trail Wisdom, and Hike-ku are trademarks of The Trailmaster, Inc.

Library of Congress Cataloging-in-Publication Data

McKinney, John
    The joy of hiking : hiking the trailmaster way / John McKinney.— 1st ed.
    p.   cm.
    Includes bibliographical references and index.
    ISBN 0-89997-385-X
    1. Hiking--Guidebooks. I. Title.
GV199.5.M387 2005
796.51—dc22
                                2005002376
                                CIP

Notice: Although Wilderness Press and the author have made every attempt to ensure that the information in this book is accurate at press time, they are not responsible for any loss, damage, injury, or inconvenience that may occur to anyone while using this book.

Acknowledgments

For their companionship and inspiration on the trail and off, I thank Gordon Black, Bill Cullison, Penny and Terry Davies, Michele De Rosa, Jane Fleischman, Clara and Harry Goldstein, Barbara Hill, Bob Howells, Ruth Kilday, Elizabeth Kuball, Milton Love, Shelly and Ann Lowenkopf, Larry Mantle, Milt McAuley, Bob McDermott. Tim McFadden, Helen and Jim McKinney, Bill Meller, Fotine O'Connor, Warren Olney, Mike and Vivian Pahos, Susan Petty, Alan Pinkney, Don Robinson, Susan and Marc Sazer, Terry Schroeder, Susan Smartt, Patti Stathis, Will Swaim, Mike Takeuchi, Marianne Wallace, Hélène Webb, Ron Webster, David Werk, Mary Westheimer, Ray and Mary Wolpert, and Michael Zolkoski. Thanks also to my son Daniel and daughter Sophia, who are great trail companions and offered a kid's-eye view in the "Hiking with Children" chapter, which Sophia co-wrote.

I also extend my thanks and want to voice my appreciation for the many rangers and administrators of America's national parks, national forests, BLM lands, as well as various state and regional parks across America, who generously contributed knowledge and expertise along the way. Many equipment makers and outdoor retailers were very helpful to this project and the time they took answering my questions about hiking gear and apparel is greatly appreciated.

For some of the inspirational quotes used in this book, a big thanks to *Trail Quotes: From Advocacy to Wilderness*, 2001, Jim Schmid, editor, South Carolina Department of Parks, Recreation and Tourism, Columbia, SC. Another tip of the hiker's cap to Jim Schmid for the assorted trail definitions and terms he compiled in *A Glossary of Trails, Greenway, and Outdoor Recreation Terms and Acronyms*, 2001.

*"Walk out the door and
find good health. There is no fever
that a 10-mile hike can't cure."*
—GARRISON KEILLOR

Contents at a Glance

Part 1: Hiking The Trailmaster Way

Part 2: Hitting the Trail

Part 3: What to Take

Part 4: Taking Care on the Trail

Part 5: Hiking Near and Far

Contents

PART ONE
Hiking the Trailmaster Way

Chapter 1 The Joy of Hiking

J OHN, I REALLY LIKE HOW YOU WRITE ABOUT HIKING. BUT I WAS JUST curious: What do you do for a living? I know you write about hiking, but seriously, what's your real job?

If I had a pound of trail mix for every time I've been asked that question, I'd have a ton of GORP.

The fact is, hiking and writing about hiking is my job—and has been for more than 20 years. I've hiked from youth to middle-age, and plan to continue hiking until I'm carried off the trail.

They say, "Do what you love and the money will follow."

Uh, not always, but I still feel blessed to be able to share my passion with countless hikers and would-be hikers. I wouldn't trade my job—taking a hike and writing about it—for all the money in the world. Wandering the world's trails looking for lonely beaches, desert dunes, dramatic summits and meadows ablaze with wildflowers is a dirty job, but somebody's got to do it.

My unusual career path began when I was a Boy Scout in Troop 441 in Downey, California. I lived for the monthly hikes in the mountains, deserts and forest around California, and for weeklong summer hikes in the San Gabriel Mountains and the High Sierra. Hiking was far and away my favorite merit badge earned on my way to becoming an Eagle Scout. (It should have been a tip-off that I wasn't cut out to be a Wall Street mogul when I needed three tries to pass the test for the Personal Finances merit badge.)

When I was fourteen, my parents sat me down for what they characterized as a frank discussion about my future.

"John, your mother and I appreciate how fun this hiking-camping-outdoors stuff is for you," my father began. "But let's face it, you're not going to be doing this as an adult."

"When I'm a grown-up, I'm going to keep hiking." I declared.

"What your father's saying," my mother chimed in, "is nobody makes a living by hiking."

"You need to take up a sport that will help you in the business

In This Chapter
- My life on the trail
- Get more out of life
- Hike safely and happily
- The Trailmaster way

world," my father continued in the persuasive manner that garnered him salesman-of-the-year honors at the huge corporation he represented. "So we've decided to help you out by—"

"Not another tennis racket," I whined.

"No, you're going to be surprised," mother cautioned, as my father disappeared into the next room, soon re-emerging with. . . .

"Golf clubs," I said glumly.

"And a certificate for eight lessons at the club," father enthused.

My heart sank. I had been hoping for a new backpack. I took the golf lessons to please my parents, but my heart wasn't in it. For me, golf was a good walk ruined, years before I ever heard of the Mark Twain quip.

My studies for a degree in broadcast journalism from the University of Southern California proved to be somewhat useful to my life's work; more so were my collegiate extracurricular activities. I helped found, and lead hikes for, the U.S.C. Hiking Club.

For a while, I did the Hollywood hustle, working as a location scout and nature film writer by day, writing the Great American screenplay at night (If you know a producer interested in biopic about John Muir, "John of the Mountains" is a great script . . .)

While the industry never came through with those six- and seven-figure offers I thought my screenplays deserved, I was pleasantly surprised to learn that magazine editors would pay me three and four figures to write about hiking and the great outdoors. Readers of *California, Sunset* and *Los Angeles Times* magazines enjoyed my hiking stories while *Islands* magazine sent me from Fiji to Kauai to Corfu to hike around the world's islands and write about them.

My articles about hiking caught the attention of legendary California publisher Noel Young and his Capra Press, who signed me to write *Day Hiker's Guide to Southern California.* This title is even more popular now than it was 20 years ago, and remains one of the best-selling trail guides of all time.

In 1986, a *Los Angeles Times* reporter interviewed me for a story he was writing about hiking. In mid-interview, he stopped and declared: "Hey, you should be writing about this subject. Let me introduce you to the editor."

So began my 18-year stint as the newspaper's hiking columnist. The weekly column proved tremendously popular. Maybe the Missing Persons song lyric, "Nobody Walks in L.A." is true; however, it seems most everybody hikes. Local parks had to assign extra staff on the weekends following one of my hike write-ups because so many hikers turned out to hit the trail.

They even turned out in droves when I made a mistake. One March I took a hike out in the desert at Antelope Valley California Poppy Reserve. It was rainy and very cold on my hike with the park ranger, who pointed out the multitude of poppy buds, sure to put on a spectacular show in a few weeks—waves of orange flowers as far as the eye could see.

My column about the joys of hiking through wondrous fields of poppies ran three weeks later. Scores of readers drove out to the desert to delight in the pathways through the poppies.

Unfortunately, a searing heat wave occurred a couple of days before my column appeared and toasted just about every poppy in the reserve. Readers found brown hills instead of orange ones, desiccation instead of lush beauty.

Some hikers were understanding about the vicissitudes of nature and took it in stride; others wanted to boil me in poppy seed oil and demanded I be fired from my position for wasting their time. Thankfully, my editor realized I had no control over the weather and kept me on the trail.

My *Times* readers liked my accounts of regional hikes but soon requested that I go farther afield to detail hikes. So off I hiked, around the West, across the East, and to intriguing hiking locales all over the U.S. I compiled the trails I described for the *Times* and other publications into a dozen guides, including *Great Walks of New England* and *Great Walks of the Pacific Northwest*.

Of the many lands that have called to me, spoke to me, my home shoreline and coastal mountains have called the loudest. I answered the call by agreeing to the California Coastal Trail Foundation's request to pioneer the California Coastal Trail. And so I took a little walk—a 1,600-mile hike as it turned out—from the Mexican border to the Oregon border along California's diverse shore, through the coast range and redwood forest.

It was a life-changing hike for me, as I transformed from a sportsman with something to prove to a traveler with something to learn—and share. I wrote a narrative, *A Walk Along Land's End*, that chronicled my adventures and the unique people and places I encountered.

Meanwhile, even my social life revolved around hiking. I must confess I took my dates on (sometimes too) rigorous hikes and I'm sure more than one woman not-so-fondly remembers not only a bad date but the hike from hell. Fortunately, I met a gal who could not only keep step with me on the trail, but surpasses me in every other way. Cheri and I have been together since our first hike, uh, date.

Heart pounding (from nervousness, not the climb), I proposed to her on the trail, just as we reached the summit of Little Pine Mountain. We started our life together with a honeymoon hike.

These days I enjoy family hikes and sharing the trail with my daughter Sophia and son Daniel. I've learned as much from my children as they have from me, and I'm delighted by the opportunity to share what we've learned together in the "Hiking with Children" chapter of this book.

I MIGHT HAVE GOT IT BACKWARDS, but I got it. I began by telling readers where to hike, then how to hike, and finally why they should hike. Perhaps I should have started with some inspiration, next imparted the practicalities, and concluded with where to go to find the best hikes.

Nevertheless, as I discussed where to hike I got lots of questions from my readers about basic hiking lore and answered them one letter, one phone call, one e-mail at a time. Here are a couple of typical questions:

Dear Trailmaster:

I'm a longtime walker but new to hiking and am looking for my first pair of boots to take short hikes in the nearby mountains. I was pleasantly surprised to find that the price of hiking boots was really low at the local chain sporting goods store. Can you get a good pair of boots for $40?

New Hiker

Dear New Hiker:

It's unlikely you'll get a good pair of boots for $40 unless the store is selling an $80 pair of boots for half price or a $160 pair at 75 percent off. The Trailmaster has tested a lot of cheapo-boots and, while they look okay when you're knocking around town, they perform poorly on the trail because they generally lack good support, get wet easily, and fail to make the grade for various technical reasons.

For an acceptable boot at a modest (but not cheap) price, go with a pair made by an athletic shoe manufacturer such as Nike or an entry-level boot made by a good specialty shoe company such as Timberland. For optimum savings, look for last year's models or discontinued styles.

Dear Trailmaster:

Thank you for your hiking suggestions. You have given me many hours of great adventures at places new to me and my family.

My 9-year old son got a compass for his birthday in one of those "Hiker Kits" for kids and asked me how to use it. The directions aren't much help and I'm really embarrassed to admit I know how to use one.

Seeking Direction,
Lost with a Compass

Dear Lost with a Compass:

You're not alone. Most hikers don't know how to use a compass. And thanks for stopping to ask for directions—something most of us guys can't bring ourselves to do.

If you want to start learning on your own, buy a little how-to book about using a compass, get a topo map of an area familiar to you (like a park near your house) and start practicing. Better yet, sign up for an orienteering class (they're often a really fun day outdoors). Check with the Sierra Club in your area or with an outdoor equipment retailer such as REI for the availability of compass classes.

Questions to The Trailmaster have by no means been confined to practical questions about where to hike and how-to-hike. I've fielded questions (or tried to) about relationships and spiritual growth and their connections to hiking. Many people have written to me or told me what they think about on the trail, what they feel on a hike.

The Joy of Hiking answers many of the questions hikers have asked me—in person, over the airwaves or on the trail. Hiking is a vast subject area—witness the seven million Google entries on the popular search engine—so I was compelled to narrow the field a bit.

The Joy of Hiking is a book first and foremost about hiking ("walking through the countryside" as it's most commonly defined by dictionaries). This is not a backpacking manual, which would necessarily mean lengthy explanations about overnight gear, camp cookery, and camp-craft. And this is not a book about walking, a fabulous form of exercise, one that I encourage at all opportunities. (I gathered so much information over the years and talked to so many intriguing people that I may just write books about the joys of walking and backpacking.)

Backpackers, who comprise 10 percent or so of the hiking population, will find almost all of the offered hiking advice relevant and may particularly enjoy some of this book's unusual where-to-hike suggestions and accounts of America's long-distance trails. Walkers will discover how easy it is to make the transition to hiking—and some walkers may realize they're already hiking without knowing it!

Get More out of Life

Hiking is one of the most natural forms of exercise, a gregarious activity for those desiring companionship, and a contemplative one for those seeking solitude. I wrote *The Joy of Hiking* to inspire, inform and entertain hikers of all ages and abilities, particularly newcomers, and to heighten awareness of the world around them. Hiking promotes increased awareness of the natural world and our moral obligation to become better stewards of it.

If the reason for taking a hike (if indeed a reason be necessary!) is the hope for mental-spiritual-physical rejuvenation, or to take time to contemplate where you've been and where you're going in this confusing world, then a hike in nature can help make sense of it all. Of course a more simple reason for taking a hike is that it's fun to do.

At times, I challenge you to reach inside yourselves and get more from your hikes. I've dropped in some inspirational quotes, "Trail Wisdom," "Trailmaster Tales," and "Hike-kus" to help motivate, empower, amuse, uplift and comfort hikers on this amazing path we call life. If you're a hiker, it's altogether natural for you to regard life as a long hike with ups and downs and points of interest along the way.

Trail Wisdom: Walk with Laughter

MAYBE it's the outwardly stern image of the serious exercise-walker, striding with erect posture, a jabbing arm swing, and unsmiling face that suggests walkers can't walk and laugh at the same time.

Ha! A good laugh and a long walk are two terrific cures for what ails us; in tandem, they are doubly powerful.

Humor is a barrier-breaking, rapport-building, mood-elevating, healing and revealing exercise.

Like walking.

Genesis records that when Sarah gave birth to a son at age 90, she said: "God has brought me laughter and everyone who hears about this will laugh with me." She and her husband Abraham, then 100, named their son Isaac, which means he laughs.

Ever since Norman Cousins' landmark book, *Anatomy of an Illness*, health professionals, as well as many ministers and rabbis, are rediscovering the healing power of humor.

Research published in the Journal of the American Medical Association actually scientifically proved what Cousins and countless generations of anecdotal evidence had pointed out: laughter is useful in fighting serious illness.

During a hearty laugh, the diaphragm, heart, lungs, thorax. abdomen, and even the liver and kidneys are given a gentle, even therapeutic, massage. Cousins calls laughter "Internal Jogging." With all due respect to Cousins, who wrote his book in the 1970s at the height of the jogging boom, perhaps we should instead call laughter "Internal Hiking."

Walking and humor have one more use in common: each fights pain. Laughter, like walking, activates the human brain's secretion of morphine-like molecules called endorphins, which in turn override pain, perk us up, and can give us "athlete's high." The retreat of pain is accompanied by an increase in mobility. So the more we walk and laugh, laugh and walk, the better we feel.

Only when faith falters, when heart and step are unsure, are we afraid to laugh. A person without a sense of humor is like a tender-footed hiker, wincing at every pebble in the path.

Walk with laughter.

Enjoy Better Health

I wrote *The Joy of Hiking* to share the health benefits of hiking: to inspire hikers of every interest and intention—from those embarking on weight reduction or stress management programs to already dedicated exercise walkers and gung-ho trekkers. Hiking can assist those recovering from illness—for individuals determined to "get back on their feet."

This book is encouragement for those taking their first steps toward a healthier lifestyle, coax the leg-weary, stressed and fatigued, and reinforce the commitments of already devoted walkers.

A good hike is a tonic for our stressful lives. As French hikers put it: *Un jour de marche, huit jours de sante*. A day of walking, eight days of health.

Hike Safely and Happily

Long before I took to the airwaves to spread the The Trailmaster gospel, I often gave talks and slide shows (such as "Hiking the Desert" or "Great Walks of New England") at outdoor retailers and bookstores. Sometimes my audience enthusiastically embraced the topic and our hour together passed quickly; other times, the audience enjoyed the presentation all right, but had scores of questions about hiking that were far from the advertised topic of my talk.

One fine spring day, for example, I appeared at an REI store to talk about hiking in national parks. Realizing it was John Muir's birthday, I launched into an impromptu talk about the great naturalist's life and work, rhapsodized about the wonders of wilderness hiking in the High Sierra and figured I just about moved the audience to tears.

I figured wrong. When I opened the floor to questions, it was clear that my audience of (mostly) novice hikers was more interested in self preservation than in wilderness preservation.

First question: How do you safely cross a fast-moving stream?

Second question: Can I hike alone?

Third question: How sick will I get if a tick bites me?

I stayed for another hour, answering questions and improvising a Hiking 101 class.

While writing this chapter of *The Joy of Hiking*, I got a call from a radio talk show producer who wanted to do a special program about outdoor safety. The theme of the show was a kind of emergency response to news of a half-dozen California hikers perishing within a month of exposure to cold, falls from cliffs, slips on icy slopes and getting lost.

The talk show host, Warren Olney, wanted to know why there were so many hiker accidents. "John, why are so many hikers getting hurt, even dying in the great outdoors?"

My answer was a simple two-part one.

"Well, Warren, more people are hiking than ever before, in California and in every other state. Some 64 million Americans say they like to hike. Unfortunately, more poorly prepared hikers are hitting the trail than ever before."

Most hiking accidents can be prevented. National Park Service studies of accidents that required the agency to launch a search and rescue operation determined that 99 percent of these accidents could be prevented by rudimentary outdoors knowledge, better preparations and the proper gear.

Hiking on a trail is one of the safest activities you can pursue—as long as you plan well, learn the basics about this rewarding outdoor activity, obey human and natural laws, and use common sense.

Almost every page in this book could be considered to offer some kind of safety advice because the more you know, the safer hiker you'll be. Master the basics and you'll be a confident (but not overly confident) hiker.

The Trailmaster Way

If, with a wave of a magic hiking stick, I could have my way, I'd hike with you, not write to you. The best way to experience the joy of hiking is to take a hike!

It's been my pleasure to lead a diversity of hikers down the trail: First-graders on beach hikes, Rotary Club members on wildflower walks, middle school students into the mountains. I've guided hikers, aged 30-something to 70-something, on weeklong hiking holidays for an upscale walking vacation company.

I plan to continue leading hikes for a very long time, but I can't take very many of you to very many places. Instead, we'll have to use our imaginations. I imagined you were with me on the trail as I wrote this book.

I imagined that I was taking you on one of my favorite hikes in the mountains near my home. I'd check to see if you had packed your ten essentials, snacks and lunch. We'd check the weather, and talk about layering and what to wear. We'd also talk about mileage, pace and the elements of a hike that you find most pleasing. Then we'd hike up Rattlesnake Canyon Trail, whose very name might prompt some questions about dangers on the trail. We'd enjoy companionship, as well as some solitary thoughts, as we hiked through a place far more inviting than its name. (Never judge a trail by its trailhead or by its name, we'd agree.)

About noon we'd reach what I call Lunch Rock, a large flat boulder in the middle of a frisky creek. We'd rest here, listening to the soothing sound of the cascades, eating our snacks and trail mix, letting our thoughts drift from trails past to this wonderful day to trails ahead.

Join me now in these pages as we hike together to Lunch Rock and beyond. I wish you more joy in every hike, wherever and whenever you roam.

Chapter 2 Hiking for Good Health

NEARLY 20 YEARS AGO, MY FATHER-IN-LAW, AN OVERWEIGHT and over-stressed engineer, saved his life by following his doctor's orders to walk. In preparation for quintuple bypass surgery, his cardiologist advised Ray to lose 30 pounds and walk 30 minutes three times a week. Ray responded in his typical overachieving fashion by dropping 50 pounds and walking five miles a day. His heart doctors were amazed at the corollary arteries Ray grew and enlarged by his ambitious walking program. He now has many grandchildren he's lived to enjoy, and he's still walking—three to five miles a day.

Innumerable research studies have demonstrated that regular physical activity, particularly walking and hiking, is directly related to a happier, healthier and longer life.

Walking is by far the best way to get into condition for hiking; in fact, at certain points, these healthful activities merge. For example, a walk along a greenway that gets away from the 'burbs and into the woods is a hike in my book. A walk that includes a neighborhood jaunt and a riverside ramble could be called a walk or a hike—your choice.

A vigorous, even modest walk, three or four times a week for a half hour to an hour is sufficient for an adult to enjoy all the advantages that exercise offers for good physical and mental health. Whether the hike you choose as part of your weekly exercise routine is a moderate one-hour ramble along a local greenway or through a park, or a more vigorous 30-minute hike with some elevation gain, hitting the trail means big-time benefits for your body and mind.

In This Chapter
- Walking is good for the body
- Walking is good for mental health
- Hike off excess weight
- Hike for a stronger heart
- Hiking slows the aging process

WHEN IT COMES TO WORKING HARD, most Americans are the busiest of beavers but when it comes to exercising hard (or even moderately) most Americans are the most sedentary of sloths. According to a recent report by the U.S. Department of Health and Human Services, only a paltry 15 percent of U.S. adults engage in an adequate amount of physical activity.

The average American's apparent aversion to exercise is not for lack of information. Study after study, going back decades, has found that regular exercise boosts a person's health and well-being and results in a longer life.

"Painful" and "boring" are the two most common excuses offered for not exercising. While I won't attempt to defend "go for the burn" 90-minute aerobic classes or treading a treadmill from the charges of causing pain and boredom, I can attest that few hikers encounter much pain or boredom on the trail.

Certainly the no-pain-no-gain philosophy of various sports and exercise regimens is also part of the hiking world. Anyone who's hiked a steep trail at high altitude knows the meaning of some pain to get that elevation gain. With hiking, however, there is a reward beyond better muscle tone: a view from the top, a new perspective, satisfaction in the going there and getting there.

Hiking boring?

Not!

I suppose someone could take the same hike on the same trail at the same time and cover the same distance, day after day in an attempt to make hiking boring. But even here, hiking conspires against boredom. Seasons change and so does the natural world along the trail. Nearly every trail has an optional route; even doing a loop trail backwards adds a new perspective.

Walking is Good For the Body

Walking is good medicine, the most prescribed exercise for post-operative patients, particularly for those recovering from a variety of heart ailments and from open heart surgery. Walking, literally opens up new lines to the heart, cardiologists attest. A strong heart, in turn, promotes oxygen delivery to active muscles. Much of the unheralded work of returning blood back up to the heart is accomplished by the calf muscles, which squeeze the veins and force the blood upward against gravity as they expand and contract. Walking, because it works all the leg muscles, has an integral role in increasing circulation; for this reason, walking is often called the "second heart," by doctors and exercise physiologists.

Walking promotes healing. We often hear someone say, "I'm walking back to good health." Doctors urge hospital patients to get out of bed and walk as soon as they are able. A patient in a weakened state takes a child-like satisfaction in shuffling down the hospital corridor. Complete strangers will speak encouraging words to such patients, as they trail IVs and all manner of machines behind them. Sometimes we don't recognize the value of walking until we're ill and immobilized.

Increasingly, we are learning other benefits for walking: mental flexibility, as well as emotional and spiritual strength. Walking, as all the latest scientific research has quantified, improves cardiovascular efficiency, burns calories and reduces stress.

As recently as the 1970s, walking was regarded as the exercise of last resort, fit only for those too unfit to do anything else. Now walking is the exercise of first choice—for health, for fitness, for exploring the world around us, far and wide.

Walking is Good for the Soul

When I struggle with my writing, I walk. When I'm entangled in a business dealing, I walk. When I have a parental decision to make, I walk. When my wife and I have an issue of the day—great or small—to discuss, we walk.

Walking unburdens the heart. While it's true that a light heart lightens the step, it's equally true that a light step lightens the heart. The kindergartner, sullen teen or elderly parent who won't speak while seated on the living room couch is apt to do some talking while walking.

Expanding with each step, our whole beings—body and soul reach farther horizons, greater possibilities. As we walk, we integrate the positives, and possibilities become probabilities.

While I have been fortunate to journey afoot in more parts of the world than most, some of my best thinking occurs on hikes close to home—along the beach and in the mountains.

Walking. We do it every day. We just don't do enough of it.

So walk. Contemplate what makes you happy and what would make you happier still. Walk. Think about what you can do to expand your life, what you can do to simplify it. Walk to remember. Walk to forget. Walk and talk with God. List what you want your walking to manifest in the material, emotional, and spiritual realms. Walk. Enjoy the beauty of providence. Walk.

In a life that takes us almost anywhere, we can walk almost anywhere. Walking means continuing to walk: Today, tomorrow, and for the rest of your life.

Healthful Benefits of Hiking

Hike off excess weight Hitting the trail is a superb means of shedding weight and surely more satisfying (and if you keep at it) and permanent way to lose weight than going on a crash diet, the latest fad diet, or ingesting one of those available-only-at-this-toll-free-number chemical formulas.

I'm not dissing diets. Many of them work quite well for those who get on them and stay on them, even if those diet books on the

Hiking is Good for You, and Blood Tests Prove It!

In 2005, Austrian researchers announced the results of an intriguing study demonstrating that different types of hiking have different influences on the fats and sugars in the blood. For the study, participants took three- to five-hour-long hikes in the Alps, sometimes hiking uphill and riding a ski lift down, sometimes taking the ski lift up and riding down.

Hiking had a healthy influence on certain blood levels, cardiologists found, and further, the benefits varied depending on whether hikers trekked uphill, downhill, or varied their outings.

Researchers found:

- Hiking uphill is more effective at removing fats from the blood.

- Hiking downhill is best for removing blood sugars (welcome news for diabetics).

- Hiking either uphill or downhill lowers bad cholesterol levels.

New York Times bestseller list seem to offer contradictory advice. (Eat more meat! No, eat less meat!)

While diet and hike are just four-letter words to those who disdain both, a healthy diet with a hiking-centered exercise program can greatly assist losing weight and keeping it off. A 150-pound hiker, sauntering along the trail at a two-miles per hour pace, burns 240 calories in an hour according to the American Heart Association. Hiking with a ten- to fifteen-pound day pack increases the calories burned by ten to fifteen percent. Add some hill-climbing and pick up the pace, and you can increase the calorie burn even more.

Hike for a stronger heart Heart disease is caused by many more factors than inactivity, but one's odds of falling victim to what is the leading cause of death in America (every half-minute or so another American dies from cardiovascular disease) can be significantly improved by taking regular walks or hikes.

Those failing to walk, hike or exercise regularly are twice as likely to have coronary heart disease.

Hiking helps reduce cholesterol, a leading factor of heart disease. In addition, hiking increases high-density lipoprotein (HDL), the body's so-called "good cholesterol" which assists removing bad cholesterol from artery walls.

Hike for lower blood pressure Hypertension (high blood pressure) affects millions of Americans. Physicians almost reflexively prescribe medications, some mild, some strong, many effective, some not. For some individuals there is an alternative to such medications in the form of regular exercise. A walking/hiking program has been shown to reduce systolic and diastolic blood pressure. Specifically, what hiking does is lower a hiker's plasma norepinephrine which corresponds to a lowering of blood pressure.

Hiking helps prevent osteoporosis A bone disease caused by calcium deficiency, osteoporosis affects a large number of (mostly) older women. This calcium deficiency reduces bone density and makes bone more brittle and likely to break. Older Americans suffer some 1.5 million fractures a year associated with osteoporosis, resulting in more than $6 billion a year in medical care costs. Hiking can help stop, even reverse osteoporosis by slowing calcium loss and increasing bone density.

Hiking helps prevent and control diabetes Hiking, as much or more than any other form of regular exercise, can help prevent diabetes and assist in the well-being of the large number of Americans who already have the disease (some 15.7 million Americans—nearly 6 percent of the population).

A program that includes a healthy diet and a walking/hiking regimen can reverse the course of diabetes for those with Type II (non-insulin dependent) diabetes. For those with Type I (insulin-dependent) diabetes, hiking can reduce the required amounts of insulin.

Hiking reduces the pain of arthritis It seems like the most natural human response: if a body part hurts, don't move it. However, responding to arthritis pain by ceasing or decreasing movement is a bad move, and can worsen joint problems.

The muscle-strengthening benefits of walking/hiking are numerous, particularly for the legs. Stronger leg muscles assist arthritis sufferers in the knees and ankles because these muscles lessen the pain cause by bones rubbing against one another.

Hiking relieves lower back pain The alleviation or elimination of lower back pain is the most widely reported and best documented health benefit of walking/hiking. And for that reason alone, many more former back-pain sufferers have become hiking advocates.

Not much of what we do in the workplace is very good for our backs, whether it is standing in one position or sitting down. Ergonomically designed chairs and work stations may help, but not nearly as much as taking a walk!

Jogging and many kinds of aerobic classes are high impact on the lower back; hiking, by contrast, is low-impact on the back, both literally and figuratively.

Contact a physician before you decide to hike away your back problem because certain conditions could be aggravated, not helped, by hiking.

Hiking slows the aging process Major declines in physical activity and strength—once commonly believed to be the inevitable results of growing old—need not accompany aging, the latest medical research tells us. Studies lasting more than 20 years followed some middle-aged men who walked for exercise and some who did not into their senior years and found that the active men lost only 13 percent of their aerobic capacity while the sedentary men lost more than 40 percent.

Those seniors who take a hike and declare "it feels good" and "it keeps me active" now have confirming evidence for their gut instincts: aging per se doesn't markedly decrease one's desire or ability to be active, strong and healthy. Alas the converse is true: inactivity actually accelerates the aging process.

Hike for Improved Mental Health

Stressed? Depressed? You could lie on a couch and talk to psychiatrist. Or you could take a hike. Hiking prompts the release of endorphins, soothing chemicals that serve to calm us.

Perhaps as a holdover from the early days of the human race

Not Your Routine Walks

Boredom thwarts our best intentions to exercise—including going out for a walk. The same neighborhood loop day in and day out can dull the motivation of even the most diehard walking enthusiast.

To keep the spring in your step, try a different route. You might be surprised what a little research might uncover in the way of walking routes in your area. Reinvigorate your walking by relocating your usual walk. Here's some relocation advice:

- **Play postman.** A walk to the post office to drop off a letter can give you a little exercise.
- **Meander down by the riverside.** The sound of running water is particularly restful to us. De-stress by walking alongside a river.
- **Make tracks.** The Rails-to-Trails Conservancy, along with assorted governmental agencies has converted thousands of miles of out-of-use railroad tracks to walking paths. Check to see if there's a trail near you.
- **Walk with the animals.** Nearby wildlife refuges, estuaries and bird-watching sites often have trails leading to, or around them.
- **A walk in the park.** Away from the maddening crowd, city and suburban parks are islands of greenery and nature.
- **Walk U.** College campuses offer safe walkways, athletic tracks, fitness trails, even gardens and nature paths.
- **The Great Indoors.** Shopping malls aren't exactly high adventure but they do offer safe, weatherproof walking.
- **Busman's Holiday.** Take a bus to the edge of the city and walk back.

when homo sapiens were NOT at the top of the food chain and often chased by predators, our modern bodies still produce lots of adrenalin, which helps us with our fight-or-flight responses and in a less dramatic way assists us with getting through tense meetings and getting over tall mountains. Adrenaline, if not periodically released, accumulates, tensing muscles and contributing to feelings of anxiety.

Taking a hike gets every part of the body moving—and dissipates anxiety-producing adrenaline.

Trail Wisdom: Walk until You're 99

WHEN Abraham was 99 years old, the Lord appeared before him and said: "I am God Almighty, walk before me and be blameless."

According to Genesis 17, the Lord assigned old Abraham some enormous tasks; he was to become the father of many nations and to take everlasting possession of the whole land of Canaan for himself and his descendants. Further, in order to keep covenant with the Lord he was to circumcise all the males in his household as well as all other males in the area.

Abraham complied with all of the Lord's commands but was taken aback by one last request: Create a son with his wife Sarah. At this point in the conversation the Bible reports that "Abraham fell face-down and laughed."

"Will a son be born to a man a hundred years old?" asked Abraham when he pulled himself together. Then he remembered his wife—at 89 not exactly in her prime child-bearing years. "Will Sarah bear a child at the age of 90?" Virility and fertility proved not to be problems and a son was born a year later, as the Lord had promised. Abraham not only fathered Isaac, but founded the Jewish nation.

As Abraham demonstrates, there is old and there is old; that old adage "you're only as old as you think," has been proven time and time again since Abraham was born in 2166 B.C.

Recent gerontological studies confirm that older walkers are far more fit and of far more cheerful disposition than their sedentary counterparts.

Gerontologists and sociologists categorize the years from 60 to 75 as the "young-old," from age 75 to 84 as the "middle-old," and age 85 and over as the "old-old."

The young-old benefit greatly from walking because it makes them stronger, both physically and mentally. Walkers in this age group face such potentially fatal and serious ailments as heart disease, cancer and strokes. A daily walk helps seniors by increasing their strength and elevating their spirits—useful in the fight against any illness.

The middle-old and the old-old also benefit physically and mentally from a regular walking program. Certainly for these senior seniors, walking, both literally and symbolically, represents mobility and independence for a group that is often incorrectly characterized (by younger generations and by themselves) as frail and helpless.

Many older folks are wrongly convinced their need to walk diminishes with age, a survey conducted by the President's Council on Physical Fitness reports. Many seniors are also apt to exaggerate the dangers of walking and their inability to walk.

Walking is a way for seniors to stay out in the world. To best resist the many paralyzing effects old age, seniors would be wise to combine the body, the mind and the heart—keeping all vigorous by continuing to walk, to learn, and to love.

Almost anyone at any age can walk—and will feel better for it. At God's request, Abraham began walking among his people, among the lovely oak grove of Mamre, and across the desert plains of the Holy Land. Abraham, who did not receive God's call to walk until he was 99, lived to the ripe old age of 175. Walk until you're 99—or older!

Chapter 3   Hiking in Good Spirit

FRESH AIR, GREAT EXERCISE, COMMUNION WITH NATURE . . . hiking offers all this—and more. Some hikers have discovered that getting outward bound helps them with an inward journey.

If you want to learn about on-the-trail technique and gear, and hold off on any kind of cosmic discussion about the value hiking may have to your inner self, higher self or the world at large, skip this chapter and turn to the dozen that detail all the practicalities. This discussion can certainly wait. I hiked for many years before giving my interior world on the trail—or anyone else's—much consideration.

I really started looking at hiking a bit differently after making a Pilgrimage with a capital P and hiked around the Holy Mountain of Greece. Journeying to the remarkable Mt. Athos, home to twenty Orthodox Christian monasteries, where the monks live and work today as they did in the Middle Ages was a profoundly moving experience: Architectural treasures; trails that have been isolated from the world for a thousand years; the wisdom and the spirituality of the monks; a place where no females are allowed, that fact alone focused my attention inward and to a contemplative place. Here was an other-wordly place that stirred my soul.

I feel very lucky and very blessed to have experienced such a remarkable place, but you certainly don't have to hike a holy mountain in Greece, Peru, Tibet or anywhere else to lift your spirit and nourish it. Scores of hikers have told me how they've discovered a greater sense of spirituality on trails near their homes. I believe nearly every hike has the potential to be a mini-pilgrimage if approached with the right spirit.

This chapter is different than the rest. Instead of giving instruction as I do elsewhere in *The Joy of Hiking*, I'm asking questions. I'm musing, and hope you'll muse along with me.

One of the most powerful tools for spiritual renewal is so simple, it's frequently overlooked: hiking. To hike is to receive a continuous

> *"Our walking is not a means to an end. We walk for the sake of walking."*
>
> —Thich Nhat Hanh

intake of new images which, in turn, prompt new thoughts and spark new feelings. Step by step, thought by thought, hiking shapes our bodies and souls, and helps create and alter our life paths. We can hike our way out of a problem and into a solution. We can hike from questions to answers. We can hike from "Can I?" to "I can" to "I will."

Walking is the exercise of choice for millions of Americans and also a scriptural term in many religions commonly used to describe an individual's earthly pilgrimage. Similarly, hiking is the outdoor recreation of choice for millions of Americans and also opens up new paths for growth.

A good hike can spiritually strengthen us in our three most important relationships—with other people, with nature, and with a higher power. In short, hiking can be a form of meditation. A good hike is most enlightening—a merging of the visible and invisible worlds.

I TRULY WISH I could report that the impetus for looking at hiking and finding something more came to me while on a hike to some ancient holy shrine—or even on a nature trail in the local mountains—but in fact it came under the hot glare of the lights in a television studio. Back in 1995, while on a book tour, I was interviewed on "Life and Times," a talk show produced by KCET, the Los Angeles Public Broadcasting System affiliate. My host, Will Swaim, asked questions about my book, *A Walk Along Land's End*, a narrative about my 1,600-mile hike up the California coast. I talked about both the great beauties and environmental atrocities I'd seen, the intriguing wildlife and colorful characters I had encountered. For the first three-fourths of our book chat, I was in fine form. Most of my book tour had been completed by the time I appeared on this show. I had been interviewed more than three dozen times and felt confident that I had a glib answer or an amusing anecdote for any question. That is, until near the end of this particular interview when my interviewer threw me a question I'd never been asked and—worse—had not truly contemplated.

Swaim talked about how I seemed to have grown more philosophical toward the end of my long walk and then asked if I thought walking could be considered a spiritual quest.

I froze. I was probably silent for only about five seconds, but it seemed like an eternity. (A friend later commented: "John, you looked like a deer caught in the headlights.")

I punted the question. "A long walk is a spiritual quest in many religions. Some people might discover something spiritual on a long hike."

Swaim was quick with a follow-up question. "But how is hiking a spiritual experience for you? Doesn't something happen out there that changes your way of thinking, of feeling?"

Another pause. I could feel the perspiration on my forehead, seeping through the studio makeup. I fumbled this question as badly as the first. "Well, you have to think about something on a 1,600-mile hike. Hiking brought me closer to nature, closer to the mountains and the sea. . . ."

Two more questions of the spirit followed, which I handled no better than the first two, before time mercifully ran out on the interview.

After the interview, I stormed out of the studio, angry with myself, angry with my interrogator. In PR lingo, I had lost control of the interview. I kicked the tires on my truck, pounded the dashboard, and seethed as I inched along the congested freeway during the three-hour drive home.

Calmer heads soon prevailed and convinced me that I hadn't performed quite as poorly as I thought: My publicist gave me a "B" grade on my performance, and my editor a B-minus. And Will Swaim, far from being the talk show host from hell, turned out to be a very spiritual man, educated by Jesuits.

It was Swaim who later showed me his copy of *A Walk Along Land's End*, with the more spiritual passages marked with a yellow highlight pen and Post-its. He suggested I begin preaching what I was already practicing: "John, you know the power of a good hike. Why don't you help hikers out with the process? Give them something to think about on their own hikes."

So that's how someone very slow on the spiritual uptake, who always figured he had better developed thighs than thoughts, began wondering how to get something more than fresh air from my time on the trail.

What do hikers want? As a "hiking writer," as an acknowledged hiking expert, I thought I knew the answer to that question. I had dispensed my share of how-to-hike advice in the form of newspaper and magazine articles and I had provided way more than my share of where-to-hike advice in the form of hundreds of articles and a dozen books.

Certainly a lot of other experts think they know what hikers want. Homebuilders and realtors report that the most commonly requested "amenity" in new subdivisions is a walking path (homebuyers prefer hiking trails and greenways to tennis courts and golf courses by a wide margin). Tour companies say the walking trip business has expanded exponentially during the last decade. Manufacturers and retailers view hiking footwear, apparel and equipment as big business.

But while the consumer needs of hikers are certainly being met, what about their inner needs? Do hikers even have any inner needs? Are most hikers as out of touch with the meditative aspects of a hike as we so-called experts?

Apparently I had intended to explore for years, perhaps on a subconscious level, to explore this "What do hikers want?" question at some later date. I discovered in the depths of filing cabinets and on

> *"I like to walk about amidst the beautiful things that adorn the world. . . ."*
> —George Santayana

Hike-ku
"Walk on," said Buddha
words of wisdom he taught us
with his dying breath

long-forgotten computer disks such intriguingly named files as "God," "Walk Back from Cancer," "Desert Monks," "Eco-rabbi," "Around the World on One Leg," "Christian Conservationists," "100-Year-Old Hiker," and a few dozen more.

As my filing system illustrated, I had quite literally maintained a strict separation of church and state, the body and the spirit, in my work. But what I soon discovered is that while separation of spirituality and practicality may indeed be necessary in some aspects of our everyday lives and in our nation's governance, such separation on our hikes, is not necessary at all. In fact, hiking serves to integrate, not separate, the material and spiritual worlds.

While seeking hiking wisdom, I became acquainted with the writings and teaching of an array of walkers that included Charles Dickens, Jesus of Nazareth, Johann Goethe, Apostle Paul, Henry David Thoreau, Harry S. Truman, Johnny Appleseed, Buddha, Norman Cousins, Immanuel Kant, Jane Austen, Lao-Tzu, William O. Douglas, Ralph Waldo Emerson, Will Rogers, Gandhi, Wolfgang Amadeus Mozart, Socrates, and dozens more. The Bible, both old and new testaments, proved to be a particularly rich source of walking wisdom, as have the literature of eastern religions and traditions.

Along with the great number of hikes I've taken to great destinations, I've managed to work in a few spiritual pilgrimages as well. I hiked with Greek Orthodox monks atop Mt. Athos, the Holy Mountain of Greece, walked where the Transcendentalists walked in New England, hiked with a Cistercian nun through a logging-threatened redwood grove that she and her order were attempting to save.

As we hikers know, what goes around, comes around. Midway through my research, my parish priest, Fr. Paul Paris of the St. Barbara Greek Orthodox Church summoned me to his office. "John, you're out there and hiking all the time. Do you ever think anything spiritual on your hikes? Is there a point to hiking?"

I'm getting better at answering those kinds of questions, though I still have far more questions than answers about sojourns of the spirit.

I've sprinkled some "Trail Wisdom" meditations in *The Joy of Hiking*, a kind of trail guide for the soul. The meditations aren't destinations; they're departure points. They suggest where you can go, not where you should go, on your hike. There are as many directions to travel as there are hikers. You'll find your own direction, your own path. One step at time.

Hiking is a Spiritual Path

From culture to culture, continent to continent, walking is an ancient and literal way of pursuing a spiritual path. English pilgrims sojourned to Canterbury, Native Americans walk to sacred places on vision quests, Australian aborigines wander into the outback on walkabouts. Jesus of Nazareth walked into the desert for 40 days and 40 nights to pray and to prepare for his future struggles.

Muslims travel to Mecca on their annual Hadj and the Mahatma Gandhi more or less mixed spirituality with politics when he began the famous march to the sea to protest British salt taxes.

But we don't have to hike to or through a holy land in order to make a pilgrimage. By combining the outward-bound momentum of our bodies with the inner voyaging of our souls, we have the makings of a mini-pilgrimage every time we step out the door.

Many great poets, those explorers of the soul, have been great walkers. One of William Wordsworth's biographers calculated that the English poet laureate walked some 185,000 miles during his lifetime. Samuel Taylor Coleridge walked ten miles a day. Passionate poets John Keats and Percy Shelley took long walks during their short lives.

Truly the rambling British bards of the nineteenth century and their ancient and modern counterparts would seem to have little to offer us today. And yet philosophically and historically viewed, I believe that walking in the great outdoors can properly be considered one of the finer arts. Walking, by its rhythmic nature, by awakening our senses, makes all of us poets. We see aspen leaves flicker in the wind, a squirrel scurry up a tree, a child run across a meadow. Life hums to us as we invite it in by venturing out into it.

Certainly beauty inspires, elevating a good walk to a great one, but we don't need to ramble the Cotswolds, hike the High Sierra or saunter the beaches of Maui to draw inspiration from our environment.

Some may avoid hiking because it doesn't lead anywhere—except to better health perhaps. Sure it's good exercise, but it's dismissed as a mere pastime, a leisure class luxury, an idle recreation.

Some very busy folks I know say: "Every week I hike up to Inspiration Point, come back home and nothing's changed except I got two hours of exercise." To view hiking solely as a physical activity is to completely miss the point.

Hiking, like life itself, is both an interior and exterior process. Our search for meaning and meaningful change requires seeing things in a new light. Hiking provides that new light by opening us up to the world. Fresh images help us change our personal power point presentations and get on with the show.

The great nature writer John Muir, who literally hiked across America, recognized that we have vast interior landscapes to discover and to study. "I only went out for a walk," wrote Muir, "and finally concluded to stay out till sundown, for going out, I found, was really going in."

A good walk is transcendent, enabling us to cross the bridge between the visible and invisible worlds—and back again. When we get back, we've seen things in a new light.

By picturing the ideal, we can transform it into the real. What we can sort out, we can work out. What we can configure, we can figure.

> *"Walk on!"*
> —BUDDHA
> His last words to his disciples

Artists call it chasing the muse, Gestalt therapists call it reaching the *aha!* moment, business strategists call it getting to yes. I call it another way of finding *The Joy of Hiking*, a way of hiking that allows our internal boundaries to expand with our external ones enabling us to enjoy more creative and fulfilling lives.

Hiking at its most personally satisfying is the body and mind together, in motion. The two elements interact with each and foster creativity. Movement aids creativity and when you channel your creativity on something, you prompt movement. Once in motion, roadblocks become apparent, alternate paths reveal themselves.

Such hiking is not "inner-hiking"—something of a contradiction of terms because hiking can never be only a mental process. Inner-hiking reduces hiking to mere metaphor—not our goal at all.

It is the combination of our unusual, two-legged upright mobility and the evolution of our capacious brain that makes us unique among mammals. Our curious bipedal locomotion dictates what we can do long-term for exercise and our big brains what we will do. It seems we may just be too smart to continue with unnatural boring activities for very long. That's the beauty of hiking. It's never boring.

Hiking can encourage interactions with our subconscious, involving our senses and emotions in our great thoughts of the day. Hiking gives the intuitive side of the brain a chance to interact with the rational sides.

Sometimes the two sides seem at 180-degree opposites, destined never to intersect, much less interact. Ah, but if we keep hiking we discover that the right and left sides of our brains, like our right and left legs, provide not only energy, but synergy, creating a force more powerful than the sum of its parts.

Here's a recent "conversation" between my left brain and right brain that took place on a recent hike in the foothills near my house.

Rational Brain: Interest rates are so low, it looks like it's time to re-finance our house and get a better mortgage payment.

Intuitive brain: Look at the mountain lilac in bloom. Clouds of blue blossoms floating atop the ridge.

Rational brain: If I go for a 15-year fixed loan instead of a 30, I'd save thousands in interest, but the payments would be more each month.

Intuitive brain: The coastal fog is lifting, the foggy curtain is parting, just a glimpse of Santa Cruz Island floating on the horizon.

Rational Brain: The loan application must be 20 pages, all those credit checks, taxes...the bank bureaucrats...

Intuitive brain: What a pungent aroma! The black sage is really flowering this year. (Sneeze!)

Now at first glance, what possible linkage could there be between these two resolutely parallel dialogues going on inside my head?

Actually, as it turns out, a lot.

My walk helps me realize that home is not simply the old 1912-vintage Craftsman house that's located on a residential street near downtown, it's my whole environment: the mountains, ocean, churches, schools, malls, movie theaters, family, friends, neighbors, the Mediterranean flora, the Riviera and the flatlands, the soft south light. From the perspective of my hilltop vista, that bank building way down there no longer looks very intimidating. Put in perspective, I realize that a loan is but a necessary obstacle to hurdle in order to enjoy my hometown, home mountains, and home shore. The sights and sounds gathered while getting "the big picture" of my environment will strengthen me and help focus my mission as I do battle with the bank's loan examiners on the subjects of points, interest rates, and a far-from-perfect credit report.

Hiking, aerobics experts say, generates alpha waves which are distinguished by their creative nature. These creative ideas, these creative solutions to problems that these alpha waves seem to prompt, often seem superior to those ideas produced by ordinary thinking.

Truth is, the simple act of taking a hike can be a life-changing activity, one step at a time. For me, hiking is a path to increased serenity, creativity and physical well-being, as well as a connection to something far greater than myself. It may be for you, too.

Ten Ways to More Joyful Hiking

- A journey of a thousand miles begins with a single step.
- Walk boldly in the direction of your dreams.
- The map is not the territory.
- Don't judge a trail by its trailhead.
- Take the trail less traveled.
- All who wander are not lost.
- Hike your own hike.
- Two steps forward, one step back.
- Summit fever is contagious.
- Leave only footprints.

PART TWO
Hitting the Trail

Chapter 4   Getting Ready

As self-appointed president and sole member of the Brotherhood of Trail-guide Writers, with a dozen guidebooks to my credit, I hereby order you to buy a shelf-full of guides. You need to understand that the price of a pound of trail mix has risen faster than the cost of a gallon of gas and that our publishers never pay our royalties on time, so my fellow hiking scribes and I need you to stock up on guidebooks. You need to have a guidebook for every trail you plan to hike.

Nah, I'm just pulling your leg. Consulting a good guidebook (and I'll explain how to choose and use a good one) is one way to get ready for a hiking adventure, but there's lots more preparation involved. You need to know what to pack, how to ready your vehicle, and become familiar with backcountry rules and regulations. And you need to ask yourself what you really want to get out of a hike.

These days it seems everyone goes online to research hikes or parks. The web is great for gathering information about trails, but don't stop with a down-load. I've discovered several lost souls on the trail scratching their heads at poor maps and chamber of commerce descriptions downloaded from a website that inadequately detailed a particular hike.

After your web research, follow up with a call to park authorities or to hiking organizations to get the true story behind a trail. Often the enthusiastic employees at an outdoor retail store will have some great tips about local trails.

In This Chapter
- Researching a hike
- Planning ahead
- Equipping your car
- Backcountry driving
- Trailhead parking precautions

W**HAT'S A GREAT HIKE?** It's a question as difficult to answer, as unanswerable perhaps, as "What is great art?" or "What is great music?" Objectivity in these matters is impossible, statistical analysis inappropriate, a rating system downright ridiculous.

Some insight into what comprises a great hike comes from my range of field experience. I've explored considerably more than a thousand trails in America, plus many pathways abroad during a 25-year span as a "hiking writer." Most, if not all, of these trails had one or more distinctly pleasurable sights and at the very least offered some good exercise.

I've also discussed the notion of a great hike at some length with dozens of trail builders, fitness consultants, park service professionals, and experienced hikers. No two experts agreed what defined a great hike, of course, but some common themes emerged.

Elements contributing to a great hike are:
- Unusual landforms
- Forests, ancient or at least mature
- Wildflowers, intriguing flora
- Splendid views
- Lakes, rivers, ocean shores
- Tranquility and solitude
- Wildlife-watching
- Cultural or historical interest

To help pick the best hikes in a region, I rely heavily on the advice of National Park Service rangers, Forest Service naturalists, Sierra Club outings group leaders, nature center directors, professional tour leaders, and many local hikers. Nevertheless, I always make it clear that the final selection of the hikes included in my hiking guidebooks is mine and the many outdoors consultants who aided me should be thanked for their invaluable expertise and be held blameless for my admittedly subjective decision-making process.

Quite apart from my not-very-scientific criteria, a great hike often depends on what a hiker brings on the hike. No, I'm not referring to a hiker's day pack packed with lunch, water bottle and compass, but to the point-of-view a hiker brings to the great outdoors. Some hikers are looking for romance, some for trout, some for leg-stretchers to break up a vacation drive, some for a week-long hike that's a vacation from driving.

A great hike for a family might be one in which baby can come along, perched happily in a backpack; or one that tires out a four-year old so he'll nap in the car during the two-hour drive back to the motel; or a stirring sojourn that puts a smile on the face of even the most sullen teenager.

For Happy Trails, Choose Your Hiking Experience

Choosing what kind of experience you wish to have on the trail—is just as important as selecting a trail to hike. Ask yourself these questions:

- What kind of social experience am I looking for—solitude, first date, male-bonding, girlfriend gabbing, grandparent-grandchild nurturing, romance?
- Is watching wildlife a goal? Want to photograph a moose, ID a dozen species of water birds?
- What's my interest level in flora and flowering plants?
- How out there do I want to get? How remote a trail do you want to hike?
- How far, how long do I want to travel to the trailhead?
- What ancillary activities do I enjoy on the trail—swimming, fishing, photography, rock scrambling?

Choosing a Trail Guidebook

When selecting a guidebook, check to see if the guidebook highlights the best hikes in a region or tries to list all of them. When I write where-to-hike guidebooks, my goal is to increase the odds for my readers to have a great day in the great outdoors, so I leave out many walkable but not-so-wonderful trails. As you might imagine, a "professional" hiker like myself encounters a lot of turkey trails; that is to say, paths that start nowhere and go nowhere, trails battered by nature or neglected by park officials to the point where I decided that they are too unsafe for you to use.

Even if the guidebook author is an enthusiastic field-tester and updates frequently with the help of park authorities, perfection is not possible. Trails change over time. Like every hiker, I hate seeing a good trail go bad, but regrettably it happens. The ravages of fire and flood, rampant real estate development and bureaucratic neglect can ruin a favorite path.

While you're out hiking, if you happen across a neglected, hazardous or overgrown trail, please report it to the relevant ranger or administrator. Only if you make your concerns known will conditions improve. It's up to all of us to preserve our trails—and the precious wild lands they help us explore.

Of course in selecting a guidebook it helps to first decide where you want to hike. A palm oasis? An alpine meadow? A deserted beach? Consult an area map. Once you've narrowed down a locale that you want to explore on foot, look through the guidebook to see if it has interesting hiking trails in your geographical area of interest, then turn to the corresponding hike description in the main body of the book. If the guidebook tells you what you want to know about where you want to hike, buy it.

Getting the Most from a Trail Guidebook

Every hike in a guidebook has a soul and a goal. You provide the soul; the guide provides the goals. Let's face it, we're a goal-oriented society and we hikers are no exception. We hike for majestic views

Hiker Safety (before you go)

- Plan ahead (your pre- and post-hike plans, too)
- Be prepared
- Ready your vehicle
- Prevent problems before they occur
- Know your limits
- Dress your best
- Map it
- Know strengths and weaknesses of your companions
- Check the weather
- Food and water
- Ask questions

Gear to Keep in Your Vehicle

- **Flashlight** Bring extra batteries, bulb.

- **Phone** Cell phone coverage is expanding rapidly but don't count on reaching out from every remote mountain locale.

- **Extra food and water**

- **Emergency Supplies** Waterproof matches, fire-starting tablets, a well-stocked first-aid kit and a couple of blankets. Replenish as needed. One of the best ways to be prepared in a medical emergency is to have taken a Red Cross First-Aid CPR class.

- **Toilet paper and tissues**

- **Sunscreen** Get the SPF rating that's right for you, and use it. Reapply frequently.

- **Lip balm** To protect from chapped lips, look for one containing a sunscreen for best protection.

- **Camera** Always bring more film than you think you'll need, along with an extra battery.

- **Insect repellent** Keeps the critters off you.

or for the best fishing spot, not just to be out there. Some day hikers collect peaks the way motorhome drivers collect decals.

Most guidebooks list mileage, expressed in round-trip figures, at the top of the page beneath the hike name or trail name. Hikes in most day hiking guides range from one to twenty miles, with the majority in the five- to ten-mile range. Gain or loss in elevation usually follows the mileage. In matching a hike to your ability, you'll want to consider both mileage and elevation as well as condition of the trail, terrain, and season. Hot, exposed slopes or miles of boulder-hopping can make a short hike seem long.

You may wish to use the following guideline: A hike suitable for beginners and children is less than five miles with an elevation gain of less than 700 to 800 feet. A moderate hike is considered a hike in the five- to ten-mile range, with less than a 2,000-foot elevation gain. You should be reasonably fit for these. Preteens sometimes find the going difficult. Hikes longer than ten miles, and those with more than a 2,000-foot gain are for experienced hikers in top form.

Season is the next item to consider. Guidebooks often offer seasonal recommendations or suggestions by the month, such as "Best from May through October." Seasonal recommendations are based partly on hiker safety, comfort and perhaps even for legal restrictions, such as wildfire season closure or access restrictions because of endangered birds nesting near the trail.

After the just-the-facts introduction, the best guidebooks offer an introduction to each hike that describes what you'll see along the trail: plants, animals, panoramic views. You'll also learn about the geologic and human history of the region.

Directions to the trailhead take you from the nearest major highway to trailhead parking. For trails having two desirable trailheads, directions to each should be given. A few trails can be hiked one way, with the possibility of a car shuttle. Suggested car shuttle points should be noted.

After the directions to the trailhead, you'll read a description of the hike. Important junctions and major sights are usually pointed out, along with options allowing you the choice to climb higher or farther or take a different route back to the trailhead.

Whether you follow a guidebook to the letter, hike the length of a trail and every one of its options, or snooze under the first sycamore you find, is your decision and no one else's. There's enough regimentation in your life without some guidebook author telling you exactly where and how you must hike. A hiking guide is merely a way for you to plan your day in the backcountry.

Planning Ahead

Traveling without detailed maps, high-tech equipment, or freeze-dried foods, the pioneers still managed to trek through the wild. Today we enjoy the benefit of all sorts of undreamed-of modern accoutrements that make journeys more comfortable than they were in days past. But the most important aids to backcountry travel remain as simple as they were 200 years ago—common sense, advance planning and packing the right supplies.

Individuals accustomed to spending their days in temperature-regulated homes and offices are in for a surprise when they venture into the great outdoors. It's often an environment that demands adaptation by inhabitants and visitors alike. Daily extremes of hot and cold are the norm; a 100-degree day can become a 50-degree night. A 50-degree day can become a 15-degree night. It's important to be prepared—not simply for comfort, but for survival.

Planning ahead is the first rule of backcountry travel. Study maps and know where you're going. Become informed about weather patterns, and know what temperatures and climatic conditions to expect. Use this information to plan your trip.

As you study your maps, determine where to obtain services—food, water, gas, ice, etc. Anticipate when you'll need to replenish fuel and supplies, and purchase them whenever you have the chance, since gas stations and stores are usually few in the vicinity of most remote parks.

Before you depart on a hiking journey, leave a detailed itinerary with a friend or family member. Be sure to indicate when you expect to return; call later if your plans change.

Backcountry Driving

Because there are so few amenities available in and around the more remote parks, you must not only bring your own supplies, but consider your vehicle a self-contained "survival module." Be certain that your vehicle is road-worthy and capable of withstanding whatever conditions you might face—a bumpy dirt road to the trailhead, high altitude, a rainstorm, etc. In case of emergency, your safety could literally depend on it.

I understand why the image of bouncing over a dusty road in a vintage auto has some romantic appeal; it symbolizes the highly cherished notion of the freedom of the open road. I've never let having an old car stop me from getting to the trailhead. Ever since my college days, I've driven across the desert, high into the mountains and from sea to shining sea, and to trailheads in vehicles made in Germany, Sweden and America—some with considerably more than 100,000 miles on their odometers.

Most hikers, though, will probably be more comfortable driving a well-maintained, comfortable and reliable vehicle, one that provides a sense of confidence and security—and a real measure of safety as well.

Naturalist Joseph Wood Krutch described venturing into nature as "rewarding travel in an unfrequented land." Such travel is rewarding for a number of reasons, not the least of which is the fact that many of our best hikes are across an "unfrequented land". We drive

Gear to Keep in Your Vehicle
continued . . .

- **Sewing kit** Buttons pop off when you least expect it.

- **Notebook or journal and pen** A good place to scribble your thoughts and take notes about your nature observations.

- **Binoculars for bird-watching.**

- **Prescriptions** If you're prone to hay fever, don't forget your medications.

- **A good book** The perfect companion during fair weather or foul, on the trail and off.

> *"Trails urge people to slow down, not to speed up."*
> —DAVID BURWELL

to remote trailheads on lonely roads that are part of the solitude that America's wildlands offer.

But in an unexpected situation, such as a vehicle breakdown, that feeling of peaceful solitude can quickly become a fearful experience in a hostile environment. Therefore, driving a road-worthy vehicle is of utmost importance.

The perils of driving include extreme heat and glare (especially when driving east in the morning or west in the afternoon); winter cold, ice and snow. Long, straight roads can become monotonous and sleep-inducing day or night. Dirt roads require special driving skills, and the unfamiliar territory demands navigational expertise. Weather conditions, including dust, wind and thunderstorms which can cause flash floods, are other difficulties faced by drivers.

Consider Alternate Transport to the Trailhead

Getting there can be part of the fun. When you take a bus through a scenic area, you'll often find that the driver is an enthusiastic local who is proud of the region and eager to share an insider's insights and tell you what not to miss.

Public or private transport that serves multiple trailheads might enable you to take a one-way hike—where you're dropped off at one trailhead and picked up at another.

Local businesses, particularly hotels, gas stations and outdoor stores offer parking/transport; in fact, often for a modest fee, you can pay someone to give you a lift to the trailhead.

In some national parks, free shuttle buses depart from large parking and staging areas and deliver hikers to trailheads. Other parks and popular hiking areas have private shuttle services to trailheads. By all means take advantage of them.

One of my favorite private shuttle services serves Zion National Park; the outfitter offers an early morning van ride to the top of Zion Canyon. You then hike down (and splash through) the Virgin River, squeezing through the Zion Narrows and emerging in the heart of the national park.

In Grand Canyon National Park, I've enjoyed the option of taking a private shuttle that services the south and north rims of the Grand Canyon. Hikers can do a one-way hike: down the South Rim and up the North Rim and get a ride back to the South Rim.

I took advantage of a van ride and jet-boat service to travel up Oregon's Rogue River. I then hiked from lodge to lodge (pretty cush, huh?) down the Rogue River National Recreation Trail. Contouring over bare canyon walls, the path offers dramatic views of the river and the rafters below and of high canyon walls towering 1,500 feet above the trail. Rogue River Trail is well worth hiking more than once, but with limited time, I appreciated the transit-assisted opportunity to hike it one-way instead of out-and-back.

One of the great pleasures of hiking in England is the availability of public transportation. In regions such as the Cotswolds and the Lake District, you can hike half a day or all day from point to point and catch a bus or taxi (don't laugh, taxis are easy to hail and not all that expensive) to take you to the beginning or pick you up at the end of a footpath. British rail service is excellent, too, and can be used to take you to or near a trailhead. Train from town to town, take a hike, and return.

On one of my favorite Euro hikes, I used a bus and a ferry to get to the trailhead and back to town. The adventure began when I boarded an early morning bus on the island of Crete. We stopped for breakfast (delicious yogurt and honey, fresh orange juice and strong Greek coffee), then continued into the dramatic White Mountains. After hiking through the famed Samaria Gorge ("The Grand Canyon of Greece"), I boarded a ferry for transport back to the coastal town where I was staying. Getting there and getting back was indeed part of the great day.

For a change of pace, try leaving your car in the garage and using the alternative transport options near home. Metropolitan transit systems in Boston, Seattle, Philadelphia or even Los Angeles are surprising in their scope and get you to some surprisingly remote parks and trails.

In terms of trails and transit to trailheads, San Francisco leads the way among American cities. A far-reaching bus system, along with a subway under San Francisco Bay and ferry service across the bay, enables hikers to access a spectacular network of trails.

"Tourons"

Stupid is as stupid does. Especially in the great outdoors. Despite the best efforts of the National Park Service and veritable thickets of warning signs, this summer you can bet at least one RV owner will attempt to drive a twelve-foot high vehicle under a ten-foot bridge; at least one warning-sign-disdaining visitor will test the temperature of a geyser to see if the water really is that hot; at least one hiker will start a midday hike across Death Valley; hundreds of visitors will feed the birds and bears.

Park rangers contrived the word "touron" (a combination of tourist and moron to describe these dummies). The origin of the term is uncertain, although rangers at Yellowstone National Park, which attracts more than its fair share of tourons, are sometimes credited with coming up with this word. The term has spread from coast to coast—at least among park personnel.

To avoid being branded a touron—or worse yet, stepping off a 2,000 foot cliff, carried out to sea by a riptide or stomped to death by a bison—use some common sense and follow park rules.

Sad to say, but day hikers account for a significant share of touronic activity in our national parks. Unprepared visitors get into big trouble on little hikes. Day hiking is not an inherently dangerous

> "The civilized man has built a coach, but he has lost the use of his feet."
> —RALPH WALDO EMERSON

Trailhead Parking Precautions

- Ask parkland managers about the safety of a particular trailhead.

- If a trailhead has a recent history of break-ins, plan to park elsewhere or arrange for a drop-off and pickup.

- Note the trailhead's appearance. Graffiti, broken auto glass, piles of beer cans or suspicious characters loitering about are clues to park elsewhere.

- Leave valuables at home (best idea) or lock them in the trunk (second best idea). Bring your wallet and keys with you rather than hiding them in your vehicle

- Hide a spare key under your car if you wish. Just remember that car thieves know all the easy places, so hide it in a greasy, grimy, difficult to reach spot.

- If you have a choice of trailheads, know that more formal trailheads tend to be safer than wide spots in the road, pullouts and dirt lots hidden from the highway.

activity, but a small number of casual hikers who abandon their common sense at the park entry station, who choose to tempt fate and break rules, give hikers a very bad name—tourons.

Trailhead Safety

Returning to the trailhead after a joyful day on the trail to find a car window smashed and the laptop computer and down jacket that you left on the back seat missing, can really make a day hike memorable—but not for the reasons you want it to be. Trailhead safety—for both vehicles and visitors—can be increased with a little knowledge about who is likely to do what where—and what you can do to prevent it.

The biggest (and almost only) bummer about hiking in Hawaii is the number of car break-ins at trailheads. With lots of visitors who like to hike, lots of rental cars and lots of un-patrolled trailheads, there are beaucoup break-ins. I don't mean to pick on the Aloha State because such trailhead break-ins occur in all 50 states. Break-ins are also a problem for New England hikers, who often cross state lines to take a hike; cars with out-of-state plates parked at rural trailheads are particular targets.

My friend Doug's old Volkswagen camper was the victim of one of the worst incidents of trailhead vandalism that I can remember. The V.W. was selectively stripped of knobs, hubcaps, a sun visor, a seat and much more—apparently all the parts the thief needed for his V.W. camper. The cost of the camper's replacement parts actually exceeded the value of the V-dub.

Surely some of the strangest occurrences of "vandalism" occur at the Mineral King Trailhead in Sequoia National Park. Rangers and fellow hikers report that for reasons unknown the local marmots have developed a taste for rubber. During spring and early summer, they sometimes gnaw on vehicle belts and hoses. Hikers either pray the critters leave their cars alone or park further down Mineral King Valley where the marmots are less numerous and walk up to the trailhead. Rangers advise hikers to check their engines before departing.

Some statistics are emerging that suggest that after three decades of "Lock your Car and Take Your Valuables with You" signs and campaigns, hikers are finally heeding this safety advice and locking their cars and taking their valuables with them. The result? Fewer reported car break-ins.

Anecdotal evidence supports another reason for a trailhead crime decline: the widespread acceptance of hikers and hiking. Years ago more tension existed between hikers (usually urban-dwellers) and rural locals, who felt resentful that land was taken out of productive use for something as silly as a park or trail. The economic benefits of visiting hikers are now more fully appreciated by rural chambers of commerce and most locals; hikers are apt to be warmly welcomed these days with helpful information and improved trailheads.

Still, if you have any suspicions (gut instincts are worth heeding as well) about parking at a particular trailhead, call a local ranger station or hiking club and inquire if any vandalism has occurred at the site. If you have any concerns, park in town or somewhere else.

If, despite all precautions, your car is broken-into or vandalized, report the incident to regional park authorities and/or the local law enforcement agency.

The Hiker's Checklist

- ❑ Day pack
- ❑ Boots
- ❑ Socks
- ❑ Underwear
- ❑ Pants or shorts
- ❑ Long-sleeved shirt or sweater
- ❑ Parka or windbreaker
- ❑ Hat
- ❑ Water in plastic bottles or canteen, and water filter (if you aren't packing all your water)
- ❑ Food
- ❑ First-aid kit
- ❑ Map and compass
- ❑ Sunglasses
- ❑ Sun block
- ❑ Insect repellent
- ❑ Pocket knife
- ❑ Flashlight
- ❑ Matches and fire starter
- ❑ Plastic bag

For Overnight, Add

- ❑ Large pack
- ❑ Ground cloth
- ❑ Tarp or tent and accessories
- ❑ Sleeping pad
- ❑ Sleeping bag
- ❑ Stove
- ❑ Cooking pots
- ❑ Eating utensils
- ❑ Food containers
- ❑ Toiletries
- ❑ Trowel (for digging latrine)

Chapter 5   All About Trails

LET US NOW ACKNOWLEDGE TRAIL-BUILDERS, OF THIS GENERATION, generations past and generations to come. The trail-builders art—and it is an art as well as a science—is vastly under-appreciated, even by seasoned hikers. Who blazed the first trails? Who builds trails today? How are they built?

Trail-builders themselves, most volunteer, some professional, are a very special, dedicated people. I've watched trail-builder Ron Webster practice his craft all over the mountains of Southern California for some 20 years. He brings some solid contractual and people skills to the job, including the ability to do cost-breakdowns and construction estimates for trails, and to manage crews from a diversity of back-grounds. My friend Ron is good at working with trail crews composed of at-risk youth. He teaches young men and women to be part of a team, to take pride in their work and to master many other social skills that will benefit them in their work and personal lives.

I particularly admire how the master trail-builder designs the route for a trail. After spending many, many hours on the slopes to be crossed by a new trail, he goes into what he calls "Alignment" in which he envisions the trail upon the mountain. It's a combination of a Zen state and a construction blueprint.

I love a hand-built trail, one that goes easy on the land, one that seems almost as much a part of the geography as a streambed. A good trail is like a good guide, subtly pointing things out and picking the very best route from place to place.

The idea of a grizzled old ranger, with pick and shovel and mule, heading into the wilderness to scratch out a new trail is romantic and colorful, but not how trails are made these days. Sophisticated trails advocates press their case in the strange speech of the land-use plan-ner, a jargon sprinkled with terms like viewsheds, visitor use days, greenbelts and easements.

To aid trails-ignorant urban planners, enthusiasts sometimes refer to the main trails as "freeways" and narrower connector trails as "on-

In This Chapter
- Trail-building yesterday and today
- Trail design
- Trail term glossary
- Trail signs
- Economic benefits of trails

ramps." The modern trail-blazer cuts deals with local politicians and isn't afraid to go eyeball-to-eyeball with developers to demand paths.

THE FIRST TRAILMAKERS were wild animals, breaking down brush as they journeyed to and from water. Prospectors used bear trails to get over the mountains, and many of today's best recreation trails are superimposed over miner trails, picked out by old bruin long ago.

Native Americans used game trails and fashioned new ones for trade and travel. Such trails rarely climbed via switchbacks; instead, they took the steepest and direct route. Out in what would become the Southwest part of the U.S., the Spanish blazed few new trails, contenting themselves with Indian pathways.

Anglo-Americans were tireless trailmakers. They hurried into the mountains to dig for metals, graze cattle and chop trees. They needed trails and they needed them right away. Trees were felled and brush cleared. Gunpowder was rammed in holes drilled into rock and the most immovable granite was blown to smithereens.

The years between 1890 and 1930 were a wonderful time to hit the trail. Historians call it in some parts of the country the "Great Hiking Era." Trail camps, fishing camps, and resorts were established and soon the mountainous regions were crisscrossed with trails.

An astonishing number of miles of national park and national forest trails were built by the young men enrolled in the Civilian Conservation Corps between 1933 and 1942. The Corps completed trail and conservation work that would be valued today at many hundreds of millions, if not billions, of dollars.

Trails Today

Trails, to the modern trail-builder and trail-planner, are no longer solely the lonely wilderness path of the mountain man. Nature trails, riverside promenades, suburban greenways and historical paths are a few of the more popular trail projects. Some trails groups are busy converting abandoned rail lines to trails while others are working to provide trails for the disabled.

Trails are not an end in themselves, trails advocates emphasize. They must be viewed within the broader context of the environment through which they pass, whether that environment is a remote wilderness or an urban gateway. And any cost of the path must be measured against what is lost by losing the trail AND the land.

Often it's not just a path that's endangered by insensitive development, but the whole damn place. In addition to providing an obvious recreational value, a trail is often an indicator of environmental conditions. When people walk a streamside, oceanside or mountainside trail, they likely form a constituency that cares about the past, present and future of the land this trail crosses. Conversely, when people can no longer walk a trail, it's likely some land misuse or abuse has occurred or will soon follow.

Trails are a precious resource, and we shouldn't shy away from the cost of building and maintaining them. They're a way for people to get out of the traffic and into our green spaces and wilderness. Most important of all, trails help keep a little green on the map.

The Art and Science of Trail-building

The science of trail-building is better known than the art. Trail construction and re-construction is often a contract to a contractor. The ranks of those who volunteer seem swollen by engineers and those from the building trades—people who like to build things. In Pasadena, California, employees of JPL (Jet Propulsion Laboratory) are avid hikers and turn out to help the trail system in the mountains next to their workplace—the San Gabriel Mountains. Yes, even rocket scientists like to help out here on earth.

Certainly there is a science to trail-building. I've read the contractor's specifications for building new trails and was surprised at how exact they are—spelling out the regulation tread width, grade and much more. Governmental agencies often conduct exhaustive environmental studies before allowing a shovel to hit the ground.

There is an art to trail-building, too. A well designed trail is a kind of living sculpture. Some modern trail-designers practice feng shui, the Chinese art of arranging elements (indoors or outdoors) in order to create flow and harmony.

True, few trails were designed with feng shui, but many of the best trails have it—a harmony with the landscape, its features and attractions, a pleasing arrangement of color and texture, form and lines.

A hand-built trail goes easy on the land. Even if it's just been completed, a hand-built trail has a way of looking like it's always been there.

A good trail designer has the eye of a landscape painter—or at least a landscape architect. Landscape, at least the way a trail designer uses the word means the sum total of an area's characteristics, particularly those that distinguish it from another area. The landscape's distinguishing patterns include its natural features—geography and flora—and may include its cultural landscape and structures as well. These landscape features, combined with the four basic elements of color, texture form and line, create an area's landscape character, which distinguishes it from its immediate surroundings.

Hikers are a visually oriented bunch. What you see on a trail is what you get and what you get from the hiking experience is often determined by what you see. And exactly what a hiker sees on a trail is often created by the trail designer.

One element of view is called sightlines—the forward view and rear view seen by a hiker on a given part of the trail. A good trail has good sight lines—that is to say, the path, real or imagined, that a hiker's eye follows when perceiving changes and contrasts in color,

"The laying of a trail . . . becomes not only a pleasure in itself, but an inducement to plan a better way of life, to contract worthwhile things, or to weave a better product in the loom of our being."
—EARLE AMOS BROOKS
A Handbook of the Outdoors

texture and form. A landscape itself has lines in it in the form of ridgetops, city skyline, the border between floral communities or between the natural and built worlds.

How the trail designer shapes the trail can shape a hiker's experience. Choosing when a trail should be contoured around a slope or switchback up it and switchback down it, can give two entirely different hiking experiences.

Workin' on the Trail

Most hikers take trails for granted. They figure some governmental agency is in charge of keeping pathways maintained. But in most cases, it's not park employees but trail users themselves that have "adopted" trails and the responsibility for their upkeep.

A trail (as well as those who hike it) benefits enormously if an organization, sometimes known in the hiking community as "Friends of the Trail" assumes stewardship for a path. Some Friends are informal hiking clubs while others are private non-profit organizations. Such groups advocate for a trail during the political process or when it's in the grasp of a government bureaucracy and also gather work parties to construct or maintain a trail. Sometimes a Friends of the Trail group will have full responsibility for a trail, while in other instances Friends supplement or support the trail's management by a public agency.

Trails need repair for two chief reasons: brush and erosion. In many regions of the country, brush or various forest "understory" plants grow quickly and can crowd the sides of a trail until the way becomes first narrow, then impassable.

Two of the worst hazards for both trail users and trail workers are poison ivy and poison oak. These three-leafed menaces can quickly close down a trail, at least to those bipeds allergic to them.

Erosion is the other enemy of trails and affects what is called the "tread"—that part of the path trod by hiking boots. Under compaction by boots, hoofs and mountain bike tires, the tread becomes so hard that it can't absorb surface water and erosion begins. Water travels about 15 times farther and faster on a compacted trail than natural soil; the resulting rivulets tear the trail and wash away the surface. Erosion then is what causes a trail to become rocky, dusty and scarred by deep gullies.

The trail-builder fights erosion by building water bars which drain trails and keep water from puddling up or running down the trail. Logs, rock piles and railroad ties are used to prop up the trail. A good trail has good drainage. Often trails are built with lots of switchbacks, in order to fight erosion.

Trail work is hard work. Volunteers work on the trail tread with pick and shovel, cut back brush with pruning shears. Workers construct and clean waterbars, paint trail markers, build bridges and rock walls. They master the cross-cut saw, the mattock, the axe, the hoe, the measuring wheel, the crowbar, the come-along. Some workers like the social aspect: volunteers come from all walks of life and are usually a friendly, conservation-minded bunch.

Above all, the volunteer trail builder learns about the environment and how to respect it. The hiker who works half a day with a hoe repairing an erosion-damaged path will never shortcut a switchback or an S-curve again.

As an investment in the future of our forests and parklands, and as a commitment to ensuring that the next generation has the opportunity to hike to the same places that you now enjoy, volunteer a little time to help build or maintain a trail.

> *If there's one essential ingredient to creating trails and trail systems, it's people. All the land and financing in the world won't blaze a trail if there aren't people championing the project.*
>
> —Bay Area Ridge Trail Council, In Support of Trails: A Guide to Successful Trail Advocacy

Trail Terms

alignment The layout of the trail in horizontal and vertical planes. The bends, curves, and ups and downs of the trail. The more the alignment varies, the more challenging the trail.

bed The excavated surface on which a trail tread lies.

brushing To clear the trail corridor of plants, trees, and branches, which could impede the progress of trail users.

brushing-in To pile logs, branches, rocks, or other debris at the start a closed trail to prevent it from being used.

center line An imaginary line marking the center of the trail. During construction, the center line is usually marked by placing a row of flags or stakes.

crown (crowning) A method of trail construction where the center portion of the tread is raised to allow water to disperse to either side of the trail.

crowned trail A trail bed built up from the surrounding area and sloped for drainage (usually by excavating trenches parallel to the trail).

flagging Thin ribbon used for marking during the location, design, construction, or maintenance of a trail project.

grade The amount of elevation change between two points over a given distance expressed as a percentage (feet change in elevation for every 100 horizontal feet, commonly known as "rise over run"). A trail that rises 8 vertical feet in 100 horizontal feet has an 8 percent grade. Grade is different than angle; angle is measured with a straight vertical as 90 degrees and a straight horizontal as 0 degrees. A grade of 100 percent would have an angle of 45 degrees.

grub (grubbing) To dig or clear roots and tree stumps near or on the ground surface of the trail tread.

gutter A trough or dip used for drainage purposes that runs along the edge of a trail.

maintainer A volunteer who maintains a section of trail as part of a trail-maintenance program of a trail organization.

maintenance Work that is carried out to keep a trail in its originally constructed serviceable condition. Usually limited to minor repair or improvements that do not significantly change the trail location, width, surface, or structures. Involves four tasks: cleaning drainage, clearing windfalls, brushing, and marking.

pruning The removal of normal vegetative growth that intrudes beyond the defined trail clearing limits.

read(ing) To study the terrain and obstacles to determine a course or possible locations for a trail through the area.

reconnaissance (recon) Scouting out alternative trail locations prior to the final trail route location being selected.

rehabilitation (rehab) All work to bring an existing trail up to its classification standard, including necessary relocation of minor portions of the trail.

rut Sunken groove in the tread, perpendicular to the direction of travel, usually less than two feet in depth.

trailbed The finished surface on which base course or surfacing may be constructed. For trails without surfacing, the trailbed is the tread.

tread The actual surface portion of a trail upon which users travel excluding backslope, ditch, and shoulder. Common tread surfaces are native material, gravel, soil cement, asphalt, concrete, or shredded recycled tires.

waterbar A drainage structure (for turning water) composed of an outsloped segment of tread leading to a barrier placed at a 45-degree angle to the trail; usually made of logs, stones, or rubber belting material. Water flowing down the trail will be diverted by the outslope or, as a last resort, by the barrier. Grade dips are preferred on multi-use trails instead of waterbars.

waterfall Steep descent of water from a height.

Trail Tools

ax (axe) A tool with a long handle and bladed head (single bit— one sharp side or double bit— two sharp sides) for chopping deadfalls from trails, shaping stakes for waterbars, and cutting notches for structures made of timber.

bush hook Used for clearing brush, briar, or undergrowth too heavy for a scythe and not suited for an ax. The bush hook with a 36-inch handle and 12-inch hooked blade (sharpened on one side) cuts easily on the "pull" stroke.

come-along A strong cable fitted with a ratchet to gain mechanical advantage for moving heavy objects over the ground with comparative ease. It is often used in trail work to move large rocks or bridge timbers.

clinometer A hand-held instrument used for measuring percent of trail grade. The user sights through the clinometer to a reference (usually a second person) and reads the measurement directly from the internal scale.

grub hoe A tool with a blade (various weights) set across the end of a long handle used in building and repairing trail tread and digging trenches.

loppers Better known by the suburban gardener as pruning shears, this long-handled tool with two opposing blades (by-pass or anvil) is used for cutting the limbs of heavy vegetation.

mattock A sturdy two-bladed tool with an adz blade that can be used as a hoe for digging in hard ground. The other blade may be a pick (pick mattock) for breaking or prying small rock or a cutting edge (cutter mattock) for chopping roots.

McLeod A forest fire tool that looks like an over-sized hoe with tines on the opposite blade. In trail work it is used to remove slough and berm from a trail and to smooth the tread.

measuring wheel (cyclometer) A device that records the revolutions of a wheel and hence the distance traveled by the wheel on a trail or land surface.

pick (pick-ax, pick-axe) A tool with a 36-inch handle and a head that has a point at one end and a chisel-like edge at the other. Used to loosen soil or rock.

pole saw (tree pruner) A pruning saw with a telescoping handle to trim branches that would otherwise be out of arm's reach. Some models have built-in loppers that can be operated from the ground with a rope.

Pulaski During the early 1900s, U.S. Forest Service Ranger Edward Pulaski of Idaho needed a good tool for grubbing and chopping fire lines, so he welded the blade of a pick to the back of an ax head and created what has come to be known as the "Pulaski." The modern Pulaski combines an axe bit with an adz-shaped grub hoe and is a very popular tool among trail-builders.

rock bar (pry bar) A four-foot bar of steel weighing 16 to 18 pounds with a beveled end used to move rocks.

shovel A tool with a broad scoop and a long handle for lifting and moving loose material.

Swedish safety brush axe (Sandvik) A machete-like tool with a protected short, replaceable blade and a 28-inch handle used to cut through springy hardwood stems.

trail dozer Bulldozers built specifically for trail construction. The pint-sized dozers are plenty powerful, able to remove most rock and roots from the trail bed, leaving a smooth trail surface.

weed cutters (weed whip, swizzle stick, swing blade) Tool with a serrated blade at the end of a wooden handle, used to clear trail corridors of succulent vegetation.

Kinds of Trails

access trail Any trail that connects the main trail to a town, road, or another trail system.

backcountry trail A primitive trail (can be open to motorized or nonmotorized users) in an area where there are no maintained roads or permanent buildings.

connecting or side trail Provides additional points of access to

Trail Days

By some hikers' reckoning, Trails Days, at least how we think of them now, began in California's Santa Cruz Mountains. Skyline to the Sea Trail, a gem of a 35-mile footpath that travels across redwood-forested slopes and through fern-filled canyons to the great blue Pacific, needed some maintenance and it turned out, this gem of a trail had many friends.

During one weekend in 1969, dedicated members of the Sempervirens Fund and the Santa Cruz Trails Association turned out more than 2,000 volunteers to dig, clear, prune and otherwise improve the path. Area volunteers put together an annual Trails Day that became a model for trails organizations statewide and planted the seed for a National Trails Day.

The American Hiking Society produces and promotes National Trails Day, an annual celebration held the first Saturday of each June with thousands of events across the U.S. to encourage hikers and newcomers to appreciate, preserve and maintain their local trails.

major trails—in particular the nation's national recreation, scenic, or historic trails per the National Trails System Act.

destination trail A trail that connects two distinct points (a trailhead and a point of interest) the destination. The trail user returns by the same route.

directional use trail A path designed in such a way as to encourage hikers to travel in one direction.

feeder trail A trail designed to connect local facilities, neighborhoods, campgrounds, etc. to a main trail.

extended trail Trails over 100 miles in length (as defined in the National Trails System Act).

hiker-biker trail An urban paved trail designed for use by pedestrians and bicyclists.

hiking trail Moderate to long distance trail with the primary function of providing long-distance walking experiences of a mile or more (often much more).

interpretive trail (nature trail) Short to moderate length trail (usually a quarter mile to one and a half miles long) with the primary function of providing an opportunity to walk and study interesting or unusual plants or natural features at user's pleasure. Interpretive signs or numbers corresponding to descriptions in a pamphlet often provide information about features found en route.

fire road Unimproved dirt road that allows fire fighting and ranger vehicles access to the backcountry.

frontcountry trail Less emphasis is put on minimizing contact with signs of the civilized world. The main objective is to provide enjoyable trail experiences within the vicinity of developed areas by utilizing the scenic and interpretative features of semi-urban, rural, and natural environments.

long distance trail In general a trail best characterized by length (more than 50 miles), linearity (follows a linear feature), and diversity (geographic and political).

loop trail: Trail designed so that the route is a closed circuit connecting a number of points of interest, giving hikers the option of not traveling the same section of trail more than once on a trip.

multiple-use (multi-use) trail A trail that permits more than one user group at a time (equestrian, hiker, mountain bicyclist, etc.).

out-and-back trail A one-way trail on which you travel to a destination then backtrack to the trailhead.

rail-trail A multi-purpose public path (paved or natural) created along an inactive rail corridor.

recreation trail A trail that is designed to provide a recreational experience.

side trail A dead-end trail that leads to features near the main trail.

single-track trail A trail only wide enough for one user to travel. Requires one user to yield the trail to allow another user to pass.

single-use trail One that is designed and constructed for only one intended use (i.e. hiking only).

spur trail A trail that leads from primary, secondary, or main trails to points of interest such viewpoints and campsites.

trail Route on land with protected status and public access for recreation or transportation purposes such as walking, jogging, hiking, bicycling, horseback riding, mountain biking, and backpacking.

way trail (social trail) Unplanned/unauthorized trail that develops informally from use and not designated or maintained by a governmental agency. A good way trail might lead to a pleasant off-the-main trail surprise; a bad way trail is one made by hikers who cut switchbacks.

> Do not tread, mosey, hop, trample, step, plod, tip-toe, trot, traipse, meander, creep, prance, amble, jog, trudge, march, stomp, toddle, jump, stumble, trod, sprint, or walk on the plants.
>
> —SIGN AT MT. RAINER NATIONAL PARK

Trail Sign Language

A trail sign is a board or a post of wood, metal or some kind of synthetic material that displays written, pictorial or symbolic information about the trail and/or the surrounding area.

A good trail sign boosts a hiker's safety and peace of mind. An unclear or misleading sign can stress, mislead, even endanger a hiker. A bad sign is worse than no sign at all.

To most hikers, a sign is a sign is a sign, but others in the field—trail-builders, park designers, pathway policy wonks—distinguish among five different kinds of signs, each having a distinct purpose.

Directional Signs help the hiker navigate from Point A to Point B. They provide the names of points-of-interest or destinations, as well as the mileage to those destinations. The way mileage is expressed varies by park agency and geography. Older signs tend to express mileage in fractions (DEER MEADOW 2¼) while newer ones use decimals and tenths (DEER MEADOW 2.2). When fractions are used, quarter-mile increments are usually the smallest trail measurement, though occasionally eighths and even tenths are used. When trail distances are expressed with decimals, the smallest measure is usually 0.1 (one-tenth of a mile), though a few signs use one-hundredth of a mile increments (DEER MEADOW 2.25).

Cautionary Signs warn of potential trail hazards such as poison ivy, bears or errant golf balls.

Regulatory Signs are the do-this and don't-do-that placards that encourage certain behaviors (OBTAIN WILDERNESS PERMIT) and discourage others (NO BICYCLE RIDING).

Interpretive Signs explain a natural or historical site (WORLD'S TALLEST LODGEPOLE PINE, THREE-FINGERED JACK'S CABIN) along the trail or near it.

Objective Signs give information about trail conditions (TRAIL NOT MAINTAINED) including the type of trail surface or warn about obstacles (BRIDGE OUT, 1.5 MILES).

Cosmic Signs are definitely not yet acknowledged by park official and sign-makers, but I'd like to see them added.

If, for example, lightning strikes a tree in front of you, that's the universe telling you to get off the mountain. Cosmic signs can also arise from cosmic thoughts and be put on signs, just like mileage markers. God, Mother Nature, great authors and poets often provide inspiration for cosmic signs. My friend Glen Owens occasionally puts up a sign deep in the Angeles National Forest that makes hikers stop and think beyond themselves and everyday concerns.

Marking the Trail

Modern trail way-marking divides into at least two camps with plenty of hikers in the middle. Safety-first trailmarkers believe in lots of signs. Their mission is to keep hikers on the trail so the more markers the better. Trail-marking minimalists say too many markers detract from the wilderness experience. Sign a few crucial junctions and call it a day, they say. Some of the most radical wilderness travelers advocate for the removal of all signs, knocking down all cairns and say let each hiker find his or her own way.

Blazes Increasingly rare, a blaze is cut (usually by an axe—ouch!) into a tree to indicate the trail route. Blazes are cut on both sides of the tree trunk so the hiker can see them coming and going. Woodsmen of earlier eras used blazes (most likely to be spotted these days along old trails) to mark paths in the eastern U.S. and Canada.

Cairns, ducks, monuments Stacking rocks along a treeless, rock-covered route guides hikers over terrain when a trail is not visible and placing a sign impossible. Often cairns are used above treeline on high slopes and mountain passes. Duck-placing is an art. A strategically placed cairn must be seen by both ascending and descending hikers. Too many ducks in a row makes hiking look like child's play and takes all the challenge out of route-finding, while too few can lead hikers astray.

Paint Ugh! Paint on rocks and trees waymarks the trail in some U.S. and European parks and forests. Hues are often color coordinated to particular trails. Instead of following the yellow brick road, you follow the orange paint blazes. Blazes can be squares, circles, triangles or a simple brush stroke.

Discs Modern markers of metal or plastic are affixed to trees, sometimes to rocks. Used sparingly, they're not too intrusive and keep hikers on the trail at confusing junctions and show where to cross a stream and where to rejoin the trail on the other side.

Trail Right-of-Way

You've probably seen those triangular yield signs posted at the trailhead for a multi-use trail. Arrows go around the triangle from symbols of a hiker to a horse to a bicycle.

It's a common symbolic presentation of trail right-of-way-rules: Hikers yield to equestrians, bicyclists yield to both equestrians and hikers.

The same rules apply when different users encounter each other going uphill or down. When two trail users from the same group meet—two hikers, for example—the uphill traveler yields to the downhill one. (Most uphill hikers are happy to pause to let descending hikers pass—if only for the opportunity to catch their breath.)

On Mountain Bikes

I'm often asked to weigh-in on the hikers-versus-mountain-bikers issue. I wish it wasn't a one camp versus another situation. But all too often it is. And I wish it wasn't such a hot button emotional issue. But it is.

It's even a hot-button issue for me when I recall the half-dozen times my companions and I have had brushes (literally) with careening mountain bikers. I try to remember that the great majority of mountain bicyclists aren't speed-crazy morons hell-bent on tearing up the terrain.

How big a deal is mountain bike use of the trail anyway?

It certainly varies greatly from park to park, mountain to mountain, path to path. On a wide, flat dirt road, no big deal. On a steep narrow path—a very big deal.

The happiest trails for me—and judging by the mountain of mail I've received about this issue—for most hikers, are those free of mountain bikes. I totally support the creation of more trails for everyone—for hikers, horseback riders, for cyclists, for walkers, for the disabled. But favoring trails for everyone doesn't mean I support everyone using the same trail.

Have I had happy hiking on multi-user paths? Of course. Many, many miles of it. Have I ever gone mountain biking? Yep. Our family of four owns four of them, and we go cycling on dirt roads and bike paths. Mountain biking is a great recreational activity, a fine family outing.

Some trails can accommodate hikers and cyclists—or even hikers, mountain bicyclists and equestrians. Provided that these multi-user trails are designed for, and can handle different users, they have my full support. But multi-user trails are not hiking trails because the recreational experience offered by these trails is different from—and usually incompatible with—that of a hiking trail.

A hiker's pace, far slower than that of mountain bicyclist, is in tune with the rhythms of nature. Hiking is a silent, low impact entry into the natural world—one free of machinery, including mountain bikes. Pathways designed for foot travel should be for foot travel only.

I support the American Hiking Society's philosophy, policies and positions in regard to mountain bikes.

- Hiking trails, or foot-only trails, are pathways developed and managed for quiet, slow travel and the enjoyment of nature away from mechanical conveyances, including bicycles.
- Trails should be managed for the primary purposes for which they are designated.

- No mountain biking in designated wilderness areas and areas under consideration for wilderness designation.
- Current National Park Service policy restricting off-road bicycle travel in national parks should continue.

Accessible Trails

A few years ago, when I was signing my newest hiking book at a book festival, a young man in a wheelchair quietly waited his turn. Shyly he said, "I used to love to hike, but since my accident I can't get out on the trail. Do you have any suggestions about wheelchair accessible trails?

It was one of the few times I've felt uninformed and unable to help someone interested in hiking.

"Well, I saw a guy with a wheelchair on a trail in one park, let me remember where that was," I began. "I know there are some accessible trails, but I'm not sure where."

I'll never forget the look of disappointment on his face.

"You might try some nature trails," I added lamely.

I ended up picking a half-dozen or so trails out of one of my guidebooks that I figured that a fit individual in a sports wheelchair could negotiate. Still, this man was a true hiker and needed some trail advice I couldn't provide very well.

Since then, I've learned about a modest—and growing—number of trail offerings to differently enabled hikers. Some 53 million Americans have disabilities, so an acute need exists for accessible trails. Such trails are crucial to ensure quality recreational opportunities for these many individuals.

Many local, state and national parks—including such crown jewels as Grand Canyon, Rocky Mountain, Yellowstone and Yosemite—have accessible trails. The free Golden Access Passport is available to permanently disabled individuals and their families.

Thanks to technological advances and good old ingenuity, beach wheelchairs have recently been introduced, allowing disabled individuals access to beaches, coastal paths and shorelines on both American coasts. They have been extremely popular wherever they have been put into use.

The U.S. Access Board is the federal agency that established guidelines and standards for accessible environments. Guidelines include provisions for the types of surfaces required for accessible trails, an unobstructed width of at least 36 inches and many more specifications.

Many state and private nonprofit groups push for improved outdoor recreation opportunities. Recreational Outdoor Accessibility for the Disabled (ROAD) mainstreams people with disabilities into Sierra Club activities, teaches outdoors skills to people with disabilities, tests accessibility of trails and recommends improvements. It also teaches club members how to assist people with disabilities on outings and educates the general public.

Along with pushing for more and better accessible pathways, we should all—challenged by a disability or not—work to ensure that everyone gets a chance to hit the trail and enjoy the pleasures of the great outdoors.

Trails Make Dollars and Sense

The hiking industry? Well, some would say it's an industry, or at least part of one. The outdoors recreation industry is a large one and growing. Outdoor-goers purchase some $10 billion worth of apparel and products per year.

Industry groups such as the Outdoor Recreation Coalition of America, the Sporting Goods Manufacturers Association's Outdoor Products Council and the Outdoor Industry Association produce enough annual statistics to make a hiker's head swim. Americans buy about $213 million worth of hiking boots and $284 million worth of backpacks each year. Los Angeles County (where urban legend has it that no one walks, much less hikes) supports a $300 million hiking equipment industry.

Three cheers for the American Hiking Society for being in the forefront of pointing out the economic benefits of hiking trails, a long-overlooked subject.

A Hike in Business: Hikers, while usually down-to-earth and unassuming as individuals, are also often a more upscale-than-average population. And they tend to spend money when they embark on a hiking adventure.

A study of Rio Grande National Forest visitors (more than half of whom listed hiking as their primary activity) revealed that each visitor spent about a thousand dollars for food, drink, and gas within a 50-mile radius of forest recreation sites. The National Visitor Use Monitoring Project 2001, as the study was known, also estimated that each visitor spent nearly $4,000 per year on outdoor recreation activities.

National Park Service studies have shown the many positive economic impacts of long-distance trails. A popular national park such as Everglades may generate $100 million or more for businesses located near the park.

Shorter trails through or near towns and cities have also proven to boost the local economy. Business owners near the 35-mile long Missouri River State Trail are pleased by the increased revenue brought by users of that popular pathway.

Urban and suburban trails can lead visitors and residents alike past historical and cultural sites as well as by cafés, shops and B&Bs. Trailside or trail-related businesses can reap increased revenue when linked—literally or figuratively—to a nearby trail.

A Hike in Home Values: A trail is now highly regarded as a neighborhood asset by homeowners. Recent housing industry surveys suggest a nearby walking/hiking trail is now a more desired amenity for homeowners than tennis courts or a golf course.

Economic Benefits of Trails

- Consumer spending on hiking gear
- Commerce and jobs created by hikers visiting recreation areas
- Property appreciation
- Traffic congestion relief
- Low-cost "health care"

—AMERICAN HIKING SOCIETY

Realtors in progressive communities are convinced a home located near a trail is easier to sell. Homeowners, too are convinced that living near a trail increases the value of their homes. Even apartment owners have found that location near a trail makes an apartment more attractive to would-be renters. In the real estate world, a walking/hiking trail is widely regarded as a valuable "lifestyle enhancement."

Studies by the cities of Denver and Seattle demonstrated the positive influence on property values brought by municipal walking/hiking trail. In Boulder, Colorado, the relationship between a home's proximity to one of the area's trail-laced greenways and home values is nothing less than astonishing. A recent study showed home values declined for each foot of distance from the trail. The average value of a home right next to a greenbelt is 32 percent higher than a similar home located 3,200 feet away from the greenbelt!

Trails Everywhere

American Trails, a nonprofit organization that promotes the creation, conservation and enjoyment of trails, envisions:

- Trails and greenways that are a part of everyday life, a quality system accessible to all people including a broad range of abilities, economic and cultural backgrounds within 15 minutes of every American home or workplace.

- A diverse trail system serving urban areas as well as wild and rural landscapes.

- An interconnected national system of trails and greenways used regularly by Americans and foreign visitors.

- Quality trail and greenway experiences that enables the appreciation of natural beauty, cultural and historic connections, and brings people back in touch with special places in the outdoors.

- Trails and greenways that promote the conservation of resources with a system that optimizes wildlife preservation and land and water stewardship.

- Trails and greenways that promote economic development, enhancing property values, business opportunities, tourism and marketability of communities.

- A trail and greenway system that is durable, affordable to maintain with a sustainable commitment of resources.

Chapter 6   On the Trail

GET TO KNOW YOURSELF AS A HIKER. IN THIS CHAPTER, I'LL SHARE the hiking world's collected wisdom about how average hikers traveling at an average pace over average terrain in average climatic conditions will arrive at their destination in an average time.

Of course there's no such thing as an average hiker. Every hiker is unique. That's why you have to get to know yourself and discover your personal pace and capabilities. The best hikers are not necessarily the ones who hike the farthest in a day, but the ones who know themselves, who stay within their limits, who truly enjoy happy trails.

I've learned that getting to know yourself as a hiker means not only knowing your good qualities, but also looking at parts of yourself that might be far from perfect. Naturally, this kind of self-examination isn't easy—but it will make you a better hiker.

For example, I'm proud of my trail-reading ability and endurance, but a bit dismayed by the amount of urban-life impatience I bring with me on the trail. You'd think I would mellow out after all these years of hiking or that I would instantly de-stress and adapt to nature's rhythms the instant I reached the trailhead, but the fact is it still takes me a while on the trail to mentally slow-down and to appreciate where I am in the moment.

As you get to know yourself as a hiker—your physical condition and limits, pace, moods and mental outlook—you'll have a more satisfying experience on the trail.

In This Chapter

- Determining your pace
- Evaluating a trail's difficulty
- Trail ethics and courtesy
- Hiker safety

SOME—OKAY, MANY HIKERS—are goal-oriented; they want to explore the entire length of the trail, climb every mountain, ford every stream, and take in every sight along the way.

Other hikers want to sleep in, start late and feel that one of the great pleasures of hiking is taking it slow and easy, savoring a welcome break from our over-scheduled lives.

Dawdling down the trail or sprinting to the summit are fine ways to go—as are a dozen different speeds in between. For safety's sake, at whatever your chosen pace, you need to be able to estimate your hiking speed and estimate how long it will take you to complete your hike. It's also helpful to understand how a trail's grade affects your hiking time and how park authorities determine how to rate a hike's difficulty—easy, moderate, difficult.

Timing is Everything

When does darkness fall? No this isn't a cosmic question; it's a highly practical one.

If it gets dark at 6 P.M. and you start what should be a three-hour hike at 1 P.M., you should be okay because you've left a two-hour cushion. If it gets dark at 5 P.M. and you started what turns out to be a ten-hour hike at 9 A.M., you might find yourself in serious trouble.

Day hikers lose track of time just about as often as they lose the trail. Rangers say that beginning and intermediate hikers rarely lose the well-traveled, well-signed footpaths in state and national parks; however, they frequently underestimate the length of time required to travel a particular trail.

Day hikers who miscalculate their time on the trail are sometimes unable to return to the trailhead before dark. This miscalculation can mean spending the night in the great outdoors (usually without the proper gear). Provided it's not ultra cold and you have the Ten Essentials with you, this could simply result in spending one uncomfortable, never-to-be-forgotten night of your life sitting by the trail, eagerly awaiting dawn's first light. (See Chapter 10, page 119 for more about the Ten Essentials.)

Or, absent the right gear, in bad weather, an unexpected night on the trail could be a disaster. For your safety, you need to learn to estimate how long a hike will take you to complete.

In the interest of full disclosure, The Trailmaster must confess that his very worst habit as a hiker is cutting things too close—that is to say, staying on the trail until the last rays of day. Curiosity, I suppose. I just have to see what's on the other side of the mountain. While I've never been caught out after dark, I have had to sprint back to the trailhead in the twilight more times than I care to remember or admit.

If you get an early start and by noon you're only halfway to your destination, re-evaluate your goal. Either you've underestimated the length of the trail, misjudged the difficulty of the terrain, or over-estimated your pace. For whatever reason you end up on the trail far

> *"Adopt the pace of nature:*
> *Her secret is patience."*
> —RALPH WALDO EMERSON

longer than you anticipate, it can be discouraging to say the least and, quite possibly dangerous, to so miscalculate.

Another factor in timing a hike is your energy level. If you use up two-thirds of your energy getting to the hike's halfway point, what happens? Sometimes you can reach down inside yourself and come up with some reserve steam, but sometimes you just can't. Avoid putting yourself in the position of having to muster every ounce of strength just to get back to the trailhead.

Pacing Yourself

- Choose the pace that's best for you.
- Rest once an hour for five to ten minutes. To keep your momentum and to avoid stiffness, several shorter rest periods are better than one long one.
- Set a steady pace, one you can keep up all day.
- Wear a watch, not because you have an appointment with a waterfall and you have to be punctual, but because a watch gives you some idea of pace and helps you get back to the trailhead before dark.

No less an authority than the U.S. Army figures that a male soldier hikes about 100 steps a minute and a female soldier hikes about 120 steps a minute to maintain a three-mile-an hour pace. (Of course, average number of steps per minute and per mile have to do with size differences not gender differences. Men and women of the same size have about the same size stride.)

Leave it to the Army to quantify everything for us. Let's remember that the military's stats are based primarily on hikers aged 18 to 22, who are likely in better physical condition than the population at large.

Adding up the Miles

Beginning hikers in particular can get overly obsessed by mileage, sometimes equating a hiker's success with mileage covered. Those who run for exercise and pay close attention to their miles jogged per week often bring a goal-oriented, gotta-do-x-number-of-miles mindset to their hikes.

Of course a hike's "success" can be measured in many more ways than miles covered: the number of bird species counted, finding one rare wildflower, exploring that side trail to a hidden waterfall.

Your friend who's been hiking for years might consider 15 miles a modest day hike. You might think five miles is an ample amount of ground to cover.

Judging a Hike's Difficulty

A trail's degree of difficulty—also called its difficulty level or difficulty rating—can greatly vary hiking time.

Park agencies and guidebook writers often assist hikers by rating

Miles per hour, minutes per mile

Some fitness experts divide walking into three speeds:

Strolling: 20 minutes per mile, low-key exercise.

Brisk walking: 15 minutes per mile, the pace of the vigorous exercise walker.

Aerobic walking: 12 minutes per mile, for very advanced fitness walkers.

Exercise walking speed is much better defined than hiking speed, which is influenced by many variables. Here are three speeds for the sake of discussion:

Hiking on level or near-level ground: 2 to 3.5 miles per hour

Hiking uphill or at elevation: 2 miles per hour

Cross-country travel or steep climbs: 0.5 to 1.5 mile per hour

the degree of challenge a trail presents to the average hiker. Of course the "average" hiker varies widely as does the average hiker's skills, experience and conditioning. No matter how skilled the trail-evaluator, "degree of difficulty" for a particular hike or trail is inevitably subjective.

A path's elevation gain and loss, exposure to elements, steepness and the natural obstacles a hiker encounters along the way (boulder field, six creek crossings, etc.) figure prominently in the hike difficulty equation, too. High or low temperatures and common climatic conditions also influence a hike's difficulty rating.

During my 20 years or so of making difficulty evaluations, I've rated hikes with a modified easy-moderate-difficult system. My day hike rating in brief is:

Easy Less than 5 miles with an elevation gain of less than 700 to 800 feet. An easy day hike is suitable for beginners and children.

Moderate 5 to 10 miles with less than a 2,000-foot elevation gain. You should be reasonably fit for these.

Difficult Hikes over 10 miles, and those with more than a 2,000-foot elevation gain.

I often qualify the basic ratings (easy—except for the steep side trail to Trillium Falls). Sometimes a hike's difficulty doesn't fit neatly into one category so I'll combine ratings, as in "moderately easy" or "moderately difficult." I've been known to add a personal touch to my ratings, too: easy—a walk in the park. Difficult—a challenge to mountain goats.

During my long tenure as the *Los Angeles Times* hiking columnist, one editor, for reasons that I never fully understood, insisted that I substitute "strenuous" for "difficult," so during his editorship of my column, I rated my hikes easy-moderate-strenuous.

Some guidebook authors use graphics such as a one-to-five star method or a one-to-five hiking boots system to rate a hike's difficulty; others use a numeric hike rating system from one (easiest) to ten (brutal).

The U.S. Forest Service (and other park agencies) uses a level of difficulty system that seems to rate the hiker as much as the hike:

Easiest A trail requiring limited skill with little challenge to travel.

More difficult A trail requiring some skill and challenge to travel.

Most difficult A trail requiring a high degree of skill and challenge to travel. Such a hike may be at high altitude, be extremely rugged or have a major elevation gain.

Some hiking guidebook writers and park agencies dodge the whole "How difficult is this hike?" question entirely and instead state the time it will take to walk the trail, (i.e. 2.75 hours). Guesstimating a hiking time for someone else usually irks hikers far more than giving a particular hike or a trail a rating and is often considerably more inaccurate.

Easy? Moderate? Difficult? It's difficult to be objective even if, as I have, you've rated hundreds of hikes. I've done hikes when I was feeling very low-energy and (until I double-checked mileage and elevation gain with rangers) was ready to pronounce them more difficult than they really are. On the other hand, I've had high energy days, when I charged up 3,000 feet in 5.5 miles and nearly gave the hike a moderate rating until I looked at the elevation gain figures.

Making the Grade

Grade is the amount of elevation change between two points on the trail over a given direction. This elevation change between points is expressed as a percentage (change in feet in elevation per 100 horizontal feet of trail, known to trail-builders and engineering types as "rise over run"). What you and I call uphill and downhill, trail builders call positive grade and negative grade.

To determine the grade of a trail, divide the number of feet of ascent by 5,280. (The hiker who can work such problems in her head while walking a trail has my admiration; the rest of us will probably need to pause here and use pencil and paper.)

Let's say you're hiking exactly one mile from the trailhead (elevation 1,200 feet) to the top of Inspiration Point (1,412 feet). Subtract the trailhead elevation from the destination to get the trail gain in feet. Next divide 212 feet by 5,280 feet in a mile. You get about 0.04 or a 4 percent grade—a very modest grade.

After a while you'll start calculating your hiking speed and grade automatically just like most guidebooks and park agency publications do.

Try it again. Let's say you're bound for Eagle Roost, a 4-mile round trip hike with a 1,000 foot elevation gain. That's a gain of about 500 feet per mile, or a 10 percent grade. Most national park trails, as well as those trails of many other park agencies are designed to a maximum 10 percent grade, which presents a mildly aggressive but not too difficult pace.

Lots of trails in lots of places were built before this 10 percent grade standard was widely adopted, so if you find yourself breathless on a 15 percent, or even steeper grade don't be surprised.

Estimating Hike Time

Those new to hiking and/or want to be sure to stay out of trouble, can use a very conservative formula. Figure your average hiking pace at two miles an hour and then add an hour for each 1,000 feet of elevation gain.

Returning to our hypothetical example of that 4-mile hike to Eagle Rock with the 1,000-foot gain. We figure two hours for the distance (2 miles an hour) plus another hour for the 1,000-foot elevation gain. Estimated hiking time is three hours.

Here's what you might read in a guidebook and how you can do the math:

> "Commonly we stride through the out-of-doors too swiftly to see more than the most obvious and prominent things. For observing nature, the best pace is a snail's pace."
>
> —EDWIN WAY TEALE

Eagle Roost Trail

Pine Camp to Eagle Roost
4 miles round trip; 1,000 foot gain

Miles ÷ Miles per hour = Hours for mileage
4÷2 = 2 hours

Elevation ÷ 1,000 = Hours for elevation
1,000 ÷ 1,000 = 1 hour

Hours for mileage + Hours for elevation
2+1 = Estimated hiking time = 3 hours

During my 20-plus years of chronicling hikes, no reader has ever complained to me that a hike I described was too easy.

The worst and most frequent complaints about mileage come not, as you might expect, from tenderfooted newbies, but from fitter-than-average individuals who walk or jog regularly—usually on flat terrain and on even surfaces such as city streets or the track at the local high school. A typical complaint: "Trailmaster, I run five miles a day, five days a week and I know what five miles is and believe you me, that hike you described was no five miles. It had to be seven miles at least, maybe eight."

Gently I respond to such a complainant by telling him how pleased I am that he is out there enjoying nature. I then point out how every hiking step, because of the uneven surface of the trail and its ups and downs, is just a little bit different from the last; a jogger on the track has a much more measured gait. That hike might have *seemed* like eight miles, but it measures only five. Really.

On Switchbacks

You don't know what you've got 'til it's gone and I never fully appreciated the switchback until I hiked in New England.

Let me explain.

As a Californian, I was brought up hiking in the local mountains—the San Gabriel and San Bernardino ranges—which reach 10,000 feet. Later in my youth, I hiked the High Sierra, the Cascades and the Rockies.

My first (hiking) trip "back East" as we say in the West, occurred during the summer between my freshman and sophomore year in college. Before I hit the trail, I wondered what challenge the relatively low mountains of New England could present to one used to scaling high mountains. How difficult could it be to summit a 3,000-foot peak?

Quite difficult indeed, I soon discovered. Short in stature the East's mountains might be, but the trails sure are steep, and often left me gasping. After my Eastern friends took me hiking on some

> "Mountains cannot be surmounted except by winding paths."
> —GOETHE

switchback-less trails in the Appalachian and White mountain ranges, I felt like a whipped puppy.

The reason? Few or no switchbacks. I learned by experience: It's lots easier zigzagging up the shoulder of a mountain than taking a straight line up it!

It seems many Eastern pathways were in use several hiker generations before switchbacks became integrated into trail design. From homesteader times to the early recreational hiking era, trails extended from point to point without a zig or a zag.

Meanwhile, west of the Rockies, trailblazers took a different approach. Many now-popular pathways were first prospectors' trails constructed with switchbacks for the use of pack animals. This switchbacking tradition continued when trail use changed from business to pleasure. Traditionally, Western land has been cheap and there's been plenty of room to roam, so that a trail builder can afford "the luxury" of long, gentle switchbacks.

Many years after my rude awakening to a mountain world without switchbacks, I returned East (several times in fact) to do field research and write a book about the great hikes of New England. By this time I had learned my lesson: never underestimate the difficulty of a trail without switchbacks.

In the more densely populated East, with a tight mix of private property and public right-of-way, trails often needed to follow property boundaries. Nowadays most new trails are constructed with switchbacks, so Eastern parks and preserves are closing the switchback gap.

England, like New England, has a similar switchback shortage. From the Cornwall Coast to the Yorkshire Dales, Ye Olde Trails were designed centuries before the "invention" of the switchback. Hiking from the car park to the top of those pastoral-looking hills often proves harder than it looks on a pathway built in the 18th century.

Time and trail design marches on. Let us salute the switchback, one of mankind's most useful inventions.

Tangible and Intangible Factors Affecting Hiking Speed

Trail tread (detailed in "All About Trails" chapter) is another determining factor in hiker speed. Obviously a brisk pace is easier to maintain on a smooth and wide trail than on rocky and root-covered one, when it's necessary to look down at your feet just to stay upright.

Hiker biorhythm Not to get too New Age-y on you, but every hiker has a different biorhythm—you might be a "morning person" and your best friend a night owl. We all have different internal clocks and different energy levels on the trail.

I'm an early morning, crack-of-dawn kind of hiker—provided I've had a cup of coffee before I hit the trail. Bottom of my biorhythm is midafternoon, 2 to 3, when my usually frisky self slows to a

Hike-ku
Thighs burn on switchbacks
no stairs escalator here
quads don't fail me now

Elementary Trail Courtesy

- Leave your electronic music machines at home.

- Dogs, depending on the personality of the individual pooch, can be a disruption to hikers and native wildlife. Be warned, many state and county parks, as well as national forest wilderness areas, don't allow dogs, either on or off a leash.

- No smoking on trails.

- Resist the urge to collect flowers, rocks or animals. It disrupts nature's balance and lessens the wilderness experience for future hikers.

- Litter detracts from even the most beautiful backcountry setting. If you packed it in, you can pack it out.

- You have a moral obligation to help a hiker in need. Give whatever first aid or comfort you can, and then hurry for help.

- Don't cut switchbacks.

Leave No Trace

Plan ahead and prepare
- Know the regulations and special concerns for the area you'll visit.
- Prepare for extreme weather, hazards, and emergencies.
- Schedule your trip to avoid times of high use.
- Visit in small groups. Split larger parties into groups of 4 to 6.
- Repackage food to minimize waste.
- Use a map and compass to eliminate the use of marking paint, rock cairns or flagging.

Travel and camp on durable surfaces
- Durable surfaces include established trails and campsites, rock, gravel, dry grasses or snow.
- Protect riparian areas by camping at least 200 feet from lakes and streams.
- Good campsites are found, not made. Altering a site is not necessary.

In popular areas
- Concentrate use on existing trails and campsites.
- Walk single file in the middle of the trail, even when wet or muddy.
- Keep campsites small. Focus activity in areas where vegetation is absent.

In pristine areas
- Disperse use to prevent the creation of campsites and trails.
- Avoid places where impacts are just beginning.

Dispose of waste properly
- Pack it in, pack it out. Inspect your campsite and rest areas for trash or spilled foods. Pack out all trash, leftover food, and litter.
- Deposit solid human waste in catholes dug 6 to 8 inches deep at least 200 feet from water, camp, and trails. Cover and disguise the cathole when finished.
- Pack out toilet paper and hygiene products.
- To wash yourself or your dishes, carry water 200 feet away from streams or lakes and use small amounts of biodegradable soap. Scatter strained dishwater.

banana slug-like pace. After that slowwwww hour, I tend to get a second wind, so to speak, and resume a normal (but not as fast as the morning) speed.

Knowing my own biorhythm, I try to accomplish most of a hike's steepest climbs and elevation gain in the morning. When I hike with companions, I try to get a feel for their internal clocks as well, and pace the hike accordingly.

On the Trail

Leave what you find

- Preserve the past: examine, but do not touch, cultural or historic structures and artifacts.
- Leave rocks, plants and other natural objects as you find them.
- Avoid introducing or transporting non-native species.
- Do not build structures, furniture, or dig trenches.

Minimize campfire impacts

- Campfires can cause lasting impacts to the backcountry. Use a lightweight stove for cooking and enjoy a candle lantern for light.
- Where fires are permitted, use established fire rings, fire pans, or mound fires.
- Keep fires small. Only use sticks from the ground that can be broken by hand.
- Burn all wood and coals to ash, put out campfires completely, then scatter cool ashes.

Respect wildlife

- Observe wildlife from a distance. Do not follow or approach them.
- Never feed animals. Feeding wildlife damages their health, alters natural behaviors, and exposes them to predators and other dangers.
- Protect wildlife and your food by storing rations and trash securely.
- Control pets at all times, or leave them at home.
- Avoid wildlife during sensitive times: mating, nesting, raising young, or winter.

Be considerate of other visitors

- Respect other visitors and protect the quality of their experience.
- Be courteous. Yield to other users on the trail.
- Step to the downhill side of the trail when encountering pack stock.
- Take breaks and camp away from trails and other visitors.
- Let nature's sounds prevail. Avoid loud voices and noises.

—COURTESY OF THE LEAVE NO TRACE CENTER FOR OUTDOOR ETHICS

Leave No Trace Principles of Outdoor Ethics

- Plan ahead and prepare
- Travel and camp on durable surfaces
- Dispose of waste properly
- Leave what you find
- Minimize campfire impacts
- Respect wildlife
- Be considerate of other visitors

Taking Care of the Trail

Deadfalls If a tree falls on a trail and no one is around to hear it, was there a sound? While you're contemplating that one, consider moving that fallen tree off the trail so others may pass. If you can drag the deadfall off the trail without hurting yourself (no heroics, please) or ripping up the trail corridor, go for it. If the tree or tree limb is too heavy or too awkwardly placed to move, choose a route around it that's sensitive to the environment and the safety of your fellow hikers.

Travel in single file This one's pretty obvious. Most footpaths are made one-hiker wide and don't require widening by tromping on either side of the tread. Doubling up on a single-track trail is neither a safe nor eco-friendly way to go.

Never cut switchbacks Repeat: Never cut switchbacks. In fact, help trail maintenance crews by moving brush, rocks or other impediments to travel in order to block those shortcuts made by less eco-enlightened trail users.

Sensitive areas Staying on the trail is always a good idea, but it's absolutely essential for the protection of certain fragile types of terrain such as bogs and alpine meadows. Also be sure to stay on the trail while hiking through sensitive bird and wildlife habitat.

Muddy going We hikers have a lot to learn from six-year-old boys, especially when it comes to mud. Your basic, All-American little boy has a primal attraction to mud and, if left to his own devices, will hike right through the middle of a muddy trail. Funny enough, so should you. To best preserve the trail, hike through the mud rather than creating a new route that detours around mucky areas.

Washouts Overuse, poor design and weathering contribute to trail erosion. Step carefully across or around washouts, searching out the most secure footing. Tell the local land managers about pathways that need repair.

Hiker Hygiene

- Sometimes chemical toilets, even relatively clean ones, reek to high heaven, but use porta-potties whenever possible.
- Avoid leaving behind a urine smell for other hikers to whiff by peeing well away from picnic areas, campsites and the trail itself.
- Don't pee into the wind. Guys may, however, write their names in the dust—just because they can.
- Properly dispose of human waste. Dig a cathole six inches deep with your heel—better yet with a plastic trowel. Choose a disposal site out of sight of the trail, trail camps or vista points and at least 200 feet away from water.
- Dispose of toilet paper by sealing it in a plastic bag and packing it out. (The most eco-correct hikers use leaves to wipe themselves.)
- Wash your hands. Wash after relieving yourself and before preparing or eating meals.
- Treat all backcountry drinking water.
- Don't share water bottles, bandanas, etc.
- Towel dry. After getting wet, you can drip dry or use a bandana, but a better way to dry is to take along one of those small but extremely absorbent "hike/camp" towels that you can purchase at an outdoor retailer.
- For women only: Hiking, like other challenging physical activities, can alter your menstrual cycle. Bring necessary sanitary supplies and pack out any waste in plastic bags.

Hiker Safety

Alas, backcountry travelers are not always immune from urban attitudes, stresses and crimes. Most people you meet in the great outdoors are as friendly and as well-intentioned as you are, but it's not unheard of to meet a creep on the trail.

While most of our parks and preserves are far safer than our urban environment, hikers—particularly women hikers—must stay alert. Your "street smarts" coupled with your trail sense are two keys to avoiding trouble.

Know that national park, national forest, state park and regional park authorities are committed to protecting the public. Many of the "rangers" you see on patrol are peace officers—meaning they have the authority to write citations, make arrests, etc., just like their city cop counterparts.

Many park users—both good citizens and miscreants—don't realize that such rangers have arrest powers. A couple of times I've watched rangers make arrests, which are handled by the book just like any trained police officer, though often with the addition of an interchange something like this one:

DRUNK: (belligerently) So what if I did? What are you going to do—arrest me?

RANGER: Yes, I am.

DRUNK: But you're just a ranger. You can't do that.

RANGER: (pulling handcuffs from belt) Yes, I can.

Call on land agency law enforcement personnel if you feel at all uncomfortable about anyone/anything; they're dedicated to not only protecting the land, but public safety as well.

Safety Tips for Hikers

- Tell a trusted friend or relative where you're going. If the itinerary is at all complicated, write it down, have your friend write it down. At the very least, include a phone number for the park/place you're visiting, the trail you're taking and expected return time.
- While telling someone your plans is better than telling no one, telling someone familiar with hiking is better than dear, sweet, but trail clueless Auntie Em.
- If you're traveling a remote trail or taking an unusual route, or simply want to cover all the safety bases, leave your itinerary and an emergency contact number with the supervising ranger station.
- Sign in and out at the trailhead register. If you get in trouble, emergency workers will know where to start looking for you.
- Use caution when sharing plans with strangers. By all means small-talk about hiking or anything else, but perfect strangers don't need to know where you're spending the night or your exact plans.

Hike-ku
Lizard on the trail
going where in a hurry
where now is your home?

- Pay attention to your instincts and abandon your plan if it feels wrong. More than once I've terminated a hike when the activities of the characters nearby felt suspicious.
- Beware of anyone who acts hostile, drunk or drugged. Don't respond to taunts or provocation of any kind.
- Hiking with one or more companions reduces the potential for harassment.
- Dress conservatively (the hiker's layered look is definitely in that category) to discourage unwelcome attention.
- Hike trails away from roads and motor vehicles. Hikers are most likely to encounter harassment in backcountry accessible to four-wheel drive vehicles; unfortunately, a small minority of the four-wheelin' crowd sometimes hassles hikers.
- Have an emergency plan. Know where the nearest ranger station and hospital emergency room is located in relation to the trail you're hiking.

Hiker Myths—or Advice to Forget

Myth: Fast-moving water is the safest stream water to drink. Nope. Turbulent water keeps that nasty Giardia in suspension while slow water at least lets it settle to the bottom.

Myth: Warm someone with hypothermia by slipping naked into a sleeping bag with the victim. Better not. The sudden heat can warm the blood too fast, straining the heart and propelling the victim into shock.

Myth: Moss grows only on the north side of trees. In near-perfect conditions, moss (and lichens) do tend to thrive on the northeast sides of trees and rocks. Don't count on moss for finding your way, however, because it also grows almost anywhere that's wet and out of direct sunlight.

Myth: Treat a snake bite by making cuts around the wound and sucking out the venom. Such treatment can spread the venom and cause infection has long been medically out of vogue. Get the victim to the hospital!

Myth: Pee around the campsite perimeter to mark your territory and scare away wild animals. Sorry, it's not an effective technique and apparently not at all scary to the animals.

Myth: Lost? Hike downstream to civilization. Following a river might help you find your way out of the woods, but don't count on it. In the High Sierra, streams dead-end at glacial lakes; in Florida, streams flow into swamps and bogs. In many mountain ranges, the lost hiker would do better to follow a ridge.

Myth: Menstruating women shouldn't hike in bear country. Bear experts say there's no evidence bears are drawn to women at "that time of the month."

Trail Wisdom: Walk with Gratitude

"GOD has two dwellings: one in heaven, and the other in a meek and thankful heart," declared Izaak Walton, the seventeenth-century English writer now regarded as the patron saint of fishing.

Walton's walks by the River Dove and along the banks of many other brooks and ponds, inspired him to write *The Compleat Angler,* still regarded as the greatest book ever about fishing. His book combines practical advice on the art of angling with some highly moral and spiritual passages. Walton's gratitude for God's gifts, the beauties of pastoral England and the companionship of his fellows shines right through in his book, as popular now as it was 300 years ago.

"Nobody expresses their gratitude about anything or thanks me," you say. Likely as not, you're probably right. Try to remember the last time anyone thanked you for anything. It was probably a "Thanks-and-have-a-nice-day," at the check-out counter from a supermarket cashier or a "Thanks for your order," from a fast-food franchise. Such gratitude!

Now try to remember the last time anyone thanked you for anything important. It's a dispiriting cycle: we rarely get thanks, and we rarely give it. Even those of us who try hard not to be thoughtless are often thankless—except perhaps for the one hour a week we spend inside our house of worship.

My suggestion: On one walk a week use a few minutes of your time to exercise your gratitude while you stretch your limbs. List everything in your life that you are thankful for, and everything that you enjoy. Contemplate this list on your walk.

Warning: this exercise in gratitude might require considerable spiritual effort, may stretch, to the point of strain, a rarely used muscle. Expressing thanks might seem ever-so-saccharine; to the most curmudgeonly among us, it might elicit a gag response.

And yet walking with an attitude of gratitude takes us someplace special. The way it helps us is by bringing our life into balance. Just as walking integrates the body and mind, expressing gratitude integrates what's all right with our world with what's wrong.

Giving thanks brings our life into harmony. No wonder scripture, such as this passage from Psalm 92, often describes gratitude toward God as "singing praises."

We can be thankful for possessions and money and yet for the freedom to walk the whole earth, and for the great benefits of our creative spirit, our life and health, we consider ourselves under no obligation to express any gratitude.

By expressing our gratitude, we can walk from feeling stressed to feeling blessed. A grateful thought toward heaven is the simplest of prayers.

Walk with gratitude.

Myth: Start a fire by rubbing two sticks together. Theoretically possible, but most people will fall over exhausted before getting even a wisp of smoke. Ever watch the fire-deprived contestants on the television show, "Survivor"? Think matches and a fire-starter kit—or flint and steel if you want to play frontiersman.

Chapter 7 Hiking Solo or with Companions

WHAT DO YOU WANT TO GAIN FROM A DAY ON THE TRAIL? Happiness found? Friendship deepened? Curiosity satisfied? Calories burned?

Happiness is a particularly difficult benefit to evaluate; if we agree that humans are social animals and that happiness is a quality that must be shared, it would appear that the hiker in good company might be happier than the one who hits the trail time and again alone. If a hiker's strongest motivation is to discover what's on the other side of the mountain, such a discovery can be just as satisfying—perhaps more so—alone, as in a group.

I enjoy hiking alone and with companions. During the many years I wrote a weekly hiking column for the *Los Angeles Times*, I was required to hike—and write about—52 trails per year. Except for the times when I could convince a friend to take a day off, or was able to spring a ranger for a day out of the office, I took the great majority of my "work" hikes alone.

Occasionally I feel lonely on a solo adventure, but most of the time I'm happy keeping my own company. When I'm hiking alone, I particularly enjoy meeting rangers and passersby on the trail. As the nature writer Joseph Smeaton Chase put it: "You meet out-of-the-way people in out-of-the-way places."

I also enjoy hiking in company. I love hiking with my family, guiding groups of kids, hitting the trail with friends. When our family hosts out-of-town friends and relatives, I like to show them the wonders of our local trails.

In This Chapter
- Hiking solo
- Hiking with company
- Women on the trail
- Hiking with dogs

> *"To sit in solitude, to think in solitude with only the music of the stream and the cedar to break the flow of silence, there lies the value of wilderness."*
>
> —JOHN MUIR

HIKING ALONE OR WITH COMPANY is strictly a matter of personal preference. Each way has much to recommend it.

Some newcomers begin hiking with a group until they gain a measure of confidence and then choose to go solo.

Other newbies start walking solo then discover they enjoy sharing the way with a particular trail buddy, a group of hiking companions, or a whole hiking club. Many hikers like to alternate between hiking with friends and family and hiking solo.

Hikers have a broad range of abilities, interests and enthusiasms. The company they choose to keep on the trail reflects that diversity.

Hiking Solo

Too many so-called hiking authorities have wrongly turned a positive suggestion "For maximum safety, hike with a companion" into a negative absolute: "Never hike alone."

While there is no question that it's safer hiking with a group than solo, "How much safer?" is a legitimate question to ask.

Is the risk of hiking solo so great that each and every hiker should wait until he/she has company in order to hit the trail?

Absolutely not. Go take a hike. Alone. The risks, while often overstated, are real, and the precautions needed are crucial, but such risks and the requirement for additional precautions are not reasons to decide you can't hit the trail solo.

Having two or three in your party is a definite advantage if something goes wrong; someone can go for help. Four eyes are better than two; a hiking partner may notice a danger that you overlook. You might remember essential gear your hiking buddy forgot. This safety-in-numbers theory holds for hiking as it does for most forms of outdoor recreation from camping to kayaking, rock climbing to mountain biking.

Hiking with a group—or at least with a trail-seasoned friend—is a good idea for first-time hikers. Most inexperienced hikers are uncomfortable going solo.

Sometimes, after a few hikes, a craving for solitude develops—by which time you should be able to take care of yourself on the trail. There's a lot to be said for solitary hiking, as the writings of Thoreau, Whitman and Muir would seem to indicate.

I can speak with some authority on the subject of hiking solo since I'm often alone on the trail. Most of my friends have what they remind me are "real jobs" and can't answer the call of the wild with me in the middle of the week when I tend to go hiking.

I enjoy hiking with my male friends, with my spouse and my children or "on business" with a ranger or a trail advocate showing me a new trail. Solo hiking, however, encompasses about 80 percent of my hiking experiences.

Intrigued as I am by the natural world and grateful for the escape from everyday life, I've rarely been lonely on the trail. Not only do I value my time alone on the trail, I find that I often return with a deeper appreciation for the people in my life.

A significant number of hikers have a craving for solitude, which can only be accomplished by solo hiking. These hikers need time alone in the woods or on a mountain to recharge their spirits.

Some people need solitude occasionally, some regularly, and find the best opportunity for getting it is by taking a hike. Hiking solo serves to nurture a special relationship with yourself and with the natural world, and perhaps even provide a time to contemplate your spiritual path.

> *"The man who goes alone can start today; but he who travels with another must wait till that other is ready."*
> —HENRY DAVID THOREAU

Tips for the Solo Hiker

- **Know your limits.** No one is going to monitor you but you. Don't exceed your personal speed limit or overreach your capabilities.
- **Leave your itinerary with a trusted friend or relative.** Even better, be personally accountable by reporting your whereabouts to someone at an appointed time.
- **Adhere to your stated plans for both your hiking route and schedule.**
- **Go out of your way to contact park staff or land management personnel.** Visit visitor centers. Check-in at ranger stations. Sign-in at trailhead registers.
- **Add to your first-aid kit.** It should contain more supplies to care for yourself—over a longer length of time, since there is a greater likelihood no one will be around to help you or go for help. (See page 121 for a full discussion of first-aid kits.)
- **Carry a whistle and mirror to signal for help and assist rescuers in locating you.**
- **Stay alert.** Even a minor mishap like a slip and fall or twisting an ankle can be a serious incident for a solo hiker.

Hiking with Others

If you're accountable to someone other than yourself, you're more apt to walk the walk. When you're facing an early-morning start, weather that's hot and humid or cold and rainy, general malaise or low spirits, having someone you can depend on—or who depends on you—makes a difference.

Making an appointment with someone to take a hike keeps you accountable for actually doing the hike. All too often in our busy lives we give up what's not critical to our work or family responsibilities, and cancel something like a hike because it has no immediate benefit or practical purpose that we can see. I understand this attitude—and have struggled with it myself. However I hope this whole book refutes the notion that there's no more to hiking than putting one foot in front of another.

> *"Even when walking in a party of no more than three I can always be certain of learning from those I am with. There will be good qualities that I can select for imitation and bad ones that will teach me what requires correction in myself."*
>
> —CONFUCIUS

I'm convinced men and women are wired differently. Women can talk on the trail AND observe the scenery, while enjoying every moment of the hike. Women multitask, even on a hike.

Contrary to the teasing we get, men can walk and talk at the same time, though men also like to hike along in what I call companionable silence—together, yet a little separate, wordlessly enjoying the presence of another while simultaneously appreciating being alone with one's own thoughts, too. Men without women have been known to go primal on the trail, enjoying the simple pleasures of sweating, scratching and burping...

Finding a hiking companion means finding the right companion. Look first for a hiking companion in your spouse, another family member or a friend. One presumes you have ready access to these individuals and have something in common with them. Time on the trail can enhance your relationships. Hiking offers a great opportunity to spend time with someone you care about.

Choose your companion carefully. Not every city friend is a good trail buddy. There are many fine people who would rather slip on designer shoes than lace up a pair of hiking boots. For truly happy trails, a good hiking companion should share the same fitness goals, pace, and nature appreciation orientation as you.

Join a Hiking Club—or Start One

With a hiking group, you get the same fresh air and exercise as you do hiking solo with the additional opportunity to visit with your friends or make new ones.

Many Sierra Club chapters have ambitious outings schedules. Beginners are welcome to join the club's easier jaunts, though it's a good idea to check first with the hike leader about an upcoming hike's difficulty or newbie suitability. Don't go to socialize if the "High Peaks" section is planning a 20-mile day hike.

The larger Sierra Club chapters not only sponsor hikes of various levels of difficulty in a variety of terrains, but boast sub-chapters that appeal to different interest groups. The Club's Angeles Chapter of Southern California, for example, has hiking groups that include older singles, younger singles, gays and lesbians, desert peaks enthusiasts, dog owners, four-wheel drive explorers, families with younger children, and many more subgroups with special outdoor interests.

Walking clubs are numerous and easier to find than hiking clubs. Call them or go on a walk. Check for walking/hiking club flyers posted at sporting goods stores, sports shoe stores, recreation centers, community centers and health clubs.

Chances are some walkers in a given group are also hikers—or would like to become hikers. Another way to search for hiking groups is to call a few parks (with hiking trails) in your area and ask park staff if any organized groups lead walks.

Walking clubs vary in quality and orientation, ranging from mall walkers who do the same circuit over and over and never venture out of the shopping center to members of a particular religious faith, who find walking together deepens both fellowship and spirituality. Some clubs emphasize neighborhood jaunts and walks in the park, while others include challenging hikes in their schedules.

Look for a hiking group that has what you're seeking—i.e. weekday hikes or a women-only membership. If you don't find what you're looking for, the best "hiking club" for you may turn out to be you and couple of friends.

Consider starting your own group. A hiking club can be very simple: a once or twice a month get-together with friends on the trail. Each member can take a turn choosing a trail, varying the difficulty of the hike in order to keep fellow hikers engaged.

Along with offering a special kind of bonding that takes place only on a trail, hiking groups build camaraderie in other ways: breakfast before the hike, a shared meal afterwards, picnics and carpools to the trailheads. Experience suggests that the most successful clubs are the ones with a minimum of (non-hiking) meetings and a maximum of outings.

A few hiking clubs offer classes in hiking skills, but most teach hiking technique in far more informal ways—friendly members assisting newcomers one step at a time.

Clubs communicate to members through paper or e-mail newsletters or the old-fashioned phone tree. Some clubs have incentive programs and offer awards that hikers earn by reaching the summits of certain peaks, logging a certain number of miles or achieving other goals.

Some hiking clubs develop an ID and logo, stitch a patch on their day packs, and enjoy wearing club baseball caps and T-shirts. Other clubs "adopt a trail," support trail maintenance projects, help disadvantaged children learn to hike or raise funds for a park or nature center. Often the bonds formed while hiking together are very powerful and members become close friends who help each other off the trail in times of sickness or personal crisis.

Canine Companions

Many dogs love to take a hike and love the "quality time" with their owners. Hiking with a dog on a woodsy trail beats walking the dog around the block any day. For many hikers, a dog is man's best trail friend—particularly for those who hike solo.

A dog is an energetic hiking companion and, with a superior sense of smell and relatively low proximity to the ground, may notice things about the natural world that would otherwise escape your attention.

Take sufficient time to prepare canine companion and you'll discover that a well-equipped owner and well-trained dog will be the best of trail buddies, each enhancing the other's experience.

Organizing a hiking club

- Gather hikers and would-be hikers together and decide on the group's reason for being and hiking together: Why a hiking club? Who can be a member? How many or how few members? What exactly will the group offer members?

- Get organized. Delegate tasks: member outreach, communications, scheduling, hike leading.

- Take a hike!

Sole Sisters: The Santa Ynez Valley Women Hikers

IN some parts of the country, where the weather is often inclement and the terrain unremarkable, groups of women meet early in the morning. They lace up their footwear and walk laps around and around the local indoor mall.

These mall-walkers, as they are known, engage in this activity to enjoy the camaraderie of a group while they determinedly keep in shape.

In another part of the country—the Santa Ynez Valley to be specific—a group of women meets every week in the early morning hours; they lace up their hiking boots, strap on their day packs and head for the hills. Or they head for coastal sand dunes, oak-dotted hills, backcountry peaks—in short, the best trails on the Central Coast of California.

This group, officially named the Santa Ynez Valley Women Hikers, has discovered the natural distinction between walk and hiking. Like their sisters who mall walk, they assemble in search of fitness and companionship; their outdoor adventures into the natural landscape take them a step beyond, adding challenges that test them, body, mind and soul.

At first glance they look pretty much like any other group of hikers that I've joined, but this a group of women only. Clad in sturdy hiking boots with thick socks and cargo-pocket shorts, some sport white polo shirts with their group's logo embroidered on the left side. Warmly greeting each new arrival, the hikers apply sunscreen, put on sensible hats and pack water bottles into day packs.

With their strong bodies and animated behav-

First, make a candid assessment of your dog's energy level and condition. Not every good dog is a good hiker. If your pooch is a canine couch potato, an "indoor" dog or a chubby chowhound who has scarfed a few too many table scraps, he might not thrill to the call of the wild. Hint: The pooch who pants like crazy on walks around the neighborhood, will have a difficult time of it on the trail.

Many dogs love to hike, though, and, with some conditioning outings, will improve over time. If you have any doubts, ask the vet if your dog is sufficiently physically fit for hiking. Ask your vet to suggest a canine conditioning program. Also ask if your four-legged friend might have any limitations that might restrict his hiking abilities. Have the vet check your dog for hip, back and joint problems.

Which brings me to the ultra-hip-concept dog-hiking business I encountered in the Santa Monica Mountains on the west side of Los Angeles. Dog-walking services have been around major (and many minor) metropolitan areas for decades. But this business takes dogs on a hike.

"The owners want the best for their dogs, and that's hiking," one of the professional dog-hikers told me. "Most of the owners wish they could hike, but they have stressful jobs. It makes them feel better, knowing that even if they can't hike, the dogs are out there on the trail having a great time."

ior, they look like walking testimonials to the benefits of an active lifestyle.

By the time they arrive at the trailhead, the gray cloud overhead is breaking up. The group of 20 hikers hits the beach and easily strides along the shore. A flock of pelicans fly overhead while a few turkey vultures perch on the cliffs above. Someone exclaims, "What a gorgeous morning!" Everyone agrees. They set a brisk pace over the sand, sometimes scrambling over rocks and skirting great gobs of tar; we amiably chat about everything from our favorite hikes to the upcoming elections.

About an hour out, a sad discovery: a beached sea lion obviously in trouble, struggling to survive or trying to let go. Some offer opinions—"If he can't help himself, it just could be that this is his end." Others try to cover it with wet seaweed to shield it from the now-blazing sun. The leader urges the group to move on. "We all want to make a difference," she observes. "We're all mothers." Instinctively, the women want to protect and extend the life of this poor creature; rationally, they know they cannot.

They continue hiking along the shoreline. The sun feels hotter and the sand feels grittier now that reality has smacked them in the face.

They turn around and hike back to the trailhead, hot, hungry and tired. Chowing down on lunch—without counting calories, thank you, they've earned them—they discuss the morning's adventures. All too soon, the midweek hiking holiday is over and it's time to return home. Reluctantly, they return to their cars, hugs all around.

Side by side and step by step, these women accomplished the simple challenge they had set for themselves. Along the way they witnessed, life and death, and returned home changed. Another memorable day on the hiking trail with the group

Walkin' the Dog

Where You Can and Cannot Hike with a Dog

National Parks Dogs are not allowed on national park trails, which stops most hikers from even bringing a dog into a national park. Sure you can walk them around parking lots and down roads on a leash, but that's not exactly the kind of hiking that draws us to America's scenic wonders.

National Forests/ Bureau of Land Management In most cases, dogs are permitted on trails. Exceptions are certain posted areas, such as wilderness, sensitive habitat or special wildlife areas that are off-limits to dogs.

State Parks Each of America's 50 state park systems has its own regulations, so it's difficult to generalize about their respective dog regulations. Some state parks restrict dogs in the same strict way as their national park counterparts, while other state parks are more permissive. Some state parks allow dogs in some types of parks, such as large recreation areas, but not in others, such as wildlife areas or fragile habitats.

City, County, Regional Parks Municipal, county and regional park dog policies are as varied as the parks themselves. Call before you go and ask whether dogs are allowed on the trail and what leash policy is enforced.

- Make sure your dog has up-to-date vaccinations and current identification tags.
- Only hike where dogs are allowed.
- Help your dog out with some flea and tick repellent.
- Heed leash laws

- Bring water and a collapsible bowl. Dogs can get dehydrated and overheated, just like humans.
- Don't allow your dog to chase squirrels, deer or other wildlife.
- Clean up after your dog. If your dog brings it into the park, you need to hike it out. Use zippered plastic bags for disposal of waste. If you are far from the trailhead, bury dog poop in a "cathole," well off the trail.
- You and your dog must yield to all other trail users including cyclists and equestrians. Leash up and allow other trail users to pass.
- After the hike, check your dog for ticks and foxtails.

Trail Princesses

"All women are princesses," or so it goes in that popular story, *A Little Princess.*

The title of another popular children's book asks a question: *Do Princesses Wear Hiking Boots?* The answer in the book—and on trails everywhere—is a resounding yes, particularly "when they wish to take the scenic routes."

While referring to a woman as a princess in certain other contexts might seem a bit negative, in my experience, I've encountered many women who appreciate the term "Trail Princess." After, all, we're living in a time when some women even admit to wearing a tiara while doing housework.

Throughout history, princesses have been strong; they have known what they want, how to get it, where they want to go, and who they want to go with them—all qualities I have witnessed in women who are avid hikers.

With admiration, I attribute several characteristics to Trail Princesses: they never whine about hills, heat or humidity—though they do have a sense of humor about challenging conditions; they dress for the occasion and are always prepared. Trail Princesses have a great spirit of adventure and love to hike in places unknown—by themselvers or with a group.

Our use of the term "Trail Princess" first came into being when we began creating hats for hikers. "Take a Hike!" predictably, was a modest success, particularly with the guys. My daughter Sophia wanted something a bit more special, though, and as we hiked a trail in Zion National Park a few years ago, declared: "I want to be a trail princess."

When Sophia wore the prototype Trail Princess hat on the trail, we were surprised at who responded and why. No, it wasn't little girls or teens who wanted to join Sophia in becoming a Trail Princess, it was women—of all ages. When my wife wore hers to a book festival, she was besieged with requests—so we created the Trail Princess hat, which has continued to delight women who hike, and perhaps serve to remind men how women would like to be treated—on the trail and off.

Chapter 8   Hiking with Children

Hᴏᴡ ʟᴏɴɢ ᴀɢᴏ ᴡᴀs ɪᴛ ᴛʜᴀᴛ ʏᴏᴜ ᴄᴏɴǫᴜᴇʀᴇᴅ sɴᴏᴡʏ sᴜᴍᴍɪᴛs, explored remote canyons and partied hearty with the Sierra Club Singles after a fifteen-mile hike?

Seems like a century ago, huh?

When you have children, it can seem like the simplest hike is more difficult to organize than a Himalayan expedition.

But don't hang up your hiking boots. Tell your kids to take a hike—with you, of course. Children learn first-hand about nature and get valuable lessons in sharing and cooperation.

I got my kids started on the trail before they could walk. (Not that the daughter and son of The Trailmaster really had a choice in the matter of hiking . . .) Fortunately they both took to it very well.

I figure it's high time adults got a kid's-eye view on the subject of hiking. Think about it: Who better to share the fun of hiking with kids than an actual kid? My daughter, Sophia Rose McKinney, now thirteen, has enjoyed hiking since she was a toddler and has some very definite ideas about what's a happy trail and what's not. I therefore turn the first part of this chapter over to her.

In this Chapter

- A kid's life on the trail
- Take a family walk or hike
- Kinds of hikes kids like
- Things kids should bring
- Trail-tested tips for hiking with children
- Bringing baby

A Kid's Life on the Trail

Aᴅᴜʟᴛs ᴀʀᴇ ᴀʟᴡᴀʏs ɢɪᴠɪɴɢ ᴀᴅᴠɪᴄᴇ ᴀʙᴏᴜᴛ ʜᴏᴡ ᴛᴏ ᴅᴏ ᴛʜɪɴɢs with kids. But do they ever ask kids what they think? I don't like to see kids struggling with hiking. You know the ones; they trip and they're slow, and they have to drink or eat something every five seconds and they take a long time to go up a hill or down a hill. And they complain. A lot.

But hiking can be so much fun! I want to help kids learn to love hiking as much as I do. I've helped my friends and I'll help you with a couple tips I've picked up along the way.

—Sᴏᴘʜɪᴀ Rᴏsᴇ McKɪɴɴᴇʏ

WHEN MY MOM AND DAD FIRST MET, they hiked together all the time, and when they got married, they went on a hiking adventure in England. I guess you could say that hiking is just as much a part of my family as eating lunch or brushing your hair; it's just what we do. Hiking is much better than watching TV! You get to be part of the world instead of watching other people doing things.

We like to hike for fun, but in our family, it's a lot more than just fun. Besides being my dad, my dad is The Trailmaster, and has been writing about hiking since way before I was born. My mom says he tells people to take a hike, and they do!

I first started walking and hiking with my parents when I was just a few days old. My mom snuggled me into the front pack and would walk for two miles at the beach every day while I slept. But before long, I would look around, kick my legs and smell the fresh salt air, wave at the people and gaze at the birds in the sky.

My parents didn't only walk at the beach, though. One of my first mountain hikes was under the Hollywood sign in Los Angeles. Later, I sat in the backpack and tickled my dad's neck. I used to love to pull his hair and jump up and down because it was so exciting being up there. Once I squished a banana in my dad's hair. I didn't ride in the backpack anymore after that! Finally I outgrew the backpack, and wanted to run on the trail as fast as I could! That was sort of dangerous, so my parents taught me to slow down and be careful—but it took a long time before I did!

I've been fortunate to have teachers who like to hike. When I was in kindergarten, my teacher, Miss Lori, used to lead us on walks to the city rose garden, down to a neaby creek and all around. It was really fun, and I still do hikes with my class, and we do all sorts of camping trips and we hike there too.

In the fourth grade, we took a walk every morning before we went into the classroom. This was a quiet walk, during which we just got our thoughts centered and ready for the day. Miss EveLynn led the way, and the whole class walked single file, down to the creek near our school. One day we followed a little squirrel up a trail we had never been on before. It was a dead-end, so we had to scramble up a steep hill and help each other up to the top.

What I've learned from hiking with a class is that it's different because you don't get to lead; the teacher gets to lead, but it's fun to walk with classmates and to help the ones who are slower or who are a little afraid. Some kids are afraid because they aren't used to being outdoors, but then when they spend some time getting used to it, they're not afraid anymore because they're adventurous like I am. You can have more fun when you're adventurous because you can challenge yourself and learn to do more things.

Know what? I hope my dad doesn't read this, because I have to tell you this: I don't *always* want to go on a hike. Sometimes I'd rather sleep-in on the weekends then get up early and go hiking.

"If you would grow great and stately, you must try to walk sedately."
—ROBERT LOUIS STEVENSON
Good and Bad Children

And there's a whole lot of other stuff I'm interested in besides hiking. Sometimes I'm not in the best mood (I have major attitude!) when we're driving to the trailhead.

But you know what else? Once I start hiking down the trail, my bad attitude always goes away—even if it's rainy or the hike is hard. Getting started, that's the key. I've watched a lot of kids on hikes, like in national parks and other popular places, and I've noticed that kids whine the most in the car and at the trailhead. Once they're on the trail, moving around and experiencing things, there's lots less whining and lots more smiles.

There are a lot of good things that I have learned to do and learned about myself because of all the hiking that I have done in my life. Here are just a few:

- I am very strong and powerful and mighty and used to challenging myself. When I can hike for five miles, I feel energetic and I know that I can reach my destiny. You can do anything you want to do if you just hike!
- I think that hiking is the best thing that anybody can do outdoors. It is a gift from God and I thank God for this gift.
- I really know the land where I live—the trees, plants, flowers, rocks, bugs and even snakes! I know how to find salamanders, and even how to pick them up, and I know what poison oak looks like it—and never touch it!
- I can climb high on rocks and cliffs, run along the surf line, slide down a sand dune and hug trees in the forest. I see lots of rainbows, I'm good at finding treasures, and I imagine gnomes and fairies in special places. Sometimes I pretend I was a Native American in an earlier life, and that I knew just how to live back then—and I feel like I could live off the land now, if I had to.

Take a Family Walk or Hike

We—my mom, dad, my little brother Daniel and I—go for a walk together a couple times a week. It's a nice way for all of us to get back together after our busy days. We talk about funny things that happened during the day, or sad things, or sometimes we just walk quietly. Sometimes we walk at the beach to see the sunset or take a trail around the botanic garden or through a park. When we walk at the breakwater at high tide, the waves crash over the side and we can get soaked. When it's warm out, that's really fun, but when it's cold, it's freezing!

These walks we do calm everybody down—especially my little brother—and are very special. Know what? My brother and I get along a whole lot better on the trail than we do in the house and certainly a lot better than we do in the car on a long road trip!

I think taking gentle walks during the week helps us all know each other better and appreciate each other more so that when we

> *"All children deserve contact with nature as part of their heritage. . . . The more our children see and know of the natural world around them, the better equipped they will be to face the basic realities of life and realize the noble potential of existence this planet has to offer."*
>
> —ANSEL ADAMS

go for a real hike on the weekends, we're used to being together and walking together.

Kinds of Hikes Kids Like

When I was little, one of my favorite books was called *The Listening Walk*. It was all about a girl who walked quietly through her neighborhood with her dad. Instead of talking, they would listen to the sounds all around them.

I'm kind of a chatterbox and like to talk when we're heading down the trail (sometimes I drive my dad crazy), so a "Listening Hike" isn't my favorite kind of hike. But I have some other favorites and given them names.

Bird Hikes What birds can you see, what birds can you hear? At different times of the day you might see different types of birds. Where I hike, we see hummingbirds drinking nectar, woodpeckers rat-tat-tatting. We often see red-tailed hawks circling overhead, especially in the late afternoon. They're looking for mice for supper!

The songbirds are cool when they're singing in the woods and chaparral, but my favorites are the big water birds down at the seashore. I love seeing the egrets and the great blue herons around the lagoon and the pelicans swooping low over the waves.

Rock Hikes Can you find pretty rocks, ones that look like crystals? I really like to look for rocks that are shaped like hearts. It's amazing how many you can find. (Before you take any rocks home, though, make sure it's okay to do so and that the rocks aren't located in a place that's protected like in a state or national park. If you don't know, just leave it there.)

Beach Hikes I guess you have to live near a beach by the ocean or a lake to this kind of a hike. I like to collect stuff by the seashore and often gather beach glass (I'm really pleased when I find a rare blue-colored piece) and interesting shells. My mom and I say it's like shopping, especially after a storm.

Flower Hikes Flowers are the way plants reproduce. I like to look at the different colors, smell what kind of scents they have, see the way they're shaped, what kind of insects they have around them. Purple lupine is my favorite flower because purple is my favorite color.

Night Hikes Every month you have the chance to take a Full Moon Hike and be able to see the trail pretty well if the night is clear. Away from the city, in the desert or in the mountains you can see lots of stars—more than you can imagine. My brother likes to carry a flashlight on night walks through the neighborhood.

Nature Hikes Nature trails, those paths lined with signs that explain stuff, can be really fun or really boring. I don't like the ones that have lots of numbered stops, big signs or long brochures to read and go back to like the beginning of time just to explain why a meadow looks like it does. I like signs that just explain one cool fact about a plant or animal and trails that don't have a million stops where you have to stand there and read half a science book.

There are many more kinds of hikes—or at least special things to look for—when you're on a hike. I like looking up at the clouds. Be careful if you're hiking with your eyes on the sky. It's fun to find recognizable cloud shapes: a bunny, an old man, a bicycle or a car.

I like learning the names of the trees, too. Looking at the leaves helps you realize the many kinds of trees there are. Tree hikes are especially fun in the fall, when the leaves turn many beautiful colors—and in the spring when the buds are just starting to sprout. Even in a pine forest, you'll find different types of trees and one way you can tell the pines apart is by counting the needles. Some of them have two-needle bundles, some three, some five.

Things Trail Kids Should Bring Along

Day pack You want to carry your own stuff, especially your own water bottle. Make your parents carry all the heavy stuff, of course! Get a kid-sized version of a good adult day pack, because it adjusts to you really well and they're strong and weatherproof. Stay away from those cheesy kid's book packs with the cartoon characters on them. Some of the better school backpacks (ones with a hip belt and padded shoulder pads and strong zippers) are OK for hiking. Look around and see if you can find one in a cool color. Another cool thing to do to your day pack is get your name stitched on the back. Boys like their names in simple lettering or something like "Hike dude!" on the pack, while I've noticed my girlfriends and I prefer fancy embroidery.

Hiking boots I like the lightweight kind of hiking boots that are more like sneakers with a heavier sole. Sneakers are fine when you're just starting to hike or for short hikes. Hiking socks are better than the cotton ones. Take extra socks, by the way. If you're like me or most kids I've seen, you'll probably get wet and then you'll be happy to have dry socks to wear. I also like to wear hiking sandals, especially in places where your feet might get wet.

Top clothing Fleecy stuff looks really cool and keeps you warm. And it doesn't weigh much, so that when you take it off when you get hot and stuff it in your pack, it's easy to carry. If you're going hiking where it might rain, don't forget a rain jacket.

Bottom clothing For hiking, I like to wear what I call my zip-off pants—those long pants that convert to shorts by zipping off the bottoms. I like to wear shorts hiking. Wear a pair that has pockets and is made of strong material. Kids like to slide along on their butts and shorts made of thin material rip. Once, I was so embarrassed when my shorts ripped and I had to hang my dad's bandana over my rear to cover things up.

Hats Hats are fun to wear because they look cool and give you a little extra style. But they're important for another reason—they

A Few More Tips for Trail Kids

No whining You know how awful it is to be around someone who whines. If you feel like whining, do something else instead! Have a snack, drink some water, slow down, speed up, take a look at the view, pretend you're an animal . . . anything, but don't whine.

Bring a friend It's really fun to go hiking with a friend, and then they get to learn all about hiking, too.

Work as a team Offer comfort to your friends or brothers or sisters if they're tired or don't feel too good. Use kindness and compassion and encourage them with positive words. Help them out by carrying some of their things in your pack, or by offering water or a little snack. Think about how you would want to be treated if you felt the same way—and then do it.

Be smart Use your senses— your eyes, your ears, your nose and hands. Stay with the people you're hiking with, and pay attention. You don't want to get lost or hurt, so just do what you're supposed to do.

Be weather-wise Dress for whatever weather you're hiking in—and expect it to change.

Know where you're hiking Get a basic idea of where you started the hike from and where you're going. If you can read a map and keep oriented to north that's really great.

Have fun Hiking is so much fun and you should enjoy every minute of it. Even if it gets a little hard sometimes, you'll feel so proud of yourself once you've accomplished what you set out to do!

protect you from heat and cold because your body actually heats up and cools off through your head! A baseball cap is fine, especially if you have long hair and let your ponytail hang out of the hole.

Sunglasses Sunglasses screen out rays from the sun that can hurt your eyes. You can't see these rays but they make you squint. Get a fun pair that you really like so that you'll wear them and won't lose them. Speaking of losing sunglasses, if you attach them to a "leash," when you take them off they'll just hang around your neck instead of getting lost.

Sunscreen Sunscreen is something you should wear every time you go out hiking. There are a lot of brands made just for kids. They have numbers on the tube that tell you how strong it is. The larger the number the more the sunscreen blocks out the sun. I always wear a high number sunscreen—like SPF 45—because I have really fair skin and burn easy.

Water Drink lots of water when you're hiking. Bring your own water bottle so you don't always have to ask for a drink. If I'm going to be hiking in warm weather, I like to freeze a water bottle the night before I take a hike so it's nice and cold on the trail. Very refreshing!

Trail snacks One of the best parts of the hike is when my dad calls out, "Sweeties!" and it's time for a snack. Sometimes he has surprises in his pack, like chocolate kisses, hard candy or dried fruit. And he always has trail mix, which is great when you need some energy.

Trail mix There are all kinds of trail mixes that you can buy. Most of them have peanuts, raisins and lots of other things tossed in. I like the ones that have chocolate chips, white chocolate chips or peanut butter chips—but look out when it's hot outside—melted chips make a major mess! It's fun to make your own trail mix by combining dried fruit, banana chips and other snacks you like.

Sometimes I like to bring different cereals like toasted oat squares, shredded wheat with raisins inside or fruit loops. They stay crunchy and yummy on the trail. Crispy rice snacks made with marshmallow are another big favorite of mine, and so are energy bars.

Energy bars Some of them taste good, but some are just plain yucky. I think Luna bars have the best flavors (especially the lemon and lime ones) and they really help power you up the trail.

Whistle If you get lost or separated from your parents, you can blow a whistle so they can find you. Get a big colorful one, so you won't lose it, and if you have little brothers and sisters, they can't swallow it.

First-aid kit Make sure your mom or dad takes along a first-aid kit. My dad always carries a first-aid kit, and he takes a Red Cross course in first aid every couple of years. He's good to have around if someone gets hurt. A good first-aid kit has stuff to treat cuts and scrapes and deal with blisters.

I never knew what can really happen on the trail if you're not careful, but one time when we were hiking near Sedona, Arizona a lady slipped in a creek and fell and hit her head on a rock and was really bleeding all over the place. Gross, huh? My dad helped her and put a gauze pad on her head to stop the bleeding. I was glad my dad had a first-aid kit and he could help her so well.

And now back to my dad.

—Sophia Rose McKinney

A Few Tips for Parents

I'm very pleased that my children have learned to enjoy hiking—though there are some would say they had little choice! Nevertheless, I learned early on what a privilege it is to share the joy of time on the trail with the little ones.

Some of the most important lessons I've learned while hiking with my kids came to me when I stepped out of my role as parent and gave them the chance to lead me on their path. Along the way, they've taught me that they're well-attuned to nature's rhythms.

Parent to parent, let me caution you: the last thing children want to hear is too much information. Relax! You don't have to be a walking encyclopedia and identify every plant and animal along the way. Just keep them safe and have some fun.

Trail-Tested Tips for Hiking with Children

- Keep your children in sight at all times. That may seem obvious, but you'd be surprised how fast kids can get off the trail.
- Repeat and repeat again all instructions ranging from snack breaks to porta-potty locations.
- Choose a hike with fairly modest elevation gains. Children prefer intimate settings, such as a little creek or a clump of boulders to those vast scenic panoramas favored by adults.
- Feed the troops. Begin with a nourishing breakfast. Carry plenty of quick-energy snack foods and offer them frequently. (By the time kids tell you're they're hungry, they're often already cranky and out of energy and enthusiasm.)
- Supplement the Ten Essentials with extra snack foods, whistles (in case you and your child become separated), a book or toy for the drive to and from the trailhead. (See Chapter 10, page 119 for the Ten Essentials.)
- Check your child's temperature. While you'd think that kids would tell you if they're too cold or too hot, they usually don't. Dress them in layers and be sure to add or subtract clothing in response to changing weather conditions.
- Teach respect for nature. Enjoy but don't disturb flowers, plants and animals. Environmental education is easy and fun on the trail, so be sure to pack a good trail guide or nature guidebook and visit park interpretive centers.
- When children travel in groups, the kids motivate each other

Haikus For You

A haiku is a poem that has three lines composed of five syllables, seven syllables, and five syllables. They're fun to compose while you're on the trail. We call them *hike-kus.* Let the sights and sounds and feelings you have inspire you. Here are some of mine that I wrote on while hiking on the rim of the Grand Canyon.

Sweet nectar searching
Hummingbird zipping past us
Fairy tastes flower

Bright angel from earth
Zigging and zagging along
Careful or you're dead

Mighty river green
So rough so strong amazing
Paddle if you dare

Lovely Grand Canyon
River carved it long ago
Indians found it first

to go farther and faster. And there's lots less whining.

- If young spirits sag, try playing games to regain good humor and maintain that all-important forward progress up the trail. With younger children, play "Dog." Throw an imaginary stick to the next tree en route and have them fetch it. "One-two-three-jump" is another popular game. With a parent holding each hand the child hikes along one-two-three steps, then jumps as parents raise arms and swing the hopefully-no-longer reluctant little hiker into the air. "I Spy" is another favorite trail game: "I spy with my little eye something that is _____" (fill in the blank).
- It's much better for everyone to stop frequently and travel slowly than to try to make the kids go faster and then have to carry them. If parents know what kids can and can't do, everyone has a great time on the trail.
- Join an outings group. If you could use a little motivation to get on the trail, join a family outings group. Many parks and nature centers lead interpretive hikes that are open to both children and parents. I highly recommend the Sierra Club's Little Hikers, which welcomes families with children (newborn to pre-teen). Four- to ten-year-olds most enjoy the hikes, chosen for their level terrain as much as for their natural beauty.

Bringing Baby

- Choose a child-carrier that has good head support for the baby, and with a design that's secure but not ultra-constricting to the child. Like any backpack, a child-carrier should fit well and feel comfortable on the parent's back.
- Dress your baby warmly. Remember, the baby is lots less active than you and needs to be warmer.
- Bring all the usual baby stuff. Remember all the in-town baby essentials such as food, bottles, a toy, diapers and wipes. Take a plastic bag to carry out soiled diapers and towelettes so they can be disposed of properly.
- Stop frequently to check—or have your hiking companion check—the baby's temperature status. Make sure your baby is warm, but not overheated.
- Avoid hiking at high altitude. Babies, particularly those who live with flatlander parents, do not adjust well to increased ear pressures and other strains of high altitude.
- Take it slow and easy. Don't try to ford fast-moving rivers or descend steep grades with that bundle of joy on your back. And watch out for low-hanging branches!
- Use a jogger stroller. When baby outgrows the carrier, try an all-terrain stroller instead. These high-tech strollers with their strong, mountain bike-like tires, good brakes and light-weight construction, are highly maneuverable on flat and

Trail Wisdom: Walk as Children of Light

"WALK as children of light," advises St. Paul, the Apostle. Children enrich any walk with their own special thoughts, feelings, and sensory impressions. They bring innocence, wide-eyed wonder and enthusiasm that knows no bounds on a walk. Their small steps are accompanied by great leaps in imagination.

Years ago, one of my daughter's favorite books was *The Listening Walk* by Paul Showers. A little girl likes to take what she calls "listening walks" with her dad and notes the thhhhhh of a sprinkler, the bomp-bomp-bomp of a dribbling basketball, the creet-creet-creet of the crickets in the grass. "I hear all sorts of sounds on a Listening Walk," she says. "I listen to sounds I never listened to before."

Another favorite children's book, *Funny Walks* by Judy Hindley, opens with a question rarely considered by adults but perhaps often pondered by children: "Isn't it funny how people walk?"

One of the senses better developed in children than in adults is the sense of the ridiculous. What is a child to make of a walker with a scowl and a head bent down or one with a "thinking face" and hands in pockets? And isn't it odd how animals walk when you take the time to stop and watch?

From infants through teenagers, I've observed no single "right" or "wrong" age to take children on a walk. On a practical basis, each style of childhood offers both pluses and minuses for walking families; on a spiritual basis, the pluses prevail by far.

Practically speaking, infants are highly portable, but they require packing all this "baby stuff" to go along with them. Often they sleep a lot, but they cry a lot, too. Toddlers toddle—but only sometimes in the desired direction. Grade-schoolers take a vigorous interest in walks—but it might not be the same vigorous interest as their parents. Teens can walk long distances, keenly appreciate both cultural sites and the natural world—but they often don't want to take such walks with their parents!

I've discovered that my children have helped me become a better walker—more adaptive, more sensory, more patient. On walks near home or faraway, children are great conversation starters with strangers—particularly those with children of their own. Young walkers remind us that many of the world's most compelling sights are all around us, just waiting to be discovered.

"Walk cheerfully over the world," wrote the seventeenth-century English religious leader George Fox, founder of the Society of Friends. "Sing and rejoice, children of the day and of the light." Walk as children of light.

---

rolling terrain, on dirt roads and on selected single-track trails. We used this type of stroller for years and it gave us much more mobility than we ever imagined. It definitely allows the whole family to enjoy more time in the outdoors—and allows a four-year-old to go lots farther than four-year-old legs can travel.

Boy Scout Hiking Merit Badge Requirements

1. Show that you know first aid for injuries or illnesses that could occur while hiking, including hypothermia, heatstroke, heat exhaustion, frostbite, dehydration, sunburn, sprained ankle, insect stings, tick bites, snakebite, blisters, hyperventilation, and altitude sickness.
2. Explain and, where possible, show the points of good hiking practices including the principles of Leave No Trace, hiking safety in the daytime and at night, courtesy to others, choice of footwear, and proper care of feet and footwear.

3. Explain how hiking is an aerobic activity. Develop a plan for conditioning yourself for 10-mile hikes, and describe how you will increase your fitness for longer hikes.
4. Make a written plan for a 10-mile hike. Include map routes, a clothing and equipment list, and a list of items for a trail lunch.
5. Take five hikes, each on a different day, and each of 10 continuous miles. Prepare a hike plan for each hike.
6. Take a hike of 20 continuous miles in one day following a hike plan you have prepared.
7. After each of the hikes (or during each hike if on one continuous "trek") in requirements 5 and 6, write a short report of your experience. Give dates and descriptions of routes covered, the weather, and any interesting things you saw. Share this report with your merit badge counselor.

10 Tips for Hiking with Teens

- Be aware that teens are prone to BAS (Bad Attitude Syndrome). More than any other age group, they're apt to be lazy, sullen, grouchy or downright mean on the trail.

- Teens are human, too (really) and there's nothing like a hike to diminish BAS. In their own way, and in their own time, kids in this age group do find joy in hiking.

- Let 'em wear cool clothes. Provided teens dress in layers with the proper kinds of apparel, let them have input about colors and styles.

- Involve them in the trip-planning and they'll be happier hikers. Let them have some input about the hike's distance and destination, about where to stop for a dinner on the drive home.

- Choose hiking activities with some excitement. A swimming hole is a more appealing destination than a historic grist mill.

- Two is not necessarily better than one. Forget parent-teen quality time if you subscribe to the "They'll entertain each other" theory (effective with younger children) and let your teen bring another on your family hike.

- Challenge them. Adults are often more surprised than the teens themselves at the mountains they can climb and the distance they can cover in a day.

- They need to be walked, not wired. Under no circumstances permit them to bring any audio/video/cellular device on the trail.

- A little separation at carefully selected times/places is okay. Let them hike a little ahead of the adults—provided there's a well understood agreement to meet at a particular time or place.

- Encourage them to wear their hiking backpacks correctly (which they probably don't do with their school backpacks). Insist they adjust the shoulder straps and fasten the hip band.

PART THREE
What to Take

Chapter 9   Gearing Up

I've LEARNED TO NEVER JUDGE A HIKER'S ABILITY BY WHAT HE OR SHE wears or carries on the trail. I went on a weeklong hiking holiday with a tour group that included Minor Bishop, a 73-year old architect from Manhattan. It was a difficult week of tramping across England on the Coast to Coast route. I was shocked when Minor appeared in "hiking" garb that included dress slacks, a trench coat and slip-on loafers. He proved to be a cheerful companion who never missed a step, even on some rigorous 15-mile long days with a lot of ups and downs. When it rained, Minor pulled an umbrella from his coat, as well as a pair of what he called "rubbers" (waterproof coverings for his street shoes). He pulled more gadgets from his trench coat, including a vintage 1960s Polaroid camera, with which he recorded the hike's highlights and shared them with fellow hikers at our evening communal dinners.

I offer the story of Minor Bishop and his hundred-mile hike with the worst apparel and accessories I've ever seen on the trail, not as an endorsement of his particular hiking gear philosophy, but as a cautionary tale for all of us who take this matter of choosing gear a little too seriously.

Most hikers I know who regularly take to the trail have accumulated a collection of apparel and accessories that was carefully purchased and has been field-tested. These hikers know what they like and what works for them.

Good gear—hiking apparel and accessories—makes an important, even critical, contribution to a hiker's well-being and safety. While good gear alone doesn't ensure a good hiking experience, it certainly can enhance the experience.

Obviously you'll enjoy a hike—even a hike in the rain—if you're warm and dry rather than cold and miserable; the difference between the two is sometimes the difference between quality and inferior rainwear.

In This Chapter
- The Trailmaster's gear philosophy
- Day packs
- Clothing
- Footwear
- Accessories

> *"Then came the gadgeteer, otherwise known as the sporting-goods dealer. He has draped the American outdoorsman with an infinity of contraptions, all offered as aids to self-reliance, hardihood, woodcraft, or marksmanship, but too often functioning as substitutes for them. Gadgets fill the pockets, they dangle from neck and belt. The overflow fills the auto-trunk and also the trailer. Each item of outdoor equipment grows lighter and often better, but the aggregate poundage becomes tonnage."*
>
> —ALDO LEOPOLD,
> *A Sand County Almanac*

Apparel makers and equipment manufacturers have made tremendous strides in the evolution of fabrics, weatherproofing and waterproofing, and weight reduction. The clothing and products available to the hiker today are significantly better than they were twenty years ago—even five years ago. As a hiker who's suffered with more than my share of uncomfortable day packs, leaky rain gear and flimsy footwear, I salute the gear makers who've worked so hard to evolve their products over the years. My comfort and that of millions of hikers has increased immeasurably thanks to their efforts.

Not only has the quality of products increased, so has the quantity. For example, twenty years ago only about a half-dozen brands of lightweight hiking boots were on the market; today, several hundred models are available.

Of course, when is there too much variety, too much to choose from? Only in America can a hiker visit a large outdoor retail store and find four different tick-removers for sale, each brand with a slightly different magnifying system to find the little buggers and a different extractor system for removing them.

My concerns about gear are less about the gear itself than how it's marketed. Advertisers and the editors of the national outdoors-themed magazines target a twenty-four-year-old male. Look for the ads for hiking products and apparel sandwiched between snowboards and SUVs with mud all over them.

This youngest-demographic-possible obsession of outdoors magazines leaves the huge majority of hikers behind. Words and images are for the most part wholly unrepresentative of the people who hike. Apparently the 20-something male hikers never become 40-something or 60-somethings, never get married, become parents or grandparents. What we see in the ads and stories is a natural world without children, trails without the kind of people we know use them every day—seniors, a mom with two kids, hikers with unbotoxed wrinkles.

Good gear—particularly apparel—can be expensive, but it doesn't have to be. If cost is no object—or nothing but the highest end garments will do, spend $25 on a pair of hiking socks, $90 for a sun hat and $600 for a parka. Just know you don't have spend that kind of money. Know that a hiker doesn't have to spend like a skier or a golfer to have a good time outdoors.

When it comes to gear, hikers tend to separate by personality into two categories: Early Adaptors and Late Adaptors. In other words, some hikers like to get clothes of the latest miracle fabric and the latest electronic gizmos, while others wear out their clothes before buying new ones and the most modern electronic accessory they tote is a vintage 1988 pocket flashlight.

You'll find The Trailmaster just a bit over the line into the Late Adaptor category. While I do try out new stuff fairly soon after it comes on the market, I tend to be very slow and conservative about replacing my trail-tested items with something new.

I still carry a map and compass; not a GPS. I carry a cell phone (turned off) for emergency use and average but two calls a year from the trail. I own bladder-style packs but prefer a carrying a water bottle in my conventional day pack. I'd rather stop and drink from a bottle than sip through plastic on the run.

While leaning toward Thoreau's warning, "Beware of all enterprises that require new clothes," I nevertheless do have my weak moments when I crave the latest gear, particularly after receiving an enticing color catalog in the mail, or walking into the hiking section of an outdoor retailer during the holiday season. I particularly like purchasing hiking apparel and accessories as birthday or holiday gifts for friends and family members.

I look forward to *Outside* magazine's annual gear issue. The magazine's reviews are to the point, explain a product's technical features well, and are often quite entertaining.

Just as getting into uniforms helps team members increase their concentration on their game, hikers who dress properly for the outdoors and carry the right equipment show a certain healthy respect for the elements.

If you're going gear-shopping first before you go out on the trail, you might get lucky and get exactly what you need, but I highly doubt it. Don't try to buy everything before you hit the trail. Ask an experienced hiker what she or he likes to wear and carry. Use the checklist in this book and add to it a little at a time

Day Packs Defined

Call me Pack-Man, a guy gobbling up miles and miles of trail, always with a day pack on my back.

All too often, my aching back.

For years and years, on hikes around the world, soon as I reached the top of that peak or that beautiful lake, I literally tossed off my pack in relief. Some brands were so badly designed I was tempted to throw them off the mountain or into the lake.

Manufacturers have sent The Trailmaster an array of low-tech, ill-conceived day packs, hardly more evolved than the rucksacks I carried during my Boy Scout days, and my response has always been the same: "Hey, hiking is not supposed to hurt."

I don't know why day-pack design has lagged behind innovations in outerwear and footwear, but it has. Maybe pack-makers think that by adding pouches, pockets and an outdoorsy logo to a flimsy book-bag, they'll fool us into thinking we're purchasing a great day pack.

More recently, some good day packs have come on the market. If you know what to look for in a good pack, you'll select one that will be a welcome companion not an albatross around your neck.

"He who would travel happily must travel light."
—ANTOINE DE SAINT EXUPERY
Wind, Sand and Stars

Day Packs

A day pack is a soft frameless pack that attaches to your shoulders and usually includes a hip band or waist belt for support. A good one will last a lifetime.

High-quality day packs are made specifically for hiking so there's no need to settle for a bike bag, book bag or a pack fashioned for another sport. It's best to purchase one at an specialty outdoors store.

Padding is crucial to a comfortable day pack. Padded shoulder pads are an absolute must, and go a long way in keeping the spring in your step. A good day pack has a padded back, as well. A wide padded lumbar belt is important, too, because you want to try and put the weight on your hips and take it away from your neck and shoulder muscles.

Before you purchase a pack, put a little weight inside it and walk around the store. Check to be sure it really fits your frame. We hikers come in all shapes and size—and there are major body differences between men and women regardless of size—so be assured that there's no such thing as a one-size-fits-all day pack.

A modest-sized day pack measures about 16 inches high, 12 inches wide and about six inches deep. A larger day pack can be 18 inches or more in length, 14 inches wide and more than six inches deep.

Day pack capacity is measured in cubic inches, with 1,000 to 1,500 cubic inches sufficient for most all-day adventures. If you're the designated donkey in your hiking group or a parent toting gear for several kids, consider investing in a "weekend" day pack, one with a capacity of 2,000 to 3,000 cubic inches. (Europeans and other hikers around the world measure day pack capacity in liters. A typical day pack has between 15 and 30 liters of cargo room.)

With the Ten Essentials (see Chapter 10, page 119), extra clothing, food, water, and a camera, figure that you'll be toting 10 to 15 pounds of gear on a day hike. Sure you and the pack *can* carry more weight, but remember you're going day hiking not backpacking. Remember that the suspension system of most day packs are not designed to support heavy loads so if you put too much weight in a day pack, that load will pull on your neck and shoulders and stress your frame.

As a general rule, you can comfortably carry 10 percent of your body weight in a well-designed day pack. Consider 15 percent of your body weight or 25 pounds as an absolute maximum load, even with a superior day pack.

Some day hikers, particularly those who hike in warm weather, prefer packs with a built-in hydration system. Remember that you'll be giving up some storage capacity and have to pack around the pack's built-in bladder sleeve. Some hydration packs are all bladder and no backpack—with minimal carrying capacity for anything but fluids. Other hydration packs are a better balance between water and cargo toting capacities.

Fanny packs have their fans among day hikers. Buy a good one with ample padding and storage. Look for rugged, covered zippers and easy access to pouches. Be sure the pack you choose comfortably carries water bottles.

Rain and Your Day Pack

With all those zippers and all that stitching, day packs are obviously not waterproof—and not even the most boastful pack manufacturer makes that claim. In fact, few day packs fare well in wet weather so you need to consider how to keep your day pack's precious cargo dry.

In Europe, Australia and New Zealand, some hikers attach splash covers, waterproof material with elasticized edges that repel rain. Few Americans use the splash covers although if you look hard enough at specialty outdoors stores, you can find a waterproof nylon cover that you can fit to your pack.

A more common "splash cover," one with particular appeal to the budget conscious hiker, is a heavy-duty plastic garbage bag with slits cut out for the shoulder straps. If you're better prepared than I am, you'll cut the bag to fit your pack before you leave on a hike.

A few of my Sierra Club hiker friends are very good with scissors and by the time they finish snipping garbage bag into a splash cover it looks like a professionally made custom product. I, on the other hand, must have missed scissors class in kindergarten and can never seem to cut the shoulder strap holes correctly.

I use a second-best garbage bag method: I carry bags to line the inside of my pack when the weather turns wet.

Trail-testing a New Pack

It took an athlete, four-time Olympian Terry Schroeder, who captained the silver medal-winning U.S. water polo team in the 1980s, to redesign the day pack with a winning combination of performance and comfort. In recent years, Dr. Schroeder, now a prominent chiropractor, noticed that many of his patients—college students, exercise-walkers, hikers and people from all walks of life—were using day packs that were at best not posture-friendly and at worst a chiropractic disaster. "Could you design a better day pack?" his patients asked.

The spinal expert did just that with great results: a truly evolutionary, even revolutionary, day pack that's quite comfortable; by design it actually improves posture while it's worn. The pack's suspension system cushions and protects your back while delivering miles and miles of easy-on-the back walking. It features a unique wrap-around padding system, S-shaped straps and a strong, padded, lumbar belt that take pressure off your neck and shoulders and distributes it over the whole torso.

At Dr. Schroeder's request, I field-tested prototypes of his pack on hundreds of miles of trail from the Southwest canyon lands to the

Packing Your Day Pack

Let's not over-complicate a simple procedure. Remember just two rules about packing a day pack:

- Pack items you'll most likely use on the hike in the most accessible place.
- Pack the heaviest items at the bottom of the pack, the lightest ones toward the top.

Main Compartment Put heavier items that you won't need to instantly access (extra food and water, first aid kit) in the bottom.

Sub-Compartment Some clothing, lighter items and cell phone go here.

Top Pocket Store maps, guidebook, binoculars, insect repellent, sunscreen and other items here for ready access on the trail.

Side Pockets Mesh ones are particularly good for holding a water bottle. Easy access for snacks and a compact camera.

Yosemite high country, from Washington's Cascades to England's Cornwall coast, and found it to be the most comfortable day pack I ever put on my back. We worked together to refine the pack for day hikers, adding some Trailmaster touches: extra-strong zippers, easy-access water bottle pouch, a Ten Essentials organizer, and even a cell phone pocket!

As a result of these efforts, I learned about what a day pack should be: easily adjustable, fully featured, generously sized and as comfortable as a pack can be.

Features of a Good Day Pack
- Durable weatherproof fabric
- One-piece body construction
- Padded shoulder straps
- Padded back
- Wide, padded lumbar belt
- Sufficient pockets and compartments to suit your needs
- Side pouch for water bottle
- Strong buckles and straps
- Storm flap-covered zippers
- Strong top grab handle

Clothing: The Importance of Layering

Although meteorologists are getting better and better at predicting the weather, hikers can often be caught off guard if they rely on the weather report alone. It's critical that your wear and bring clothing that can accommodate changes in weather, and the inevitable changes in body temperature that occur from alternating between steep ascents and periods of rest.

Outdoor pros can get pretty scientific when it comes to dressing for the trail, but it doesn't have to be terribly complicated if you understand some basic principles of layering. In some respects, layering is just like it sounds—you add layers of clothing as you cool off, and you peel them off as you cool down.

What makes the concept seem so complex, however, is the dizzying array of fabrics, weaves, and types of clothing available to hikers. From polypropylene to Thermax, Polartech 100 to Capilene and polyester, there are so many synthetic fabrics on the market now, it's enough to intimidate almost anyone from taking a hike.

When not complicating your life, these new fabrics work together to provide lightweight insulation and breathability—a combination that was unheard of twenty or thirty years ago. Historically, the price you paid for staying warm was to wear heavy, bulky clothing. And to keep dry, plastic ponchos did the trick—until you started to move, of course. Once you began to sweat, you became a walking, sweat-trapped sauna. Yuck.

Another feature of the new fabrics is that they are relatively quick drying—a welcome feature when hiking in the rain, or when resting after a long uphill climb. Cotton is a great fabric to wear if you want to stay cool (on desert hikes, for instance), but, because it holds moisture, it is useless as an insulator. "Cotton kills," some outdoors experts warn.

On all hikes, it's best start out a little cool and keep your extra layers in your pack for later. You'll start to heat up as you get moving. And, if you're taking an early morning hike, chances are that outside temperatures will heat up as the day wears on.

Day Hiking on Clear, Summer Days

While weather may be fickle, most of us have a pretty good idea of the seasonal changes where we live and are likely to hike. If you are hiking in mild, sunny weather, it's silly to prepare for a blizzard (though strange things do happen!). For mild hikes, it's often good to wear lightweight nylon shorts. Some hikers swear by lightweight pants with legs that can zip off. This is a really cool feature if you want to keep yourself especially prepared.

- **T-Shirt** A synthetic t-shirt is a good first layer on top. More and more companies are making great synthetic alternatives to the traditional cotton t-shirt. You'll find zillions in any hiking store.
- **Long-sleeved shirt** Wear or bring along a long-sleeved shirt to wear on top. One that zips or buttons is best for temperature control—but it's really up to you.
- **Pants** Extra pants are also a good idea, if you aren't wearing "convertible" pants/shorts. I sometimes forget about keeping my legs covered until I reach a windy summit, and I wish I'd brought along a pair of nylon pants to pull over my shorts.
- **Jacket** No matter where or when you're hiking, it's wise to keep a lightweight rain jacket/windbreaker in your pack. It can never hurt, and will come in handy when you least expect it.

Cold, Windy Days

Layering takes on new meaning when temperatures drop. On chilly days, your first layer should fit snugly against your skin. Depending on the weather and temperature, your first layer can range from lightweight Capilene pants and top to double-layered long underwear. The job of the first layer is to keep you warm and dry. A snug fit gives the fabric a better chance to do its job, and will likely make for a more comfortable hike.

Your second layer is your major insulator. Warm fleece pants and top work well, and an extra fleece hat and pullover will keep you even warmer.

> "I say beware of all enterprises that require new clothes, and not rather a new wearer of clothes. If there is not a new man, how can the new clothes be made to fit? If you have a new enterprise before you, try it in your old clothes."
>
> —HENRY DAVID THOREAU

Rainwear

If you dress properly, a little rain shouldn't put a damper on an otherwise great hike. In many regions of the country, rain can sneak up very quickly, which is why it's so critical to keep basic rain gear with you at all times. Many manufacturers make lightweight jackets and pants that live up to the claim of being waterproof and breathable in drizzly weather. Gore-Tex is now so ubiquitous that you can find rain gear that keeps you pretty comfy and dry in anything from summer showers to chilly autumn rain.

Hats

No matter what the weather, it's important to bring a hat along with you. Wool or fleece hats help keep you warm, since most body heat is lost through the head.

On warm, sunny hikes, wear a broad-brimmed hat to keep you shaded from the sun. Light colored hats reflect the sunlight better than darker ones, and will keep you cooler. Nylon hats with mesh around the crown of the head are especially nice on a hot day. Very fair, sun-sensitive hikers might opt for the expedition type hat with a long flap that extends over the neck, offering extra sun protection.

Demystifying the Primary Fabrics

Unlike cotton, synthetic fabrics don't leave you soaked in sweat. Most are designed to "wick" moisture away from your skin so you stay relatively dry. While cotton is great for hot desert hikes (where a sweaty cotton t-shirt helps to keep you cool), synthetics are better for most other climates. When the wind picks up, or after you stop to rest after a long climb, you'll be thankful for your dry shirt.

Polypropylene One of the first to come out on the synthetic market, polypro (as it's referred to among folks in the outdoor biz) is cheap and a good, basic insulator. It's main drawback, however, is that it doesn't do very well at "wicking" moisture away from your skin. Without an absorbent layer over it, it has the same effect as the plastic poncho.

Properly combined with other synthetics, or even under a wool shirt or pants, polypro is pretty good at keeping you nice and toasty on the trail. Also, be forewarned. It can retain odor (usually the "been on the trail too long" kind), and you can't throw it in the dryer—it shrinks and bunches up, and is hard to pull apart.

Gore-Tex Invented by a guy with the last name Gore (not the brainy, former vice-president), this stuff is pretty neat. And it's all over the place. Boots, jackets, pants, backpacks, hats, you name it. The reason it's so popular is that it is—at its best—breathable and waterproof. The company claims that this is due to "patented membrane technology." What this appears to mean is that Gore-Tex consists of two (or more) layers of fabric. The outer layer is impermeable, the inner layer is semi-permeable.

In theory, Gore-Tex works like a charm. I've found that, while it does work well in most weather conditions, I get a wee bit damp in my Gore-Tex jacket, nevertheless. The jacket does "breathe" reasonably well. Hiking in the pouring rain in Gore-Tex outerwear has been pleasant enough—I've stayed warm and dry. Gore-Tex sure beats a lot of the alternatives—heavy slickers, or leaky, sauna-like nylon jackets, for instance.

Wool Unless you grew up on a small, isolated tropical island, you've likely encountered this timeless fabric. It's doesn't hold moisture, and has always been a great insulator. Historically, only the heartiest of folks could tolerate wool's scratchiness right next to the skin. Wool is still used (mostly in socks and sweaters), but several companies have been able to soften the material up a bit (blending it with synthetics, among other things), and now offer sensitive-skin-friendly long underwear. It's a good insulation choice if you're wary about all the fancy new fabrics.

Polyester While leisure suits never became popular on the trail, a lot of great outdoor clothing is made of polyester and polyester-blend fabrics. Polyester itself is useless, but manufacturers have found ways to chemically treat the fabric so that it wicks away moisture so that you stay nice and dry. There are dozens of brands and blends out there—CoolMax and Capilene are two of the most prevalent variations.

Capilene This is one of the more sophisticated insulating fabrics out there. Unlike polypropylene, it can be washed and dried (in a dryer!) a million times, holds up well, and—if reasonably cared for—doesn't get stinky. The downside is that it's a lot pricier than some of the other fabrics.

Footwear

A good pair of hiking boots can keep you on the trail for years, and a bad pair may march you right back to the store. Wearing the right boots is a critical part of the hiking experience.

Before you even think about buying, be sure to be clear about how your boots will be used. What kind of terrain are you planning to encounter? Hikes in the muddy Northwest require something a little different than desert walks do, for instance.

Not only should you take weather and terrain into consideration, but it's critical that you realistically evaluate the intensity and duration of your hikes. Boots made for extended backpacking trips are more durable, but much heavier than boots intended for day hiking.

Never rely on shoe size alone to determine what you should buy. Online boot shopping is a mistake, unless you are ordering a pair that is identical to boots you already own—right down to the size, brand and model. I'm sure it's not news to anyone to report that footwear has one of the highest customer return rates in the mail-order biz.

Hike-ku
Looking good on trails
wearing trendy hiking gear
great designer shades

Boots can vary quite a bit in terms of their construction, comfort, and durability. Until recently, all hiking boots have been made of leather. There are several synthetic options out there now that are worth checking out—many strict vegans (folks who don't wear or eat animal products) who love to hike have finally found lightweight boots that are durable and leather free.

Don't expect hiking boots to last all that much longer than running shoes. Per mile, it can cost less to keep a car running than to walk in hiking boots. Some lightweight boots on the feet of aggressive hikers offer only 300 or so miles of wear. The uppers often can go several hundred miles more, but soles lose their tread and can eventually start splitting from the rest of the boot. These days, stuff is meant to be worn out, and then thrown out.

If you are as averse to getting rid of things as I am, you can always look into resoling your boots—for the heavier varieties, not the lightweights. It's also a nice way to keep an otherwise sturdy pair around a whole lot longer.

Manufacturers can have you believing that you need a different pair of shoes for every kind of terrain you encounter. This is certainly true in some cases—warm beach walks and snowy mountain hikes each require different features to keep you reasonably comfortable, and your boots in good shape. But as a rule, hiking is hiking, and a boot either fits or it doesn't.

The other caveat to that, however, is that you need to consider how likely it is that you'll be hiking in the rain and mud. A wet hike wearing "breathable" nylon mesh and split-grain leather boots will make you utterly miserable.

Breaking them in

Experts warn not to wear boots on the trail that haven't been broken in. It's an odd piece of advice—after all, don't you need to wear them hiking in order to break them in?

The answer is, "it depends." Lots of people wear new, lightweight hiking boots straight out of the box and onto the trail. Low-top lightweight boots are especially trail-ready. Generally this works out fine, and if the boots are a good fit, you'll start out and stay blister-free.

The more heavy-duty your boots are, the more you'll need to prep them for a hike. Thick, full-grain leather mountaineering boots, for example, need a lot of break-in time before they can comfortably carry you down the trail.

Start breaking-in your boots by taking short walks around the block. Walk up and down hilly streets. Wear them and stand on your toes several times. Wear them around the house and yard, on shopping trips.

Boots generally are categorized as follows:

- **Lightweight** These are made to be worn on day hikes and light overnight trips. Also included in this category are trail-running and all other low-top trail shoes. Lightweight trail shoes/boots are usually a combination of split-grain leather and nylon mesh, and have a thinner sole than heavier boots. As a result, they don't last nearly as long as the others, but are a great choice for both novice and expert day hikers because they aren't at all cumbersome and require little to no break-in time.

- **Midweight** These are designed for backpacking trips or off-trail day hiking. They typically require some breaking in. If you have injury-prone ankles, midweight boots are also a good choice for lighter day hikes because they provide ankle support and are sturdier (but heavier) than their lightweight counterparts. The ankle support offered by mid- and high-topped boots is an especially welcome feature when traveling unstable terrain.

- **Heavyweight or Mountaineering** These are what the big cheese backpackers and mountaineers wear. Almost always made of full-grain leather, they feel like stiff cement blocks when you first put them on. Needless to say, they are very heavy, extremely durable, and take a long time to be broken in.

If the shoe fits...

- You have room to wiggle your toes, but the boots won't be so loose that you feel like you're floating in them. Tightness in the toe box can eventually lead to extreme discomfort later on, especially when hiking down steep hills.
- Your heel won't slide up and down when you walk, and stays put without feeling pinched.
- You should be wearing the type of socks that you'd wear on the trail. This helps ensure a good fit.
- You've tested several pairs already, even though the pair you choose may have been the first you tried on. It's a good idea to get a feel for fit from several different boots.
- You've walked around in each pair through the store and up and down an incline (most shoe stores that carry hiking boots have these).

All About Blisters

Blisters are one of the annoying realities of, well, wearing shoes. Most of us have gotten a blister or two at some point from ill-fitting or not-yet-broken-in boots or shoes, damp feet, or too-thin socks. Since hikers place heavy-duty demands on their feet, they need to be especially vigilant against anything that rubs the wrong way.

Blisters are the painful result of constant friction between your foot and boot. As your foot rubs against the inside of the boot, the point of contact on your foot becomes red and irritated (this is often referred to as a "hot spot"), and sure enough, a pocket of fluid—a blister—then develops under the top layer of skin.

Blister Prevention

• Wear thick socks. Or better yet, double up with thin socks on the inside and thicker ones on the outside. The theory behind wearing two pairs is that the first pair keeps your feet protected from any chafing between the second pair and your boots.

• At the first sign of a hot spot, tape the sore area with sport tape or a bandage to protect it from further chafing. Band-Aid makes "Blister Block" strips for this very purpose.

• Rub petroleum jelly on blister-prone areas. This can reduce friction enormously.

• Never start out in damp boots or socks. In addition to keeping your feet cold and clammy, damp footwear will ruthlessly chafe your poor old feet.

• Keep an extra pair of socks in your pack. If your feet get wet during the day, you can change into them.

Treating a Blister

If the blister breaks, dab the area with antibiotic ointment. When you get home, wash it well and re-apply ointment. Then cover with a bandage. For the next several days, be sure to wear a different pair of shoes than you did on the trail.

If the blister doesn't break, leave it be until you get home. Once off the trail, wash the area thoroughly, then pierce the blister with a sterile needle, drain the fluid, and follow the above directions.

During the hike, however, a bandage is unlikely to last more than ten steps before rubbing off altogether. The following treatments are better on-the-trail fixes for blistered feet:

• "Second Skin" by Spenco is one of the latest and greatest blister treatments around. It is a little like wearing a cold, wet, slimy bandage—which sounds disgusting, unless you have a blister, of course. To use, cut a piece of the Second Skin large enough to generously cover the affected area, and then seal it up with the dry and un-slimy "knit" tape provided in the box.

• "Molefoam" by Dr. Scholl's is another great blister-treatment innovation. Though it doesn't ease the pain of a blister quite like Second Skin, it certainly keeps the blister from developing any further. To use, cut a donut-shaped piece of foam so that the hole is larger (but not by much) that the actual blister. Peel off the foam backing and press it firmly to the area surrounding the blister. The theory behind this treatment is that the raised foam will protect the blister from any contact with the sock or boot.

Socks

The time-honored two-sock tradition is still a useful one for hikers. A thin, inner liner sock of synthetic material, such as polypropylene or Capilene is coupled with an outer layer of rag wool. This tandem reduces friction and thus the odds of developing blisters.

Ah, but time and sock technology marches on.

For years now, a whole lot of other hikers, including myself, have opted to one-sock it. I prefer wearing hiking-specific socks, such as those made by Thorlo, a company that weaves and markets a line of socks specifically for hikers, and even for specific kinds of hiking. I've appreciated the company's usage suggestions (i.e. "light hiking") and found these recommendations to be right on target.

A good-fitting sock should be snug, but not tight. Bring your hiking boots with you when you sock shop (and bring your hiking socks with you when you boot shop). Sock thickness can bump up your boot size a half-size or more.

Many hikers are prepared to spend the money for a good pair of boots but go into sticker shock when they see the cost of quality hiking socks. Nevertheless, don't stint on socks. Wearing cotton gym socks with your new hiking boots is almost guaranteed to make your feet—and hike—very unhappy. The new SmartWool socks are well worth their price and are far superior to the scratchy rag wool socks of the past.

Carefully check sock sizes on the package. Don't know your hiking sock size? Not to worry, neither does anybody else. (The way sock-makers size socks is truly bizarre.) Some quality European brand socks have Euro-sizes and correlating Euro shoes sizes printed on the package in much larger print than the American sizes. If your sock size is anywhere close to falling "between sizes" try the pair on! One manufacturer's size medium might be another manufacturer's large. Other sock makers put the "M" and "W" for Men and Women in a type size so small you need a magnifying glass to see it.

(Both my wife and I have failed to read the sock package fine print, which explains why Cheri has a pair of small black men's hiking socks in her sock drawer and The Trailmaster has a pair of large pinkish-purplish women's socks in his.)

Fresh feet are happy feet. On any day hike longer than half a day, consider bringing an extra pair of socks. Change socks at midday and hang your damp pair on the back of your day pack to dry.

Hiking Sandals

I admit it—I'm more comfortable wearing hiking boots than any other footwear, and that includes running shoes, dress shoes, sandals and worst of all for me, being barefoot.

My wife and kids, however, wear sandals nine months out of the year. They almost have to be coaxed into lacing up their hiking boots, and would prefer to be barefoot almost every day.

For them, and other like-minded hikers, the introduction of hiking sandals has solved a real problem. Originally designed for river-running, these new-generation sandals designed for hiking feature shock-absorbing soles and well-designed strap systems. Several boot manufacturers have gotten into the act and produced sandals that offer both support and protection.

Barefoot Hiking Advice

- Always step straight down; don't shuffle or drag your feet.
- Watch the path ahead, especially when you're hiking uneven terrain.
- Try to keep your weight on the balls of your feet and not on your heels.

Some fresh-air fiends and hikers who just prefer the freedom offered by this approach to footwear (my family members among them) swear by these high-tech hiking sandals, especially for beach walks or streamside hikes, rambles with many creek-crossings, or simply on very hot days. But for me, it's socks and boots on every hike.

Shoeless Wonders

Hiking without boots? Most of us wouldn't dream of it. There are, however, a handful of hikers out there who swear by barefoot hiking to better connect with nature and to lessen their impact on the environment.

Richard K. Frazine, author of the book *The Barefoot Hiker,* claims, "There is nothing more natural than hiking through nature barefoot. The soles of your feet and toes are wonderful sensory organs and the myriad of feelings from earth, grass, moss, pine-needles, and mud are wonderful. Many could not see hiking any other way."

If you are yearning for a barefoot trail experience, there are a dozen or so barefoot hiking groups in the United States, Canada and the U.K. Many are in surprisingly chilly locations—Connecticut, New York, Southern Ontario, and Pennsylvania, though it's likely that only the hardiest (or craziest) of these souls take to the trails in the wintertime. Take a look at their website www.barefooters.org/hikers for details.

Accessories

Walking Sticks

Hikers who carry walking sticks may not look like the toughest guys on the trails, but they are doing their muscles and joints a gigantic favor. Walking sticks and hiking poles help with balance, absorb shock, and provide much-welcomed leverage for steep ascents.

While I don't consider a staff or pole an absolute hiking "essential," I'm convinced that its utility is highly underrated.

There are several terms out there for products that serve—essentially—the same function: Walking stick, hiking stick, walking staff, hiking pole, trekking pole, Nordic pole. In my discussion, I'll used the terms interchangeably; the differences between the terms are highly debatable, if they even exist at all.

Walking sticks help a great deal with balance. Many senior hikers swear by them for this reason alone. Having a third, or even fourth "leg" to lean on can increase your confidence on the trail tremendously. And this added balance is especially critical when you're hiking over uneven terrain, on winding, narrow trails, and when crossing streams and rivers.

Walking sticks also redistribute weight from your lower body to your arms and shoulders, easing up the strain on your knees, hips, ankles and lower back. They are a blessing for those of us who are prone to aching joints. Walking sticks can help to improve posture, too, which makes breathing much less labored, especially when climbing steep terrain. And better breathing can help your endurance considerably.

Some hikers enjoy collecting the metal medallions made to affix to a wooden hiking stick. Hint: if you do a lot of hiking, fasten those medallions you purchased at park visitor centers from around the country on a second hiking stick—creating an object d'art that you can proudly display at home.

My own children felt they had truly arrived as full-fledged hikers when I purchased each of them a hiking stick. Nimble and very-well balanced without a stick, they nevertheless like carrying a stick and poking at things along the trail. And they love collecting the trail medallions from everywhere we go!

Depending on your physical and aesthetic preferences, there are (like so many hiking gadgets!) a wide variety of poles, staffs, and sticks out there.

> *"Forget not that the earth delights to feel your bare feet and the winds long to play with your hair."*
>
> —KAHLIL GIBRAN
> *The Prophet*

Wooden Walking Sticks

Wooden staffs are the true classic in this arena. Not only are they functional on the trail, but they've held a prominent place in human history—not only as primitive weapons, but also as travel aids. Greek gods were often depicted with large wooden staffs. Shepherds wouldn't be shepherds without their telltale staffs, and Egyptian hieroglyphics include countless images of travelers with walking sticks in hand. And what about the story of Moses parting the Red Sea? Or the one about drawing water from a stone?

It's unlikely that you'll be able to use your staff to get water from a rock, but it will help to negotiate steep descents and winding trails.

Walking sticks can be made from many different kinds of wood— willow, maple, dogwood, hawthorn, hickory, oak, you name it. Hardwood sticks have greater lasting power than their softwood counterparts, which have a tendency to splinter and fall apart, especially at the bottom where the stick comes into contact with the ground.

You can make a walking stick yourself (if you have the carving skills), or buy them (probably the better bet for most of us). They are sometimes difficult to find in outdoor retail stores, but there are several places online that carry—and even specialize in—walking sticks. Whistle Creek at www.whistlecreek.com appears to have the greatest selection, but look around for yourself. The internet is always changing, and you'll never know what you'll find.

The downside to buying walking sticks online is that you can't test them out to see how they feel. I know of a guy who has had considerable success using old broom sticks. He removes the bristle end and replaces it with a cane tip, and claims that the resulting "staff" is far sturdier than any that are hand-carved.

What this frugal method leaves out, however, is the importance of the walking stick's size. All the benefits of using a great stick are

Hiking Sticks Help You

- Ease your knees on steep descents
- Balance while traversing uneven terrain
- Cross fast-flowing streams
- Scare away menacing dogs
- Support an impromptu rain shelter
- Clear spider webs overhanging trails
- Probe areas where snakes are suspected

lost when hiking with one that is either too long, or too short. The perfect walking stick should be about 6 inches higher than your elbow. Any shorter, and you'll find yourself hunching over; any longer, and you'll find it awkward to climb even small hills.

The benefits of choosing wooden over aluminum hiking sticks are largely aesthetic. Some people simply prefer the rustic charm of a hand carved wooden walking stick to a straight-as-an arrow mass-produced metal one. Cost is another factor to consider when comparing the two: sticks start at less than half the price of metal poles, and require fewer parts and accessories.

Trekking Poles

More and more people are turning to aluminum or titanium "trekking poles" for support on the trail, and understandably so. Trekking poles are lightweight (compared with their wooden counterparts), sturdy, and best of all—adjustable.

Most trekking poles are made from aluminum or a titanium alloy, so they are extremely lightweight. Many of the newer poles weigh as little as 9 or 10 ounces apiece, and are usually sold in pairs.

One of the neatest things about poles is that they're collapsible. Usually two or three sections make up the pole shaft. These sections telescope neatly into one another, and make storage and travel a breeze. Three section poles are the easiest to carry or store, but are more prone to breaking than two-section poles, which have fewer parts and longer pole sections.

Virtually all poles have handles, which protect you from the cold metal of the pole shaft, and keep your hand from slipping on warm days. The most common handle materials are rubber and cork, and there are benefits to each. Cork can absorb moisture more easily than rubber, but rubber will prove far more durable in the long run.

Nordic Walking Poles

The use of Nordic walking poles is starting to catch on in North America. Like their trekking pole cousins, Nordic walking poles keep you stable and in balance on almost any surface, and help build strength.

They can be one-piece lightweight, composite poles or slightly heavier and collapsible. Nordic walking have switchable tips that work on hard surfaces and grass and sand, as well as special strapping systems and grips shaped for efficiency and comfort.

The most important factor to keep in mind when evaluating walking sticks or hiking poles is comfort. And the only person who can determine what feels good to you is, well, you. Like other products mentioned in this book, it's extremely important that you test them out for yourself. Perhaps you'll find that a broomstick suits you just fine.

Binoculars

There seems to be endless selection when it comes to outdoor gadgets and gizmos. Binoculars are no exception. Before you buy a pair, ask yourself some questions about how they will be used: How much do I want to spend? How will my binoculars be used—for casually taking in the views, or serious bird-watching? Will they be routinely exposed to rain or snow?

One thing that you'll discover when binocular shopping is that they have unique, and perhaps baffling, terminology to describe their various technical features. Here's brief explanation of the most critical terms:

• **Focus** On most binoculars, this is adjusted using a control located between the lenses. This is appropriately called "center focusing." Many of the better pairs allow you to first focus your left eye (while closing the right) using the center control, and then tweak the image by turning the right eyepiece (with the left eye closed). Once the right eyepiece (or diopter) is adjusted, it's very easy to focus the pair using the center control alone. With individual focusing models, you adjust the focus on each lens every time—this can become a major nuisance after awhile.

• **Field of view** This tells you how much you can see (in terms of area, not detail) from 1,000 yards away. Remember, the higher the magnification, the smaller the field of view. High field of view binoculars are your best bet for viewing wildlife from a distance, or for taking in the view from a mountaintop.

• **Magnification power and objective lens diameter** These numbers are listed together in model descriptions—8×25, 7×35, etc. The first number refers to magnification, and the second refers to the diameter of your objective lens. For instance, an 8×25 model magnifies whatever you are looking at by eight times, making the object appear eight times closer. It also has objective lenses (the ones farthest from your eyes) that measure 25 millimeters across.

It's pretty obvious what a higher magnification power can do for you—the greater the magnification power, the closer things appear. They also magnify your hand movements, so be careful. Without a tripod, high-powered binoculars offer a really jerky view.

With objective lens diameters, the wider the lens, the more light can enter the binoculars. A large objective lens diameter can be especially helpful in low-light conditions.

• **Exit pupil** This refers to the amount of light that reaches the pupils of your eyes. The larger the exit pupil, the more light reaches your eye, and the brighter the view through your binoculars appears. To get the exit pupil measurement, divide the objective lens diameter number (or the second number) by the magnification power (or the first number). The higher the resulting number, the better your low-light viewing though most experts agree that a 3mm to 5mm exit pupil is adequate for regular daytime use.

• **Prisms** Prisms bend and transmit light inside the binoculars, so that the images that reach your eyes are clear, bright, and right-side up. There are two different kinds of prisms to consider. While we may not be able to tell you their precise technical differences, roof prism binocs are generally most favored by hikers and backpackers. They may be more expensive than their counterparts (porro prisms), but they are considerably lighter and less bulky. Porro prisms offer a better depth of field, which, depending on your activity, may be worth the extra weight.

Heart-Rate Monitors

People wear heart-rate monitors for all sorts of reasons. Some have a heart condition that requires them to keep careful tabs on exercise, while others find them helpful for weight loss or building up endurance.

Most heart-rate devices used for exercise have a strap with built-in electrodes that fits around your chest and monitors your heart rate where it's the strongest (at your heart, of course!). Your EKG (the German acronym for electrocardiogram) signal is then transmitted to a monitor unit that is usually worn on the wrist and looks deceptively like a watch. Beyond this, heart-rate monitors vary quite a bit. You can get ones that tell you the date, time, and have a built-in stopwatch, lap timer, compass and altimeter.

Pedometers

Pedometers are groovy little devices that track how far you hike. By sensing your body motion and electronically counting your footsteps, these gizmos can inform you of the distance walked. Enter your stride length and hit the trail!

On your walks around town, a pedometer can be a great way of motivating yourself to measure your mileage. Because pedometers rely on stride-length for their calculations, their accuracy is better at measuring a pedestrian's progress on a level route around town than a hiker's mileage on an up-and-down and uneven trail.

Missed steps are to be expected. Some pedometers are too sensitive, some not sensitive enough. Recent consumer tests report that some pedometers slightly undercount and others way over-count steps. The good news is pedometers under- or over-count consistently, so you can do a little math and improve their accuracy.

Pedometer sales have soared in tandem with the popularity of the "10,000 Steps" program that promotes good health and weight-loss by counting one's daily steps with a pedometer. Ten thousand steps per day is a worthy goal for good health and weight management, particularly if half or more of those steps occur during an uninterrupted walk.

Multi-function pedometers do more than count steps and/or calculate distance. Options include clocks, timers, stop watches, "speedo-meters," pulse-rate readers and calorie counters.

Picking a Pedometer

- A pedometer should fasten securely with a sturdy clip and be comfortable to wear.

- Choose one that allows you to easily adjust stride measurement—a particularly important feature for the hiker.

- Look for one that does a good job with the basics: measuring steps and calculating total distance traveled.

- Make sure the pedometer has an easily readable display, large enough and bright enough to view, even as you're hiking.

- A built-in clock is useful if you're one of those hikers who doesn't like to wear a wrist watch.

- Consider a safety leash for your pedometer to prevent dropping it or losing it.

Chapter 10 Ten Essentials

B Y NOW, I'VE FORGOTTEN EACH AND EVERY ONE OF THE TEN ESSEN-
tials on one hike or another. And always regretted it. I've left
the trail map in the car and grabbed a bag of hamster food
instead of a bag of trail mix off the kitchen counter. I can't seem to
remember to check the freshness of my flashlight batteries and I forget to replenish the supplies in my first-aid kit. When airport security
confiscated my trusty Swiss Army knife out of my day pack, I assured
myself I could do without a pocket knife for a week of hiking.
(Naturally, I needed it several times . . .)

How many essentials are there in the Ten Essentials?

No, this isn't a whimsical question like "Who's buried in Grant's
tomb?"

Some hiking experts count twelve or even fourteen essentials.
And what about the day pack, essential to carry those essentials,
shouldn't that count as an essential? New hikers argue that a cell
phone should be the eleventh essential while veterans insist it
should be "common sense". Some Ten Essentials lists include matches and fire starter as two separate essentials, some count them as one
essential. Some lists include water, some don't. Items that usually
finish just out of the top ten but that are considered essential by
some hikers include signaling devices (whistle and mirror) and insect
repellent.

A Ten Essentials list was first circulated in the 1930s by The
Mountaineers, an outings club located in Seattle. Since then it has
become a kind of gospel among hikers and an essential teaching tool
in outdoor education programs.

In This Chapter

- The Ten Essentials
- Features of a good compass
- A hiker's first-aid kit
- All about sun protection

1. Map

Even if you're positive about where you're headed and how to get there, it's wise to bring a map with you on the trail. You can find good trail maps at specialty outdoors stores, travel bookstores and a number of on-line outlets. Use care when you select a map off the rack. Many maps sold to tourists are okay for civic sightseeing, but don't show the backcountry in the kind of detail we hikers require.

Maps in trail guidebooks and from local and regional park authorities vary in quality from great to abysmal. Funky hand-drawn maps or poor-quality reproductions are indicators that you should purchase additional maps of the region in which you intend to hike.

Forest Service maps are available at ranger stations and various commercial outlets for a small fee. They're general maps, showing roads, rivers, and trails. The Forest Service usually keeps its maps fairly up-to-date. Topographic maps show terrain (elevations, waterways, vegetation and improvements) in great detail.

2. Compass

A compass and map go hand in hand. Once you figure out how to use them together, you'll find yourself racing around the back-country with confidence.

Some of the features to look for in a good compass:
- One that registers 0 to 360 degrees with two-degree increments
- Liquid filled to protect the magnetic needle and reduce fluctuation
- Adjustable declination to be able to adjust for the difference between magnetic north and true north
- A base plate that can be used as a straight-edge for determining distances on maps
- A pop-up mirror for making sightings

3. Water

"Drink before you're thirsty" should be the hiker's mantra. Bring plenty of water for your hike, plus some extra. And drink it! As ridiculous as it sounds, The Trailmaster has observed many hikers who remember to pack water, but don't take the time to drink it.

Try to bring your entire water supply for the day with you so that you don't have to rely on trailside streams. It's still possible to drink from a very select number of backcountry creeks and springs without ill effect, but each individual water source should be carefully scrutinized.

With a few exceptions, I reluctantly advise: Don't drink untreated water. Many hikers assume water is pure and 48 hours later have a queasy feeling that tells them their assumption was wrong. Even clear-looking waters may harbor the organism *Giardia lamblia*, one of the causes of "traveler's diarrhea." Treat any backcountry drinking water with purification tablets and/or a quality filter.

4. Extra Food

Don't be shy about bringing more than you think you might eat. Your hunger—or the day's plans—may surprise you, and you'll want to be prepared.

On a day hike, weight is rarely an issue, so you can pack whatever you wish. Remember to pack out what you pack in. The day you hike is not the day to diet. Calorie counters rejoice: There's a lot of calorie burning on a hike and quite an energy cost. You'll need all your strength, particularly on steep grades. Energy bars, GORP, or trail mix, with fruit, nuts, raisins, and M&M's are good high-octane fuels. A sandwich, fruit and cookies make a good lunch. A continental spread featuring sourdough bread, a fine cheese and a splash of chardonnay is also nice.

Snack regularly and avoid a big lunch. Exertion afterward sets up a competition between your stomach and your legs and your legs lose, leading to weakness and indigestion.

5. Extra Clothes

Wherever you travel, there's a good chance you'll encounter some old timer who loves the old adage, "If you don't like the weather in (pick a region), then wait five minutes." It almost doesn't matter where you're hiking, the weather often changes quickly and with little warning. The trick is to be prepared. If you start out on a warm sunny morning, dress accordingly (t-shirt, shorts), but bring along a long-sleeved button-down shirt or pullover and a pair of lightweight pants. Vice versa, of course, if it's cold. The extra shirt is especially nice when stopping or sitting down to rest on the trail. It's surprising how chilly you can get when you stop moving, particularly when you're in dry weather, wind, or high altitudes.

Extra clothes also come in handy after an unexpected fall into a creek or on a wet, muddy trail. Depending on the climate, dry clothes might be the key to saving an otherwise lousy hike.

6. First-Aid Kit

While you don't need to lug along your entire medicine cabinet, there are a few essential items that will make any trip much safer and more comfortable. It's important to be prepared for a range of mishaps: blisters, cuts, scrapes, sprained ankles, among other things. Here's what to include in your kit:

- A small assortment of adhesive bandages in various sizes.
- Antiseptic towelettes
- Antibiotic ointment
- Sterile dressing a small roll of adhesive tape for larger cuts
- Antihistamine and ibuprofen tablets for allergies and aches
- Anti-diarrheal tablets (not a necessity, but they might make your trip a whole lot more pleasant)
- Moleskin, for blisters

- Ace bandage—really helpful in the event of a sprained ankle
- A couple of safety pins. These can help with the oddest of medical and non-medical mishaps—a torn t-shirt, a broken zipper, you name it.
- Some hikers swear by homeopathic products such as Rescue Remedy cream and tincture and arnica.

Larger injuries are less common on the trail, and for those, I suggest you consult a more comprehensive first-aid manual.

7. Pocket Knife

From slicing salami to cutting an ace bandage to rigging emergency shelter, a pocket knife is an indispensable tool on any hike. Knives really run the gamut of price, utility and style, and you can find yourself paying as little as five or as much as $70 for these gadgets. Almost any pocket knife will do on a day hike, as long as you keep these criteria in mind: your knife must be clean, sturdy, and sharp.

Few know basic wilderness preparedness as well as the Boy Scouts—and the Official Boy Scout Handbook offers guidelines for caring for your knife that are worth noting:

- Keep your knife clean, dry and sharp at all times
- Never use it on things that will dull or break it
- Keep it off the ground. Moisture and dirt will ruin it.
- Wipe the blade clean after using it
- Treat the joints to an occasional drop of machine oil so that the blades will keep opening easily.

To keep your knife sharp, you'll need to use a sharpening stone. You can find these at most hardware stores, and they're cheap—often less than five bucks. They're extremely easy to use, and they make your knife a whole lot easier to use.

8. Sun Protection

No matter where you live, or what season it is, hikers need to be take precaution against the hazards of the sun's rays. Overexposure can leave you fatigued, dehydrated, and painfully burned. A combination of a hat, sunglasses, sunblock and the right clothing can keep you properly shaded from the sun.

It's important to be extra sun-savvy when hiking in high altitudes, long stretches of un-shaded terrain, and when the sun is at its most intense—roughly between the hours of 10 A.M. and 2 P.M.

9. Flashlight

Although you may have no intention to stick around on the trail past sunset, it's a good idea to carry a flashlight or headlamp every time you head out for a hike. It's easy to underestimate just how long a particular hike might take, and you might find yourself scrambling down the mountain as dusk approaches. Without a flashlight, you're far more likely to lose your way, take a fall, or worse, panic.

Many seasoned hikers have stories about getting stuck on the trail after dark. And most will tell you that packing a flashlight is a classic case of "better safe than sorry."

It's easy to bring one with you. A light can be inexpensive, light-weight, and—if you bring along a set of extra batteries—pretty reliable. Headlamps are now more popular than ever. They're just as good (or better) than regular flashlights, and they have the added benefit of being hands-free. You'll need to make sure that your flash-light throws a strong enough beam to light up a trail in total dark-ness. Check with store clerks (or online) about beam-strength. Many of the cheaper, drugstore lights may be great for nighttime reading, but won't help you navigate a dark trail. Some flashlights, like the mini Maglite, boast a high-intensity beam that can adjust from "spot" to "flood," or from a bright, focused point of light to a wider, slightly dimmer beam—kind of like the zoom lens on a camera.

Whichever you choose, be sure that you find one that's water-proof. While you may never get stuck in the dark when it's raining (cross your fingers), it's worth the extra expense.

10. Matches and Firestarter

Firestarter is fool-proof kindling for starting emergency fires in the wilderness. Anything from rolled up newspaper, pinecones dipped in paraffin, to store-bought sawdust "nuggets" work to get flames going in a jiffy. Some backpackers recommend petroleum jelly-saturated cotton balls—stored in old film canisters, birthday candles, and paraffin-covered dryer lint. There are a zillion options.

But day hikers generally don't need to go all out with firestarter. More than likely, you'll never use it, but it's an important item to bring along in case of an emergency. Tuck one of the above men-tioned items in a plastic bag, keep it in a dry corner of your pack, and forget about it.

A handy—and necessary—firestarter companion is, of course, a box of matches. It's best to buy the waterproof or "stormproof" vari-ety for trips on the trail. Camping supply stores carry them. Keep your matches wrapped up, toss them into your pack with your firestarter, and you're set for any day trip—and unforeseen emer-gency.

Caring for Your Sunglasses

- Avoid leaving lenses face down on any hard surface

- Keep your sunglasses in a glasses case or pouch (many manufacturers provide these) when you aren't wearing them.

- Avoid putting them in a pocket where loose coins, keys or other objects may damage the lenses.

- Never leave them in or near intense heat such as the dashboard or your vehicle.

- Clean by rinsing under warm water. Dry gently with a soft clean cloth. Do not use paper towels or any cleaning agents containing ammonia.

All About Sun Protection

SKIMPING on sun protection just isn't worth it. Just ask anyone who's recently felt the sting of a bad sunburn, and they'll tell you one thing: OUCH! Not only does a sunburn feel terrible, it increases your risk for melanoma and other types of skin cancer. Given the vast array of sun protection possibilities on the market today, there's no excuse for not covering up, or slathering on sunblock when heading outside.

No matter what the weather—sun, fog, haze or snow—you'll need to take some precaution against sun damage. Wearing good, waterproof sunblock or a wide-brimmed hat is your best bet, and the combination of the two is even better.

Picking out the right sunblock can be confusing. Do you want something water-proof or water-resistant? Non-comedogenic? Something that offers UVA protection? UVB protection? Both? What does SPF mean, anyway?

Basically, UVA and UVB describe two different wavelengths of ultraviolet light. While UVB causes the most immediate and visible burn damage, both UVB and UVA rays are found in sunlight and can cause major damage to human skin. It is widely recognized that overexposure to UVA and UVB rays can dramatically increase your risk for skin cancer.

SPF stands for Sun Protection Factor, and only refers to UVB protection. It tells you how much time you can spend in the sun before your particular skin type will burn. An SPF 20 sunblock, for instance, should provide twenty times your natural skin protection against UVB damage. So if you ordinarily begin to turn pink after 8 minutes in the sun, the application of SPF 20 sunblock will theoretically give you 160 blissful, burn-free minutes in the sunshine.

But these numbers aren't always so accurate. While you can find sunblocks that boast an SPF of 45 or higher, most experts agree that there is little to indicate any real difference between an SPF 45 from SPF 30. And while a high SPF sunblock can offer great UVB protection, it doesn't necessarily protect against UVA damage—the main culprit in the premature aging of the skin.

There are, however, sunblocks that claim to provide "broad-spectrum" (UVA and UVB) protection. These are your best bets. In a recent study, *Consumer Reports* magazine found that a few sunblocks provided the promised amount of UVB protection, and offered complete (or near complete) UVA protection. Rite-Aid Sunblock (SPF 30) and Walgreens Ultra Sunblock (SPF 30) proved to offer the best bang for the buck. Both rated "Excellent" and are easy on the wallet. If you want to spring for a brand name, Banana Boat Sport Sunscreen and Coppertone Sport Sunblock rated "Excellent" as well.

Studies vary in their evaluations of water-resistant and waterproof sunblock protection. We recommend that you opt for the water-proof, and if you tend to sweat a lot while hiking, reapply sunblock every couple of hours to be safe.

Sunglasses

Most sunglasses these days offer 100 percent UV protection—a feature no hiker should forego, however cheap or cool-looking a pair of specs may be. Some of the fancier sunglasses boast scratch-resistant polycarbonate lenses, aerodynamic design, and polarization to cut down on glare.

One of the most important criteria for picking out a pair to wear on the trail is—how comfortable are they?

Ideally, you'll put on sunglasses every time you go for a hike, and end up wearing them for several hours, so how do they feel? Do they pinch the tops of your ears? Can you move around without knocking them off your head? Will they slide off your nose as you begin to sweat?

Some of the well-known brands (Oakley, Smith, etc.) make glasses that have hydrophilic rubber "socks" that cover the glasses' stems, and become tacky when wet. Many have readily-replaceable lenses, which make it easy to replace one that gets scratched, or pick another lens color. Others claim to retain their form—and not break—when sat on, stepped on, or otherwise abused.

Chapter 11 Food and Water

THE GREAT TRAIL MIX TASTE TEST WAS THE FIRST (AND LAST) publicity stunt I ever cooked up. Here was the plan: To promote my new hiking guide detailing the wild side of L.A., I would take Rich Morada, the sports reporter for KFI, a major metro news-talk station, on a hike in the wilds of Griffith Park. Rich good naturedly agreed to accompany me, as well as to judge a trail mix tasting. The four trail mix contenders were three store bought brands and my wife Cheri's special homemade blend, which I figured would win the contest easily.

The hike went very well, with birds singing and astonishing (for smog city) clear-day panoramas from the mountains to the sparkling blue Pacific, and live, lively dispatches from the cell phone back to the morning talk show host.

We reached Amir's Garden, sat down at a picnic table and Rich began to taste-test the trail mixes.

That's when the trouble began.

"I like the simple kind," the sports reporter began, giving high marks to a just raisins and peanuts variety.

Uh-oh. If Cheri's trail mix doesn't win I'll never hear the end of it. She will have been humiliated on the city's most popular drive-time radio show.

"I don't know about this one with all the stuff in it."

Enter Amir Dialameh, who tended his namesake garden on the slopes of Mt. Hollywood for three decades. "This is the best one," he pronounced, savoring Cheri's mix.

"What's this weird thing—papaya or something?" the sportscaster complained.

"Mango," Amir countered, "and it's quite delicious. Try the white chocolate chips."

"Okay, I'll defer to Amir on this one. We have a winner. What brand is it, John?"

"Amir, Rich, you have good taste. That's my wife Cheri's secret

In This Chapter

- Favorite foods for the trail
- Nutrition for hikers
- Quenching your thirst

recipe, which I will reveal to your listeners. First she takes. . . ."

That was close.

WHETHER YOU'RE A TRADITIONALIST or an experimental gourmand, you're sure to enjoy eating on the trail. Day hikers have a multitude of options when it comes to snacking. Depending on your palate and your budget, you can pack away anything from wine and fancy imported cheeses to granola bars. I know of a guy who actually packed a watermelon on a long day hike in the High Sierra. How carried away you get is really up to you and your taste buds, wallet, and in some cases, physical ability.

Most people I know tend to go pretty simple with their food on the trail. Hiking makes everything taste delicious (well, almost). The boring peanut butter and crackers that you overlook when you're home make for a tasty feast when you're outdoors.

Use common sense with your menu selections. Don't bring anything on the hike that is prone to quick spoilage, especially if you are hiking in the heat. For example, mayonnaise-laden egg salad would be a bad choice for a hot desert hike—or any hike at all!

It's important not to pack large meals, but rather, put together a variety of snacks that can be eaten throughout the day. Eating too much at one sitting can make you feel bloated and sluggish.

Favorite Trail Foods

Dried fruit Grocery stores seem to be stocking a greater selection of dried fruit these days. Places like Trader Joe's, Whole Foods and health food stores not only carry your basic banana chips and prunes, but often have more exotic dried fare like strawberries, mangoes, pineapples and blueberries. Yum. Dried fruit is easy to pack, high in carbohydrates (a good thing when you're climbing hills all day), won't spoil in the heat, and is—of course—really tasty.

Jerky Meat and meat alternatives have also gotten swept up in the dehydration frenzy. In addition to the old stand by, beef jerky, some stores and online catalogs now carry turkey, pork, clam, salmon, elk, buffalo, and tofu jerky. Yikes. You never know what they'll come up with next. The cool thing about jerky is that it has a lot of protein and gives a person a kind of Early Man experience: the chance to gnaw away at dried meat in the middle of the woods.

Cheese and crackers A satisfying protein-carbohydrate-fat combination, and a cinch to prepare and carry. Hard cheeses pack much better than the softer ones, and can withstand a surprising amount of heat. Whole-grain crackers, flatbread or even a hunk of your favorite sourdough bread are all easy to pack and great to eat.

Chocolate It tastes great at home, even better on a mountain top. But be forewarned: chocolate melts in the heat, and can turn into a gooey mess. (Many would argue that it tastes better that way.)

Cheri's Trail Mix

1 cup white chocolate chips

1 cup dried mango

1 cup dried apricots

1 cup raw almonds

1 cup dried cherries

¼ cup crystalized ginger

Mix ingredients in a plastic bag

Fresh fruit Apples and oranges are among the easiest to carry with you. They can round out a meal of peanut butter sandwiches or crackers rather nicely. Fruits like bananas, cherries, and peaches tend to bruise easily, get mushy in your pack and are best left at the trailhead for a post-hike snack. Grapes are great, as long as they're carefully packed.

Veggies Consider cut-up or baby carrots and celery. For a more exotic taste treat, try sweet red peppers or jicama.

Bars Energy bars, granola bars, protein bars, whatever you want to call them. Bar fever has hit the outdoor recreation industry like nothing else, and everyone seems to have a favorite brand and flavor. Keep a few in your pack. If you don't eat them that day, they can keep for the next hike. They're also a superb emergency-food source.

Ants on a log A favorite in every kindergarten classroom, this tasty snack is also great on the trail. If you missed out on ants on a log in childhood, fear not! They are simple to make. Cut up a bunch of celery, fill stalks with peanut butter, and sprinkle with raisins. They're a great source of protein, carbohydrates, fat, fiber and flavor.

GORP "Good Old Raisins and Peanuts," or trail mix, has been a part of the hiking experience for generations. But if GORP really only consisted of raisins and peanuts, it wouldn't be nearly as popular as it is. Hikers have added all kinds of great stuff to it over the years, and now things like M&Ms, almonds, chopped-up dried fruit, and coconut have become GORP mainstays.

Making your own GORP at home is a cinch, and it allows you to throw together foods and flavors you really love. Begin with basic GORP recipes and customize to your heart's desire.

Fuel for the Trail

"Fat," "calories," and "carbohydrates" have become dirty words these days. And for good reason. Obesity has become a widespread problem in this country, and many agree that high-calorie diets are the major culprits.

But a large part of the problem is lack of exercise. In fact, doctors frequently point to walking and hiking as two of the best ways to improve health and lose weight.

If we think of our bodies as complex machines, we need food to fuel us along. When we place strenuous demands on the body— exercise, heavy labor, cold weather activity—we burn more fuel then we may otherwise need.

Hiking is more physically taxing then many of us might think. Unlike ordinary walking, hiking often involves steep uphill climbs, rugged terrain, a heavy load, and battles with the elements. These demands on the body call for higher-calorie foods, particularly carbohydrates and fats.

With that in mind, however, hiking every now and again shouldn't be excuse to constantly pig-out. It is important to balance how much you consume with how much you exercise.

Tasty Trail Mix

1 cup dry cereal (pick your favorite!)
1 cup M&M's
1 cup peanuts
1 cup raisins
1 cup dried fruit
1 cup yogurt-covered almonds or peanuts
1 cup sunflower seeds
1 cup pretzels

Mix ingredients in a plastic bag.

Healthy (and tasty!) Trail Mix

½ cup roasted soynuts, plain or seasoned depending on your tastes
½ cup flaked coconut
¼ cup carob chips
1 cup mix dried fruit (tropical mixes that include bananas, mango, and pineapple are a good choices)
¼ cup shelled sunflower seeds

Mix ingredients in a plastic bag.

How much do we really use?

It's difficult to estimate how many calories a given person expends while hiking. The pace of the hike, incline, outdoor temperature, size of the hiker, and what he or she is carrying, are all factors that affect how the body utilizes "fuel."

That said, many agree that a 150-pound person hiking 2 mph and carrying a 20-pound pack is likely to burn about 300 calories per hour. Bigger hikers burn more calories, as do hikers who maintain a faster clip, carry more weight, or hike in cold weather. While estimates vary tremendously, this can give you a rough idea why hikers get so darned hungry. So eat up!

Nutrition Basics

- **Carbohydrates** Although low- or even no-carb eating is all the rage today, carbs have the most immediate effect on a person's energy level. They provide roughly 100 calories per ounce, and are immediately absorbed into the body as blood sugar. Simple sugars (like candy, juice, or fruit) digest more quickly than complex carbohydrates (whole grain bread and crackers) which take a couple of hours. Both have their place in a hiker's diet: choose simple carbs for quick energy and complex carbs for pre-hike breakfasts or sit-down lunches. The longer you're on the trail, the more carbohydrates you'll need to keep your energy up throughout the day.

- **Fat** Despite its notorious reputation, fat is essential to any diet. By themselves, carbohydrates offer a high jolt of energy, and then cause us to crash. Packing about 200 calories per ounce, fats digest more slowly than carbohydrates and help to even out the highs and lows from blood sugar fluctuation.

- **Protein** Protein is a critical part of any diet. Like fat, it digests slowly, and is a great complement to high carbohydrate consumption, and provides roughly 80 calories per ounce. Nuts, cheeses, jerky and lunchmeat are all great sources of protein on the trail.

- **Salt** It is difficult to avoid salt. These days, most packaged foods are loaded with salt, and many people are advised to drastically cut down on their sodium intake. It is worth mentioning here, nonetheless. Because we lose sodium and other minerals during periods of strenuous exercise, eating a few salty snacks (along with ample water) can help to keep the body's mineral balance intact.

Water 101

As you may know, hiking without sufficient water can be extremely uncomfortable, and potentially disastrous.

Individuals are constantly losing water, even at rest. Respiration, urination and perspiration are all a part of basic day-to-day functioning. And when out on the trail, hikers invariably sweat more and breathe harder than usual. This increased activity accelerates water loss, especially in hot, dry, climates and in high altitudes. Long hikes in hot weather can cause a body to lose up to two gallons of water per day.

Keeping yourself hydrated isn't rocket science. Just be sure to drink ample water before and after the hike, and on the trail. In very rare instances, people have managed to over-hydrate, but that's an almost impossible feat. For most people, the only downside to drinking excessive fluids is frequent trips to the bathroom. Or the bushes.

Many experts recommend drinking one-half to one quart of water for every hour you're on the trail. I'd say this amount is likely to be excessive for cool, low altitude hikes, so think realistically about the location and duration of your hike.

Hikers should not, however, wait until thirsty to gulp down fluids. Thirst is a sign of mild dehydration, which at best, decreases stamina and makes one sluggish. At its most severe, dehydration can impair judgment, cause severe nausea and headaches and, in extreme cases, lead to death. Not a pretty thought.

During exercise, fluids and valuable electrolytes are lost. Electrolytes contain high concentrations of sodium, potassium, and other minerals, and are critical to healthy cell functioning. Some people swear by electrolyte replacement drinks (Gatorade, Powerade, etc.) to stay hydrated. Sports drink come in crazy colors, have cool names like "Glacier Freeze" or "Riptide Rush," and are quite tasty and refreshing.

Fortunately, the kidneys were designed to keep electrolyte levels pretty well regulated. Although sports drink manufacturers might have you believing otherwise, humans have managed to survive tens of thousands of years before Gatorade was ever invented.

The good news for day hikers is that tap water works just fine—or bottled water if you're a purist. Never drink untreated water from trailside water sources (more about this later in the chapter). There are any number of ways to pack your water—in anything from fancy hydration packs, to unbreakable polyethylene containers, to old plastic soda bottles. Consider whether you want to carry a lot of water, a little water or if you want to treat backcountry water.

The most expensive option is a hydration pack—a small backpack that can hold anywhere from 50 to 100 ounces of water in a plastic "bladder" that slides right into a sleeve in the back of the pack. A tube extends from the bladder to the outside of the pack, and can be kept right at chest or shoulder level—so you can easily turn your head for a quick sip.

These packs vary quite a bit in price, but it's unlikely that you'll find anything under $60. In some cases, hydration day packs can run as much as $200. Be careful about picking one in this category that's too small. Your Ten Essentials and various personal items need to fit in the pack.

Bladder packs come in many models of sizes so try on a few varieties to see what you think and what fits well. For example, I tested

Signs of dehydration include:

- thirst
- dizziness
- confusion
- fatigue
- dry mouth
- less-frequent urination
- dry skin
- headache
- light-headedness
- increased heart rate

out the Camelbak Cloudwalker and found it to be a little skimpy for long day hikes, but perfect for shorter trips. Some of these packs are big enough to carry your refrigerator (well, almost), while others can hold little more than a granola bar and band-aids.

Backcountry Water Treatment

Hikers often encounter beautiful lakes, ponds, streams or rivers. No matter how crystal clear they might appear—DON'T drink from them. The likelihood of ingesting giardia, cryptosporida, or other nasty parasites is high, and the risk just isn't worth it. The symptoms of both giardiasis and cryptosporidiosis (the diseases caused by these respective pathogens) don't often show up right away, but they certainly aren't subtle. Cramping, diarrhea, and vomiting are the most common effects, and must be treated by a doctor.

If enough water can't be carried, you'll need to pack a water filter or water-treatment chemical like iodine. Pump-action microfilters have gotten lighter—and cheaper—over the years, and are a cinch to use. Some of the big-time filter manufacturers claim that their products can eliminate giardia, fungi, parasites, cholera, typhoid, cryptosporidia, and salmonella from even the most foul water.

These filters can clog, and become so annoyingly slow and difficult that you'll want to hurl them at a nearby tree. Remember to carry replacement filter cartridges and other parts that are prone to clogging, breaking or getting lost.

A less technical option is to treat your water with chlorine or iodine. Hiker-friendly tablets and drops are relatively cheap and easy to use. Iodine and bleach can even be used as-is to treat water, but I'd go with the pros. Over-doing it with the chemicals can be disastrous.

When used properly, chlorine and chlorine-based products kill all water pests: viruses, bacteria, you name it. Iodine, however, is ineffective against cryptosporidia, and should never be used by pregnant women or people with thyroid problems. Although chemicals and filters may treat water so it's safe to drink, it may still look and smell, well, unpalatable.

PART FOUR
Taking Care on the Trail

Chapter 12 Finding Your Way

IN AN ERA WHEN HUMANS ARE EVER-MORE ORIENTED TO *GETTING* THERE not *being* there, to highways not footpaths, to the built world not the natural one, the people who navigate by way of rivers and mountains and valleys are becoming rare birds indeed.

Count me as one modern who does his best to keep his sense of direction in this hurry-up world by staying centered, and by locating myself in relation to the natural geography that surrounds me. I don't always succeed, but I've found the effort well worthwhile.

In an attempt to encourage students to rediscover their place in nature, outdoors educators ask them to give directions to their homes using only natural landmarks in their descriptions. The students are to assume their visitors will arrive on foot. No street names or structures are permitted when giving the directions.

Poet Gary Snyder, who writes lovingly and wryly about the land and the way we live on it, asked his audience to try this exercise at a reading I attended. I've tried giving directions myself by way of natural features and it's quite a challenge. "I live at the base of the mountains, on the east side of a creek that flows to the Pacific. . . . "

I've met some hikers who have a great natural sense of direction and many more who, while lacking an innate sense of direction, have developed one by practice. A good sense of direction begins with paying attention to the geography around you—on the trail and off.

You don't have to venture into a remote wilderness to lose your way. Hikers even get lost in Rhode Island, where trails experts have figured that no state footpath is farther than a mile from the nearest road.

No one expects to get lost—particularly when hiking the well-signed park and forest trails that most hikers choose to follow. "After all," say novices, "our mountains aren't big and icy like the Rockies, and we're only out for the day."

Even experienced hikers can get lost. Getting lost is usually the result of taking a "shortcut" off an established trail. Danger is magnified

In This Chapter

- Staying on the trail
- Locating a lost trail
- When you're really lost
- All about maps
- Maps, compass, GPS
- Geocaching

> *"If you don't know where you are, you don't know who you are."*
>
> —WALLACE STEGNER

if a hiker ventures out alone or fails to inform someone of an itinerary or return time.

An early twentieth-century U.S. Geological Survey report noted, "With some persons, the faculty of getting lost amounts to genius. They are able to accomplish it wherever they are." If those words strike home, remember that map-reading and navigating are skills. And like any other skills, performance improves with practice.

Hikers can take many common sense precautions to avoid getting lost in the first place. Know your physical condition and don't overtax yourself. Check your boots and clothing. Be prepared for bad weather. Inquire about trail conditions. Allow plenty of time for your hike and allow even more for your return to the trailhead.

Unless you repeat the same hike over and over again, you really need to learn the basics of map reading and how to use a compass.

Staying on the Trail

When you're on the trail, keep your eyes open and develop a sense of where you are. If you're hiking so fast that all you see is your boots, you're not attentive to passing terrain—its charms or its layout. STOP once in a while. Sniff wildflowers, splash your face in a spring. LISTEN. Maybe the trail is paralleling a stream. Listen to the sound of mountain water. On your left? On your right? Look up at that fire lookout on the nearby ridge. Are you heading toward it or away from it? LOOK AROUND. That's the best insurance against getting lost.

- **Watch for way-marks.** Parks are marked with basic trail mileage signs and in many other ways, including blazes, disks, posts and cairns. If you're hiking a woodsy trail signed every 150 feet or so by a blue disk and 10 minutes pass without seeing one, you may have left the main trail.
- **Be aware of your surroundings.** Note passing landmarks and natural features. Stop now and then to compare your progress on the ground to the route on the map.
- **Think for yourself.** Just because you're in the middle or at the end of the line of hikers doesn't mean you can switch over to autopilot and stop paying attention to where you're going.
- **Eyes in the back of your head.** Look behind you frequently. Knowing where you come from always gives you a better feel for where you're going and prepares you for the return trip.
- **Put the trail into words.** Sharing what you see and what you expect to see when with your trail companion can confirm whether you're on the "same page" in regard to the hiking route. Two heads are better than one, four eyes better than two, when it comes to staying on the trail.
- **Here comes the sun.** Use the east-rising, west-setting sun and its respective position to the trail to help you in your orientation.

Locating a Lost Trail

How many ways can you lose the trail? Quite a few! Unsigned or poorly signed junctions, paths crowded or covered by brush, buried by rock-falls or mudslides, covered by fallen trees. . . . If you suspect you've lost the trail, stop immediately.

Ask yourself, "If I was the trail where would I go?"

Sure, it's a weird question, but if you know where you've come from and where you're going, you can often figure out how the path should take you there. Often a trail has a logic all its own and sometimes the hiker can dial into it. A trail traveling a blufftop high above the surf will rarely all of a sudden plunge down the cliffs to the sea. Chances are a path contouring gently around a mountain will not suddenly veer straight up a steep slope.

- **Return to the last point you're certain was on the trail.** You'll likely find you missed a turn or switchback.
- **Look for way-marks.** Find the last sign, blaze, disk or mileage marker.
- **Look for help.** If you're hiking with a companion and one of you goes looking for the trail, stay in voice or whistle contact.
- **Don't get more lost.** Before you wander off in search of the trail, fix your current location in your mind so you don't get more lost. Memorize distinctive features—a twisted tree or unusual rock formation, for example.

Really Lost

So you're really lost? Stay calm. Don't worry about food. It takes weeks to starve to death. Besides, you've got that trail mix in your day pack. You have a water bottle. And you have a jacket in case of rain. You're in no immediate danger, so don't run around in circle.

LOOK AROUND some more. Is there a familiar landmark in sight? Have you been gaining elevation or losing it? Where has the sun been shining? On your right cheek? Your back? Retrace your steps, if you can. Look for other footprints. If you're totally disoriented, keep walking laterally. Don't go deeper into the brush or woods. Go up slope to get a good view, but don't trek aimlessly here and there.

The universal distress signal is three visible or audible signals—three shouts or whistles, three shiny objects placed on a bare summit. Of course, you will have already tried to summon help with your cell phone, which unfortunately won't get a signal in the mountains. Don't start a fire! You could start a major conflagration.

If it's near dark, get ready to spend the night. Don't try to find your way out in the dark. Don't worry. If you left your itinerary, your rescuers will begin looking for you in the morning. Try to stay warm by huddling against a tree or wrapping yourself in branches, pine needles or leaves.

Relax and think of your next hike. Think of the most beautiful place you know—that creek, that stony mountain, a place where the fish bite and the mosquitoes don't. . . . You'll make it, don't worry.

Really Lost Hikers Should:

- S.T.O.P. (Stop, Think, Observe, Plan)
- Blow a whistle to signal you need assistance.
- Stay put. Most likely, if you've informed friends and authorities of your itinerary, a rescue effort will be launched quickly on your behalf after you fail to show at the appointed time.
- Drink enough water.
- Put on your extra clothing. Avoid getting cold, hypothermic.
- If appropriate, build a fire for warmth and as a locator. Don't set the woods on fire with your blaze.

Maps

Area Maps Before you put that trail map to good use, you need a map to get you to the trailhead. A good area map might be a county map, a city map or a Forest Service map.

Use care when you select a map off the rack. Many of the maps sold to tourists are okay for civic sightseeing, but don't show the backcountry. The American Automobile Association's county and regional maps are among my favorite area maps. I've found the AAA's maps are excellent at delineating parks and natural areas, and are consistently up-to-date and easy to read.

U.S. Forest Service Maps Many hikes take place in national forests. U.S. Forest Service maps are available at ranger stations and some outdoor retailers. They're general maps, showing roads, rivers, trails and little else. The Forest Service keeps its maps fairly up-to-date, so they're useful for checking out-of-date topographic maps. USFS maps that show a portion of a national forest, such as a particular region or a wilderness area, are more useful than the maps that put a million-acre forest on one page.

Each road and trail in the national forest system has a route number. A route number might look like this: 2S21. Signs, inscribed with the route number, are placed at some trailheads and at the intersection of trails to supplement other directional signs. The route numbers on a Forest Service map usually correspond to the route numbers on the trail, but not always; be careful because the Forest Service periodically changes the numbers.

Trails on Forest Service maps are drawn in red and black. Red trails are usually maintained and in good shape. Black trails are infrequently maintained and their condition can range from okay to faint to impassable.

By the way, don't be so quick to throw away that out-of-date forest map. Some veteran hikers swear that budget-conscious Forest Service bureaucrats erase trails from the agency's maps with each new edition. If the trail isn't on the map it doesn't exist and if it doesn't exist the Forest Service doesn't have to pay to maintain it.

I'm not saying I agree with these hiking trail conspiracy theorists, but I do treasure my collection of old Forest Service maps, some of which date back to the 1960s. And I've discovered more than a few hiking trails that disappeared from the map but may still be enjoyed on the ground.

National Park Maps These are excellent getting-to, and getting-around-the-park maps. Because the cartography and map symbols are so classic, as well as so easy to read, picking one up feels like hanging out with an old and familiar friend.

No need to wait until you drive up to a national park entrance station to get a map. Go online and look up the National Park

Service's Cartographic Resources Home Page. You can quickly review any national park map from Acadia National Park to Zion National Park and download them in a variety of formats.

Review Maps Before You Hit the Road Go over the map before you get into the car. Have a good driver-navigator chat. Certainly there is nothing more nerve-wracking or upsetting than the experience of a frustrated driver demanding directions from an unsure navigator. Not only is it frustrating, but potentially hazardous, especially when intensified by traffic, inclement weather, fatigue or confusing territory.

To avoid such disorienting and upsetting scenarios, spend time before departure planning and mapping out excursions. Write down directions, road names and numbers and pertinent landmarks to prevent on-the-road confusion. While chances are most of the main access roads on your way to the hike are well-marked, lesser roads may not be signed at all. Therefore, pay close attention to mileage on the odometer when following directions to trailheads in backcountry locations.

Blow it Up! Make your area map or trail map easier to read by blowing it up. Photocopy the map at 150 to 200 percent of original size and mark your way with a yellow highlighter.

For the many of us who need to wear glasses or contacts, are far-sighted or near sighted, this is a great tip. I'm near-sighted myself, so while contact lenses or prescription sunglasses correct my distance vision to 20-20, when I wear them, I cannot then read the fine print on a map.

Many of you have the opposite problem—far-sightedness. You see well for distance, but need glasses for reading—particularly the fine print of a map.

So enlarge the map on the photocopier. Suddenly the map's six and eight point type gets twice as big and lots easier to read. You'll have an easier time staying on the trail with a map that you can actually read.

Topographic Maps Some hikers have a love affair with topographic maps. Those blue rivers, green woods and labyrinthine contour lines are—well, artistic.

Topographic maps are valuable for any off-trail hiking or as a back-up in case of any route-finding challenges. Topos show terrain in great detail including trails, elevations, waterways, brush cover and improvements.

Topos come in two scales, the 15 minute quadrangle and the 7.5 minute quadrangle. The 15 minute series scale is approximately 1 inch to 1 mile and the contour interval (the gap between contour lines) represents an elevation of 80 feet. The 7.5 series maps have a scale of 2.5 inches to a mile with a contour interval of 40 feet. For the hiker, the 7.5 minute series is preferable.

Topos usally come in a sheet size of about 18×22 inches. If you're thinking about getting a set of topos to cover the whole U.S., you'll need a place to store 57,000 maps.

They're valuable maps all right, but sometimes even seasoned hikers tend to put a little too much faith in a topo's depiction of terrain. Some of the most common misrepresentations are the omission of creek branches and seasonal watercourses, misplaced trails and trail junctions. While the feds make an effort to update topos, some maps go decades without meaningful improvement.

During the 1980s, with hopes of shrinking the federal budget deficit, government agencies such as the U.S. Geological Survey, never known for marketing savvy or an entrepreneurial bent, came under pressure to produce revenue. The USGS began to aggressively push its product lines, from aerial photos to maps of all kinds.

One happy result of Uncle Sam-turned-salesman is that topo maps are much easier to obtain these days. A hiker can go online and locate the topographic map for anywhere in the U.S. with a click of a mouse. The USGS offers GNIS (Geographic Names Information System), a complete listing of federally recognized geographic place names, accompanied by a powerful search program that allows the user to locate maps based upon these place names. Enter any place name and the name of the map title will be listed.

Let's say your friends recommend that you take a hike to Lonesome Lake in New Hampshire's White Mountains. You enter Lonesome Lake, New Hampshire and *voilà*—the system suggests you buy the topo map named Franconia and tells you the latitude and longitude of all geographic features named "Lonesome Lake."

Lonesome Lake
44 deg 08 min / 071 deg 42 min
Lonesome Lake Hut
44 deg 08 min / 071 deg 42 min
Lonesome Lake Trail
44 deg 08 min / 071 deg 41 min

Using a Map and Compass

Some moderns argue that learning to use a map and compass is a hopelessly old-fashioned outdoors skill, akin to fashioning a rabbit snare from twigs or tying a diamond hitch on a mule. If you have a good guidebook with step-by-step directions and stay on maintained, signed trails, what need do you have for a compass? Many hikers have walked the entire length of the Appalachian Trail without consulting a compass, so why bother with one in the local mountains?

It is true many a trail has been immortalized in a trail guide, and described with step by step directions and that very few hikers ever have to depend, really depend, on map-reading skills. Still, a familiarity with a map and compass can at least help you be aware of your direction of travel. You'd be surprised how many hikers don't have a sense of direction at all. If you are on a trail, a quick map and compass consult can help you determine if you're going in the right direction. If you lose the trail, a map and compass can help you find it. If you are supposed to be hiking north on a trail to your destination and you find yourself on a trail leading west for miles and miles, a map and compass can help you decipher if you took off on the wrong trail.

One poor way to use a map is to employ it as a last resort measure after getting lost. Hikers often make the mistake of failing to consult a map at all as the miles disappear under their boots. Without stopping occasionally to match the map to the territory, hikers have no ready point of reference from which to fix their spot on the map.

These days the best backcountry navigators know how to use a map and compass, as well as a map and GPS receiver. You need map reading skills because a map—without the ability to put your finger on your position does a hiker little good. At the same time, a GPS receiver is of little help unless you can take the coordinates and then locate them, and yourself, on a map.

Hikers can put the map and compass combo to two good uses: (1) Find out where you are (2) Determine where to go. The best way to learn map and compass skill is by taking a short field course. These courses are offered by hiking clubs, outdoor retailers and community colleges. Once you learn a few basics, it's wise to practice them occasionally.

When I took my first compass class, I suspect I had the same two reactions that many other hikers have. First I was genuinely dismayed how utterly inadequate my map-finding skills were. Secondly, after mastering a few of the fundamentals, my overall confidence on the trail was bolstered.

Learning to use a map and compass is one of those things that's far easier to learn by doing than by reading about it. (Some orienteering how-to books begin with the history of latitude and longitude and make it difficult to get at the few basics that would be useful to the hiker.) I'm not going to attempt to give compass-reading lessons in the pages of this book, but I want to offer a brief overview of a few of the skills that you'll need to learn.

To find out where you are, you'll employ what's called the Triangulation Method. First you'll locate two landmarks—ideally about 90 degrees from each other relative to your position. Next you'll take a bearing for these landmarks, adjust for magnetic declination, then plot these two bearings on your map. Your position is the point where the two bearings intersect. Repeating the process with more landmarks and more bearings can improve accuracy.

To locate a lost trail, or when hiking cross-country, you'll need a precise way of determining the right direction to proceed. To accom-

> "In beauty may I walk
> All day long may I walk
> Through the returning
> seasons, may I walk."
> —NAVAJO PRAYER

> "On the trail marked with
> pollen, may I walk.
> With grasshoppers about my
> feet, may I walk.
> With dew about my feet,
> may I walk.
> With beauty, may I walk."
> —NAVAJO PRAYER

Basic Features of a Hiking GPS

- **Waterproof** (rated Submersible) It should work in the worst downpours.

- **Long battery life** You don't want to carry a lot of extra batteries—particularly on a long hike.

- **A 12-channel parallel receiver** Necessary for good reception in canyon bottoms, thick forests and rocky terrain.

- **Twenty-route capability** Usually the standard storage in the system. Having a minimum of 20 routes allows you to retrieve nearby trails and choose from a variety of routes.

- **Waypoints, lots of them** Five hundred is a fairly standard number. Bearing to the next waypoint is almost always included in the unit and absolutely essential to hikers.

- **A map screen** To ascertain your location in relation to particular reference points.

- **Maps** Built-in maps are a big help of course.

- **Topo maps** If you're a hiker who likes using topos on the trail, the GPS system should support that and display the maps well.

plish this, plot your chosen route on the map to determine you compass heading. Next you'll hold the compass at eyelevel to take a bearing to determined which landmark you wish to reach. Hike to that landmark until you reach it or it disappears from view, Keep repeating the map-compass bearing process until you get where you want to go.

GPS: Global Positioning Systems Even if you're hiking in a pea soup fog, on a moonless night or in a white-out, a GPS receiver will plot your exact location anytime, anywhere. Key to the GPS are two dozen satellites orbiting the earth twice a day, beaming time and position data.

Receiving a satellite's signal, a GPS unit calculates the time gap between transmission and reception of this signal, thus establishing the distance from satellite to receiver. Next, using data from a minimum of three satellites, the GPS receiver, via triangulation and a lot of complicated math, delivers exact longitude and latitude and a precise position fix. By making contact with a fourth satellite, the GPS receiver will display exact altitude, too.

The units can be quite useful on the trail, particularly if the hiker gets some instruction in their use. Remember that a GPS unit, like a compass is just a navigation tool, not a skill, and certainly not a substitute for common sense and trail sense.

Just like a map and compass, the main purpose of a GPS is to keep you on course as you hike to your destination. A GPS can also help total altitude gain and loss, as well as where you've been and how far you've gone. A GPS can help you locate a favorite fishing spot or a historic site, and assist you to get to the trailhead with detailed driving directions.

You can download crucial waypoints to a GPS and use them to plan your route. Once on the trail, the route can be used to estimate distance and travel time. After completing a trail, the GPS helps create a record of the hike, useful for sharing with friends or to reference on a future outing on the same trail.

What users want from a GPS varies widely. Hikers need different GPS features than boaters and motorists. In fact, hikers should steer clear of GPS units designed for in-the-car or "street" use.

A good hiking GPS is compact enough to take on the trail, waterproof, rugged, and work with the kind of software hikers need for planning, following and recording a travel route. A basic GPS unit can be turned on and, with a minimum of user input, deliver a precise position fix—a good part of what a hiker really needs.

Orienteering

If you're a hiker who knows north from south, orienteering might be a sport you'd like to try. The goal is to get from one central point to another with the aid of a map and compass. Orienteering can be enjoyed with a group of friends, a map, a compass and a picnic lunch or as a route finding/trail running competition at top speed.

Orienteering is appealing because it offers much more than a fast walk in the woods: the sport requires considerable thought and concentration. Success in orienteering depends on the ability to read a map on the run, being able to read the terrain, and relating the terrain to the map.

Letterboxing

It's quaint, as intriguing as an Agatha Christie novel and oh-so-British.

It's letterboxing, a mixture of treasure-hunting, hiking, orienteering, and even arts and crafts. The object of this pursuit is to follow a set of clues in order to locate a letterbox, hidden in the great outdoors. A typical waterproof letterbox contains a notebook, a one-of-a-kind, hand-crafted rubber stamp and an inkpad.

Clues range from the simple and straightforward: "Follow the summit trail to Inspiration Point and look under the rock cairn by the bench atop the peak," to the very complicated and the cryptic. Clues might be in the form of a joke, riddle or puzzle

Hikers who find a letterbox, stamp their own notebooks with the box's stamp and stamp the box's notebook with their own personal stamp. Victory!

Letterboxing has a number of elements in common with its high-tech cousin, Geocaching, particularly the fun of hiking along on a treasure hunt through the natural world. Geocaching clues, however, required a GPS to follow. (See Geocaching description on following page.)

Long-established in England, letterboxing was exported to the U.S. in the late 1990s. As the story goes, letterboxing began about 150 years ago when a gentleman left his calling card in a bottle by a remote pond on the moors of Dartmoor, a region in southwest England. Today, more than 10,000 letterboxes are hidden in Dartmoor National Park. Those intending to look for letterboxes can obtain a catalog listing clues to finding thousands of these boxes in the national park.

In the U.S., most clues are in a database posted on the Letterboxing North America web site, www.letterboxing.org. Some organizations, such as hiking clubs and scout troops also publish or circulate clues to letterboxes—sometimes for the hiking public, sometimes strictly for a group's own membership.

Some letterboxing etiquette includes: respect the land when hunting boxes or when hiding them; repack and hide a box in the exact place where you found it; don't violate private property or disobey park rules (letterboxing in America's national parks, for example, is strictly forbidden); don't post solutions to seeking a letterbox on the internet.

What you need to start letterboxing:

- **Clues** to find a letterbox.

- **Compass** (some clues give compass bearings or are highly directional).

- **Personal rubber stamp and stamp pad.** You can start with a store-bought one, but you'll probably want to make a custom one.

- **Map** While you're following clues, stay in touch with "the big picture" with a map.

- **Hiking garb and gear** plus the ten essentials, and all your usual hiking apparel and equipment.

Geocaching

Geocaching is a captivating outdoor adventure game for hikers who possess a Global Positioning System device. Individuals and user groups stash caches all over the world and share the locations of their caches on internet sites. After obtaining the location coordinates, GPS users then set out to find the cache.

Geocaching is a compound word comprised of Geo, short for geography (though I take a more cosmic view and consider it to be short for the Greek word for earth) and caching (pronounced cashing) for the process of hiding a cache. Those of us who have spent too much time at the computer know cache as data stored in memory enabling the machine to retrieve it more quickly, but the use of the word predates the invention of the computer and was commonly used by hikers and campers to describe a hiding place for provisions to be retrieved at a later time.

Rewards for the cache-finder are many and varied. (Of course just taking a hike in an attempt to find a cache hidden in remote and beautiful place is a great reward.) The most basic of caches are waterproof buckets holding a logbook and offer geocachers the opportunity to record the date and time of their visits. Logbooks sometimes reveal coordinates to locate other caches, and are often filled with wry observations and some pretty funny notes. CDs, maps, books, pictures...the other contents of a cache are limited only by the imagination of the cache creator. The rule is if you take something from the cache, you must leave something.

Geocaching, in theory at least, is deceptively simple. A GPS unit can pinpoint your location (to within 6 to 20 feet no less) anywhere on the planet and you start the hunt with exact coordinates, so you should know where the cache is hidden, right? Not so fast. Knowing where a cache is and getting to it is an entirely different manner. Some caches may require long and arduous hiking and skillful orienteering to find.

You can begin enjoying geocaching with an inexpensive basic GPS unit or purchase a more deluxe model complete with built-in topo maps and a compass. The best website for geocaching is www.geocaching.com. At this site, you can enter your zip code and view a listing of all cache sites in your region. In addition, for each cache site you can get the location coordinates and read a narrative account of getting to the cache site.

Geocaching isn't for everybody but can be a fun activity for hikers who want to improve their navigation skills, and provides yet another excuse—if one is really needed—for taking a hike.

Lost Coast

I HEAR the residents of Sea Lion Rocks before I see them—two dozen Steller sea lions. A mile beyond the big creatures is the abandoned Punta Gorda Lighthouse.

In 1911, after several ships were wrecked on the rocks and reefs off the Lost Coast, a lighthouse was built a mile south of Punta Gorda—whose name means "massive point."

The mouth of the Mattole River, a complication of gravel bars, marks the northern end of the Lost Coast. Sea gulls and osprey circle above me as I watch the harbor seals bob in the tidal area where the river meets the ocean. I look back into the mist at the King Range, at slopes that seem so much steeper than the angle of repose, that only by some hidden force deep within the earth keeps from collapsing into the sea.

It is not really the coast that is lost, but us. If we cannot find the coast because of the smoke of our cities, the walls we build to keep each other out, the industries we run that run us, it is surely we who are lost.

We all need one place on the map, one place in our hearts that is lost. In a wild place, lost from the mean streets, we can find ourselves, our best selves. A place that is peaceful, for prayer and for contemplation is good, a place that is wild, for challenge and confrontation, is better, a place that is both peaceful and wild, for the love of life and the passion for living, is best.

Chapter 13 Hiking through the Seasons and in All Kinds of Weather

SOME HIGH SIERRA VISITORS INSIST THERE'S LITTLE GOOD ABOUT A day that begins with frost at dawn, gets hot enough by noon to peel your nose and becomes downright chilly with the first afternoon shadows. I say autumn days are among the most magical of the year.,

I like to hike the John Muir Trail in fall. During July and August the dazzling 212-mile trail along the Sierra crest vibrates under the passage of hikers, horses and pack animals, but October brings miles of solitary walking.

I love leaf-peeping, Sierra style. Red-leaved dogwoods glow against the redwood bark of the Sierra sequoia. Along meadow rims, golden aspen flicker like fire in the wind.

But really, it's not the leaves but the light that gives autumn its color in the Sierra Nevada. The sunlight is strong, the shade deep and black, a five f-stop difference between light and shadow, the kind of sharp contrast found in an Ansel Adams photograph. Early sunsets over the summits are amazing, as the gravity-defying liquid shade flows uphill. The sun glows red, then rose, then indigo, coloring the minarets until there's no light left in the sky. Then the great daystar is replaced by a thousand constellations. Fall nights are long, but that gives you more time to gaze at the stars.

I like to hike in the "shoulder" seasons—just a little too early or a little too late for most visitors. And I like to hike some of my favorite places (the ones that aren't snowbound in winter, of course) in all four seasons and observe the changes in nature and life along the trail.

Whether you choose to hike in season, out-of-season, early in the season or late in the season, you need to know what you're getting into. Checking the weather forecast, dressing in layers and being prepared for what the season is supposed to present and what it might throw at you is the key to hiking safely through the seasons.

In This Chapter
- Splendors of spring, autumn and mud seasons
- Hiking in the rain
- Dangers of lightning and flash floods
- Hiking in cold weather
- Hiking in hot weather

I love living in a part of America that offers four-season hiking. That doesn't mean every trail near my home is accessible year-around—far from it—but does mean that at least some trails are open during each season.

Many regions in America, from Florida to the Southwestern Sunbelt that receive little or no snow, can also rightfully claim four-season hiking. Some states, such as Washington, with both snow-covered and snow-free locales, dry and very rainy areas, have regions of two-season, three-season and four-season hiking.

Some avid hikers are bound and determined to hike all year whether conditions permit it or now. Several proud Connecticut hikers insisted to me that their state is the only one in New England where four-season hiking is possible. By New England standards, Connecticut's winters are relatively mild, these gonzo hikers point out. Southeastern Connecticut is spared the worst of winter's wrath, sometimes staying snow-free for much of the winter; it's usually among the first areas in New England to burst into spring.

Hmmm… Well, three seasons are pretty terrific for hiking: a muddy, but magnificent spring, a hot, humid summer, a New England autumn with all its leafy splendor.

While I encourage you to extend your hiking season—to hit the trail earlier in the spring and stay on the trail in autumn—I don't mean to suggest that you should push your luck. After a discussion about the splendors of hiking in spring and autumn, I detail some of the precautions necessary when hiking in cold weather, hot weather and on rainy days anytime during the year.

SPRING IS THE EXACT SAME LENGTH as other seasons. But wherever you live, and wherever you hike, spring is the one season that everyone agrees is too short. Just when you notice the days are longer and the flowers are in bloom, it's summer.

April showers bring May flowers.

True enough at very particular latitudes and altitudes. In the low desert, for example, January showers bring February flowers. And in the Rockies, June showers can bring July flowers.

If an advertiser claimed "April showers bring May flowers," the government would require a lengthy disclaimer.

I'm indebted to rangers at the Sequoia National Park Visitor Center for pointing out to me that certain parts of the country—most particularly the regions around Sequoia, Kings Canyon and Yosemite national parks—have nine months of spring: January through September. These parks offer a way of resolving the national spring deficit, the rangers joke.

More accurately, Sequoia National Park has 13,000 feet of spring, interpretive rangers explain. Elevations in this park range from just over 1,000 feet to the 14,494-foot top of Mt. Whitney. For every 1,000 foot increase in elevation, there is a corresponding temperature drop of three degrees F.

So what does a change of elevation really mean? And how does it get us more spring?

In Sequoia National Park, and in other fabulous hiking areas around North America, if you're willing to gain elevation, you can partake of the joys of spring for far longer than the traditionally defined three month period between the vernal equinox in March and the summer solstice in June. In certain mountain ranges, a wide range of temperatures and elevations create a variety of habitats and climates, both macro and micro.

In the case of the High Sierra, the first flowering plants can appear as early as January in the lowest foothills that rise from California's flat Central Valley. At Sequoia National Park's middle elevations (4,000 to 7,000 feet), where the mighty sequoias thrive, spring flowers begin to bedeck the meadows in April. On higher slopes, hikers will notice the more obvious signs of spring—tender grasses and wildflowers—in June and July. In the very highest alpine ecosystems, spring comes very late— August, even September. Spring and summer are greatly compressed at such high elevation. Spring comes and goes in a matter of weeks.

In Sequoia National Park, you can drive to a 7,500-foot trailhead, gaining more than 6,000 feet and losing nearly 20 degrees F. in

> "In the high mountains, in the woods I find a little solace: every haunt of man."
>
> —PETRARCH

Trail Wisdom: Walk where Spring Lingers

DOGWOOD blooms, strawberries ripen, blue-birds and robins return. Spring is a time of flowers, singing birds, sweet-smelling air, emerald green grass and trees shimmering with new leaves.

We sense the coming of spring in our life stream. Spring reminds us of youth, of optimism, of new beginnings.

All things seem possible in the very merry month of May. Spring brings hope and spiritual renewal to the walker.

Calendars to the contrary, nature's year begins with spring in most of the world's Temperate Zone locales. If nature's year is viewed as a single day, spring is sunrise, summer is high noon, autumn is sunset and winter is night.

Scientists have calculated that spring advances up (south to north) the U.S. at an average rate of about 15 miles a day. When I learned of spring's pace, I immediately matched the 15-mile distance to that of a good day's walk.

How marvelous it would be, I fantasized, to advance up the continent, 15 miles per diem—in effect, to walk where it's always spring.

Nobody, not even the most learned scientist, knows exactly where spring begins. The season has a multitude of reference points, but no single starting point.

Spring is a splendid season for walking hand in hand, walking down the aisle, begin a great walk alone or in company. But spring also is a state of mind and one way we keep the faith is by remembering springs past and looking forward to next year. We don't have to wait for that three-month period between the vernal equinox and the summer solstice to have spring in our heart and spring in our step.

Walk where spring lingers.

Mud Season Hiking Guidelines

- If a footpath is so muddy that you must hike atop the plant life or alongside it, retreat to the trailhead and select another hike in another area.

- Observe posted trail closures. Never hike on a trail closed due to wet conditions.

- Least muddy trails are apt to be found in lower-elevation hardwood forests with southern exposure. Sunny, south-facing slopes are among the first to dry out in spring.

- Hike through the mud on a trail, not around it.

- Avoid high elevation conifer forests, alpine areas and other fragile ecosystems.

- Remember that mud season is not only a spring thing; it can occur in late autumn with lots of rain or in winter with an unusual warm spell and sudden thaw.

temperature. You can then hit the trail for the 14,494-foot top of Mt. Whitney, losing another 20 degrees F. or so as you climb to the top of the highest peak in the continental U.S. Hikers pass a lot of "spring" as they make one of America's most classic climbs.

Flowering plants are not the only life forms following spring uphill. Bears emerge from hibernation, foraging at ever higher altitude to sniff out their vegetal preferences. Birds and bees and many more creatures thrive in spring, whenever and wherever they find the season.

So, if you want to prolong spring, hike higher and higher into the high country. Pause along the trail to admire the wide variety of flowering plants that adorn different elevations.

Mud Season

It's kind of a northern New England thing, but the rest of you listen up because even if mud season isn't a defined season where you live and hike, you're apt to encounter muddy conditions from time to time.

Vermonters take a kind of perverse pride in mud season, which extends from about mid-March to Memorial Day, give or take a few weeks. Vermont's "Fifth Season"—and mud season anywhere—can be the beginning of hiking season, provided the just-can't-wait-for-better-conditions hiker chooses the right trail on the right day. (Of course if it's too darn muddy, stay off the trail; when hikers slosh across saturated soils, they damage trails and adjacent flora.)

Some Canadians trump New Englanders by claiming six seasons: spring, summer, fall, mud season, winter, and mud season again. During a year of maximum mud, the two mud seasons add up to six months, America's neighbors to the north claim.

Mud happens when water can't soak into the soil quickly enough to be absorbed. Water runs off sandy soils but not so over other soil types. When water lingers on the surface of soil, you get mud. Snowmelt, often combined with spring rains, produces the volume of water necessary to make mud.

Theories abound explaining why one mud season might be worse than another: Could severity be related to how deep the frost permeates the ground? How quickly the ground defrosts in spring? The amount of snow on the ground when it starts to melt?

Vermont is more firm about closing hiking trails during mud season than other states. Mud season hikers of years past, along with foot-traffic accelerated erosion in all seasons, have worn portions of Vermont's Long Trail down to bedrock. Some of the Green Mountain state's most famed trails, such as the ones leading up to Camel's Hump, are closed to hiking until the end of mud season.

Along with muck, mud season seems to bring more than its share of psychic misery. But don't succumb to this mud season of the soul, take a hike!

Some hikers can find beauty even in mud season. When a cold night's temperatures temporarily re-freezes puddles and creates a mirrored surface, or when water-saturated mud re-freezes, and adds a frosting of ice crystals that sparkle in the morning light.

Autumn Hiking

Autumn has its critics and its fans. Some say there's little use for a day that begins with frost, becomes hot enough to sunburn your nose by noon, and has you shivering by sunset. Wiser heads, those attached to hikers no doubt, believe autumn is the best of all seasons. The high country air is crisp, but still inviting, and the woodlands offer great opportunities for wildlife-watching. Southern regions and the high desert has cooled enough for pleasant hiking.

Some of my most enjoyable hikes have been autumn adventures. In addition to the obvious lure of colorful fall foliage displays, hitting the trail in autumn offers an insect-free environment, sparkling clear-day views and an excellent opportunity to view woodland wildlife during the "leaf-out" season.

I've found solitude in this season on trails around Europe and across America. Even the wildlands around such major tourist destinations as Aspen and Cape Cod have little trail traffic in the fall.

Planning for an Autumn Hike Fall weather often brings highly changeable hiking conditions. You could face an unseasonable heat wave or an ice storm, an Indian summer or early winter.

Check the weather forecast for the day you're hiking and, if you can, check again with local authorities on the morning you start up the trail.

Autumn days are shorter days. Remember that sunsets come earlier at this time of the year, so be sure to return to the trailhead before dark. Because of the shorter days, try to get a very early start. If you're on the trail bright and early, behold the many birds, usually most active and in best songster form during the first few hours of daylight.

Layer, now more than ever. Layering, as an outdoor dress methodology, is important in every season, particularly in autumn. With layers, the hiker can prepare for early morning and late afternoon chills and bright and sunny conditions at midday. Wear three or four layers and shed them as the temperature rises.

The autumn hiker should also remember rainwear. Pack it, even if the weathercaster is predicting a week of clear days. Fall sunlight can be intense so remember your sunscreen and sunglasses.

Autumn is the season to don those convertible pants, the ones with zip-off legs that convert to shorts. A hat will keep your head warm in the morning, cool in the afternoon.

Autumn's Special Pleasures

- **Leaf-peeping** New England is ablaze with red, amber and gold. Other regions boast brilliant, but less renowned fall foliage.

- **Wildlife-watching** Late in the fall, with the deciduous trees now bare, birds, deer and many more creatures are easier to spot.

- **Bug-free trails** No insects to plague hikers! After the first cold snap or frost, most of the little biters and stingers are dead or hibernating.

- **Solitude** Park trails are almost always uncrowded and it's possible you could have a whole mountain, small or large, to yourself.

- **Travel deals** Take a trip and take a hike. From airplane tickets to lodging at mountain resorts, travel is cheap in the fall. Be spontaneous to take advantage of last-minute deals.

Hiking in the Rain

Rain, rain, go away
Come again some other day.

That chant from childhood never works very well does it? At least not for me. Besides, some of my most memorable hikes have been rained-on. I've taken my friends and family for hikes in the rain. Hiking in the rain gives us a chance to enjoy a kind of hiking that's experiential—not goal oriented.

I've been on expensive European hiking vacations when it rained and you know what? Yes, that's right, the guest hikers had a wonderful time. The group camaraderie and bonding increases exponentially with the shared experience of hiking in the rain.

I'd rather be rained-on than rained-out.

You could stay indoors and watch the rain come down and re-schedule your hike for a clear day. But sometimes you can't re-schedule. Or your could take a hike.

Part of being a hiker is embracing all kinds of weather. Certainly the drier you are, the happier your trails will be.

It rains when the weathercaster calls for clear skies. It rains on the coast on supposedly good "beach days." It rains in the middle of a record drought. It rains in the desert where it's not supposed to rain.

Rainwear, therefore, is essential. Carry it at all times.

• **Rain jacket** No jacket is completely waterproof, but many will protect you from getting soaked for an entire day. Whatever you choose, keep your rain jacket in your day pack.

• **Rain pants** Not only keep your legs dry, but your feet as well. If they're cut a bit long (that's the proper fit for rain pants), they'll extend over the top of your boots; rather than trickling down your pants into your boots, the rainwater will flow toward the more waterproof sides of your boots.

• **Hat** Those hikers who wear prescription glasses will probably wish to avoid the surreal visions caused by water-smeared lenses. The hood of your rain jacket will keep your head dry but not your glasses. A baseball cap will help deflect rain, but eventually get soaked and a plastic visor (don't quibble about aesthetics) works pretty well. A rain hat with a wide brim (geeky but effective) is your best bet for keeping rain off your glasses.

• **Glasses** Contact lenses certainly offer hikers the best rainy day view of the world, but not everyone can wear them. Some hikers who wear glasses on a daily basis are able to wear contacts on a limited basis, such as on a day hike.

Rainbows

Rainbows have long held a revered place in religion and mythology. In the Bible, one of the very few times God speaks directly to people, it's to Noah and he talks about a rainbow. A rainbow in the clouds is the sign of the promise between the Almighty and earth.

Chumash Indians tell the Legend of the Rainbow Bridge, a glorious bridge leading across the ocean to a promised land. Those Chumash who heeded the god Hicka's warning (Don't look down or you'll fall!) reached this land, while those who looked down fell into the sea and became dolphins.

In Ireland, where there's lots of good hiking, much rain and many rainbows, stories abound about bows. The Irish believe that a leprechaun make a rainbow and puts a pot of gold at the end of it. As legend has it, whenever a leprechaun is too rich for words, he makes rain, then sun, then a rainbow and puts the pot of gold at the end.

Rainbows are one of the great natural wonders and a special treat for the hikers who see them. Like me, you might have figured that there was just one kind of rainbow, but actually there are six.

Rainy Day Hiking Tips

- **Unzip your pits.** Assuming your rain gear has armpit zippers, regulate your temperature by zipping and unzipping your pit zips.
- **Keep your map dry.** Carry a waterproof map or put your paper map in a plastic sleeve to keep it dry.
- **Keep everything else dry.** Ah, the wonder of self-sealing plastic bags. Use them to keep dry the more vital of your pack's contents—maps, camera, food and more.
- **Enough is enough.** It's fine to hike in the rain up to a point. If you get wet and cold, get back to the trailhead and hike again another day.
- **Don't be surprised.** Experienced hikers aren't surprised by sudden wet conditions. Sometimes when hiking to the coast, all of a sudden you'll experience fog so dense you might as well be walking in the rain. It's common to labor up a high and dry mountain pass, crest the range and find wet and rainy conditions on the other side of the mountain.
- **Keep snacks at the ready.** Keep food and snacks in a handy place on your person so you don't have to stop and retrieve them from the depths of your pack. If the rain is intermittent, use the dry spells to eat and drink and never mind your normally scheduled break or meal times.
- **Snack at will.** When the rain stops, take a break and start eating, even if it isn't your regular break time or meal times. Keep trail snacks handy so that you can refuel on the go.
- **Keep your clothing dry.** Carry a change of dry clothes in waterproof stuff sacks.
- **Watch out for post-rainstorm drip.** Rain-soaked undergrowth can drench the passing hiker. If you're hiking in a forest, beware of trees drizzling down on you, sometimes for hours after the storm passes. Remove your rainwear when it's dry going on the trail not the instant the rain stops.

Rainbows: Six Different Kinds

- **Primary Rainbow** The most common rainbow, this one is a broad arch of bold colors.
- **Secondary Rainbow** The second most common rainbow, it's a broad arch of rather faint, light colors.
- **Dew Bow** Sometimes a raindrop or dew drop on the ground is large enough to display a little rainbow around or through it.
- **Double Rainbow** Two rainbows—a primary rainbow and a secondary rainbow—make up a double bow. The primary rainbow is usually the one inside the double, while the secondary one is the usually the one on the outside.
- **Fogbow** The water droplets in fog are very small and unable to refract light very well so fogbows are usually white. Fogbows are usually about twice as wide as other rainbows.
- **Lunar Rainbow** You are very lucky if you see one of these faint rainbows lit by the moon—in fact seeing one is supposed to bring the observer love. Lunar rainbows appear not only in the usual color spectrum, but also in rose, pink and other pastel colors.

Lower Lightning Risk

- Carefully time hikes to high-risk regions in coordination with evolving weather patterns.
- Finish your hike before thunderstorms start.
- If you hear thunder, seek the safest terrain in the immediate area—a low area with short trees or shrubs.
- Avoid tall or isolated trees.
- Assume the recommended "lightning position."

> "To be struck by lightning: What a way to get enlightened."
> —GRETEL EHRLICH
> A Match to the Heart

Lightning

One strike and you're out, maybe out permanently, so you want to take some precautions against getting struck by lightning.

Lightning strikes hurl some 30,000 amps of electrical current at the earth. To put such a force in perspective, that amperage is two thousand times greater than the 15 amps that circulates through our homes. Imagine if 15 amps can kill us, what 30,000 can do.

The odds are comforting to the hiker, though. Odds of being struck are only one in 600 thousand. Most of the 300 or so Americans killed by lightning each year perish in cities, not in the backcountry.

Some people seem to be lightning attractors, however. Shenandoah National Park ranger Roy Sullivan was struck seven times (in the sense that he wasn't killed by these strikes, seven was a lucky number). Nature writer Gretel Erhlich was struck twice by lightning and wrote A Match to the Heart, a moving narrative about her experience and its life-altering effects. The lightning strike propelled the author to journey from one natural world to another, and to undertake a spiritual inquiry, as well.

"Quick as lightning" is an accurate description. Lightning strikes in a fraction of a second. The many branched streamers of electrical current (of which only two will strike the earth) charge out of the clouds. About 100 meters from the ground, the negatively-charged "leaders" of electrical current meet positively charged "streamer" currents rising from the closest (often the highest) grounded object. A significant charge (return strike) shoots from the ground back up to the cloud.

Calculate how far away lightning is from you by counting the seconds between seeing the strike and hearing the sound of the resultant thunder. Each five-second interval equals about one mile.

Most lightning strikes occur directly below one of those scary-looking cumulonimbus clouds but there are exceptions, including the proverbial "bolt out of the blue," a sudden, horizontally-traveling bolt of lightning that can strike from as far away as ten miles.

If you're out on the trail and no shelter is readily available, scamper off high exposed peaks and ridges and away from tall, isolated objects. Look for a low spot. If in an expansive woodland, take shelter under the shortest of the trees.

If you can hear thunder, you're the target of a lightning strike. If your hair stands on end and your skin tingles, you are in a mighty high electrical field and in a high and immediate risk of being struck by lightning.

Assuming you can't dash to a building or a hard-topped vehicle, you need to find the safest ground possible to wait out the lightning storm. As quick as you can, get off high exposed terrain and find the lowest spot—or at least a lower spot—with the most low-growing trees and shrubs. Avoid fences, poles and isolated trees.

Recent data suggests that the old mountaineer's advice about how to avoid lightning—"Up high by noon, down low by two" is still fairly accurate. According to the National Lightning Safety Institute, most lightning-caused injuries take place during the summer months between 11 A.M. and 9 P.M.

If a storm is developing, plan to get to your destination and back to a low-lightning risk spot by noon. If you're hiking above treeline and hear thunder, descend immediately.

When you've reached the best lightning-safe spot you can immediately find, assume the "lightning position." Squat or sit, balling up so you are as low as possible, in order to become the smallest target possible. Don't lie down; you want to minimize your contact with the ground.

Stay 50 feet or so away from your hiking companions. Drop or move away from all metal objects such as frame packs or hiking poles.

If one of your fellow hikers is struck by lightning and isn't breathing, immediately begin CPR. (It's just an enduring myth of the mountains that a lightning victim retains an electrical charge and is unsafe to handle). Conscious victims with lightning-caused injuries usually survive, but should have a comprehensive medical evaluation as soon as possible.

Flash Floods

When a thunderstorm breaks over the mountains and desert, rain falls fast and furious. These rains—calling them torrential is not overstating their severity—quickly spill into gullies, arroyos and canyons, dislodging and carrying along boulders, trees and massive amounts of mud. Animals—and occasionally people—can be trapped or surprised by a flash flood cascading down what was dry passageway just a short time earlier.

Flash floods are a danger in the canyon country of the American Southwest, and in many other regions of the world.

Your classic cumulonimbus, or threatening cloud, is not a subtle presence in the skies over the Colorado Plateau. When it's right over you, it appears dark and ominous, and often assumes the shape of an anvil.

While it's easy for the hiker to make a thunderstorm ID when one of those nasty-looking clouds looms overhead, the same storm cloud may look white and bright when observed from farther away. Since flash floods can roil down a canyon as a result of a storm unleashing a deluge on a mountain located many miles away, a thunderstorm need not occur directly overhead to pose a danger to hikers.

Flash floods, at least in the American Southwest where they are most notorious, can occur from isolated thunderstorms at any time, but there is a distinct "Flash Flood Season" that extends from early summer to early autumn.

Flash Flood Precautions

- Keep an eye on the sky. Watch for storm cloud patterns. Listen for thunder.

- If a storm is approaching, avoid slot canyons and other narrow canyons and gulches.

- Check weather reports frequently, particularly on the morning of your hike.

- Backpackers should camp on high ground, but avoid the crests of ridges or peaks.

TRAILMASTER TALE
Zion in Winter

FROM APTLY NAMED Canyon Overlook Trail, we behold the majesty of Zion National Park, a wonderland of sculpted cliffs and deep canyons. Before us is a kaleidoscope of dazzling desert colors, ever-changing with the angle of the sun.

"It's just like a birthday cake," exclaims my daughter Sophia. I applaud my budding naturalist's observation; in winter, the park does resemble a red-rock layer cake, topped by snowy white frosting.

"Where do the animals go when they're cold?" inquires my son Daniel.

"Powerful rocks, soothing waters, very orderly," declares Cheri, bringing an eastern consciousness to this most western of landscapes, the result of her weekend reading—a book on feng shui.

"Still the right place," I affirm, echoing Utah's motto, or at least the one newly posted along I-15 at the state line.

Alas, Utah in general and Zion in particular proved to be anything but the right place the July when I decided to introduce my family to the splendors in the park. In short, Zion was a zoo. Rangers told me that the vast majority of the park's 2.5 million or so annual visitors arrive dur-

ing this desert's hottest months of July and August when temperatures routinely exceed 100 degrees F. We watched motorists' tempers and radiators boil over as the four to five thousand cars a day entering the park competed for parking spaces around the visitor center, and lines at the Zion Canyon shuttle bus stops looked like those at Disney World. It was so bloody hot, that fifteen minutes into our first, hike my family mutinied. They sat waist-deep in the Virgin River and refused to budge.

But that was then, and this is now. Now, in winter, when nature adds snowy white to Zion's palette of pastels, is a special time indeed. Winter (and spring and late autumn I hear) are splendid times for touring Zion Canyon and other lower elevation parts of the national park: campsites and accommodations are easy to come by, the trails uncrowded, and the pace of everyone from rangers to raccoons is slow and easy.

Late autumn, winter, and early to mid-spring are the best times to visit Zion, a ranger at the information desk told me. "But summer is our busy season, when everybody from everywhere comes to Zion. I just can't understand why any-

Cold Weather Hiking

For some American hikers, the end of hiking season comes on Columbus Day, for others on Halloween. Still others regard Thanksgiving as the end of the traditional hiking season.

I say wait a while before you hang up your hiking boots. Plenty of good hiking awaits you in the woods and mountains before the snow sticks.

Apparently many hikers who live in lands of little or no snow have deep empathy for their snowbound brethren because they, too, drastically curtail their hiking in mid to late autumn. Other hikers who could enjoy cold, but snow-free, winter hiking don't. Such reluctance could be the guilt caused by partaking of the pleasures of the trail while hikers in colder climes are housebound, but more likely their reluctance is really resistance to the notion of venturing out into the cold.

Cold weather hiking has its rewards for the hiker who makes extra preparations and takes extra precautions. One reward for

one's crazy enough to come to Zion in the middle of the summer when it's 110 degrees."

"Ask him," Cheri replies, pointing at me.

Hiking is big in our family so naturally we spent a lot of time on the trail. Particularly impressive were the icicles hanging from the park's seeps and springs. We saw lots of deer browsing by the Virgin River and lizards doing their push-ups on nearby rocks.

Even in winter, there's no shortage of footpaths to explore; about 60 of Zion's 150 miles of trail are winter accessible. We hiked what are Zion's most popular trails—to Emerald Pools, Weeping Rock and along the Virgin River to the Gateway of the Narrows—and encountered few fellow hikers. We vowed to come back in the spring when the snow melts and hundreds of small waterfalls cascade off Zion's great cliffs.

Park service signs and brochures more than adequately warn of winter trail conditions. However, what rangers regard as potential hazards to visitors proved to be irresistible challenges to children: Ice is for skidding, snow is for throwing, mud is for sliding. We parents wondered if the park's leash laws applied to children.

Expect to be surprised by Zion's weather. On Saturday we arrived at the park in our cold weather gear and were surprised by a sunny day made to order for shorts and T-shirts. Then on Sunday, expecting a second mild day, we were surprised by cold and rain. It even appeared to be snowing on the surrounding mountains.

Far from the lights of the big city, the night sky above the land of Zion is a dazzling display of twinkling stars.

It's unlikely visitation patterns to Zion National Park will change anytime soon, either. The National Park Service intends to cope with the summer crush by expanding its extensive shuttle bus system, not by encouraging visitors to come during the cooler months.

Returning the park to its original 1909 name—Mukuntuweap National Monument—might discourage some summer visitors, but given the compelling grandeur of this land, probably not.

Our winter view of the Great White Throne, the Court of the Patriarchs and the other magnificent rock formations thrusting skyward high above the North Fork of the Virgin River will long stay in our memories.

By the time I drove south past Utah's "Still the Right Place" billboard, my hiked-into-exhaustion wife and children were sound asleep. Yeah, Zion's the right place, all right. As long as you go at the right time.

hiking in the colder months is more solitude on the trail. A deciduous woodland of leafless trees sure looks different in December than it does in its fully leafed-out splendor in July. The cold air is invigorating and the vistas inspiring in the clear mountain air.

Dressing for a Cold Hike Get out all the synthetic fabric clothing you have out of the closet, as well as your favorite wool items, and get ready to do some serious layering. If it's really cold, begin with polyester long johns top and bottom—a poly t-shirt if it's not quite so cold. Continue with a fleece jacket or vest and fleece pants. Top that with an outer layer of wind/rain jacket and pants and you'll be ready for just about anything.

Don't forget some kind of neck covering like a scarf or hood. Remember to wear a hat and a pair of gloves or mittens.

Weatherproof boots and warm socks are essential. Each year bootmakers make footwear more water resistant and more breathable, but a hiker's socks still get wet and sweaty. To keep your feet

"Take long walks in stormy weather or through deep snow in the fields and woods, if you would keep your spirits up. Deal with brute nature. Be cold and hungry and weary."
—HENRY DAVID THOREAU

Cold Weather Hiking Tips

- Get the latest weather report and adjust and scale your trip with regard to any approaching storms. Keep an eye on the sky and be flexible with your hiking goals and itinerary.

- Dress in layers (synthetic garb of course) and prepare for a wide range of temperatures.

- Pack waterproof outer layers of clothing.

- Wear a hat, scarf or hood, gloves or mittens.

- Practice with walks near home to determine how you and your apparel fare in cold weather.

- Drink plenty of fluids.

- Eat regularly, with lots of high-energy snacks.

- Wear heavy socks and weatherproof boots.

- Bring along a hand warmer.

- Trekking poles help hikers keep their balance on slippery slopes.

warm and happy, bring extra socks and change them out during the day. Gaiters help keep mud and moisture out of your boots.

Food and Fluids Fueling the body in cold weather is a challenging task because stopping to prepare or consume a meal means that at rest body temperature drops, often leading to stiff fingers and numb toes. Rather than stopping for a sit-down lunch, refuel "in flight," so to speak, munching along the trail. Choose "high octane" high carbohydrate/high fat snacks and stash them in your jacket pockets and pack pouches for easy access. Chocolate bars, energy bars, dried fruits and nuts are ideal snacks for this purpose.

When hiking in cold weather, you'll burn more calories in order to stay warm; however, if you're well dressed for the cold, you really won't be burning too many more calories than normal to maintain your body's core temperature.

Even in cold weather, even though you're not feeling particularly thirsty, drink plenty of water—two liters per person per day. Pack a thermos of hot tea or soup.

Dehydration increases the effects of the cold on the hiker, further exerting the heart and muscles, and contributing to fatigue.

If the temperature is below 32 degrees F., wrap your water bottles in insulated sleeves to keep them from freezing. You can also slip them inside your jacket to keep warm.

Adding a sports drink or sugary mix such as Kool-Aid to your water will lower the freezing temperature. However, if you put too much sugar into the water, you'll increase diuresis (in other words, you'll pee out more fluid than you gain)—not a good thing when you're trying to stay hydrated.

Safety Start with the weather forecast from radio, TV and the internet, but remember most of the reports are oriented to population centers. Often the park or remote wildland where you wish to hike is off the radar—literally and figuratively—of the weather service, and may have a distinct microclimate that's different from the nearest city. Call the local authorities or land manager to get more specific weather information about the terrain you plan to trek.

Hike at a steady pace, fast enough to generate some body heat, but slow enough so that you don't start sweating a great deal. Find a pace you can sustain and stick with it, so you don't wear yourself down and you don't have to stop very often to rest.

Those short autumn/winter days mean that the day hike you planned could unexpectedly turn into a night hike. Take along a flashlight or headlamp (and spare batteries) in the event your return to the trailhead takes longer than expected.

Autumn is a great season for wildlife-watching, a chance to view land birds and waterfowl, deer, moose and many more creatures. It's also hunting season in many regions of the country. To avoid being mistaken for any animal that a human needs a license to kill, wear at least one article of bright orange clothing if you intend to take a walk in the woods during hunting season.

Hypothermia

Hypothermia is the sudden cooling of the body's core temperature and the body's subsequent inability to respond by generating enough heat to make up for its loss. Many hikers have a tendency to think of hypothermia as a problem only for such hardy outdoors-folks as scientists on Arctic expeditions and snow campers, but the potentially fatal condition can result from a variety of mishaps or mistakes.

Hypothermia, rightly associated with cold temperatures and inclement weather, can also affect hikers in more moderate temperatures and conditions. Wet clothing, a plunge into an icy river, sitting atop snow and exposure of a sweat-soaked person to a cold wind are some of the ways hypothermia can strike hikers.

Hypothermia is a difficult challenge to treat, but in most cases, easy enough to prevent with some commonsense precautions and preparations. Staying dry, wearing warm, weatherproof clothing that keeps some of its insulating qualities even when wet, wearing a hat (nearly half our heat loss is through our heads) and gloves, and drinking plenty of liquids are ways to ward off hypothermia.

Often it's not backpackers but (too) casual day hikers who are most at risk. For example, that 5-mile ascent to the top of Bald Mountain looked like it was going to be a breeze until a sudden storm swoops in with a cold rain. You forgot your rain gear and are soon soaked to the skin.

You're really piling up the miles on a long day hike and decide to extend your outing a couple of miles. In mid-later afternoon, just short of Beaver Meadow, you slip off a log while crossing Wild Rose Brook, and plunge into the rushing, snowmelt-swollen waters, soaking you and all your gear. You're a long, long way from the trailhead, the sun seem to be rapidly dropping behind the mountains and it's getting cold fast.

Backpackers, with their portable camps on their backs, and often clad in better and more weatherproof apparel, can simply stop, set up camp and take the necessary steps to get warm. Not so day hikers, who must hike back out to camp, lodge, parking area or wherever they started the hike.

Many hikers try to get away with carrying the minimum on a day hike—sometimes just a water bottle and lunch—and don't even bother with the Ten Essentials. To guard against sudden weather changes, rainwear and extra layers of clothing are a must. Just pack this gear and clothing, even if the weather forecast is for a beautiful day, even if you don't feel like carrying it, even if such precautions seem excessive to you.

Having it, but not needing it, is a good feeling. When you're well

Symptoms of Mild Hypothermia

- Shivering, complaints of being cold
- Difficulty performing simple motor skills
- Apathetic behavior, apparent disinterest in taking care of personal needs
- Body temperature falls to 96 degrees F.

Symptoms of More Severe Hypothermia

- Stumbling or falling
- Slurred speech
- Irrational behavior
- Decreased pulse and respiration, possible slip into unconsciousness
- Body temperature drops below 96 degrees F.

Prevent Hypothermia

- Double-check the weather forecast. Learn about any predicted storms or cold fronts moving into the area where you'll be hiking.

- Dress warmly in layers. Be sure to pack a rain jacket.

- Pack an extra set of clothes, particularly if your hike includes creek crossings.

- Wear a hat and carry some gloves.

- Stay dry.

- Drink plenty of fluids.

- Eat high-energy foods and snacks.

prepared, you'll feel blessed in good weather, secure in bad weather.

At the first serious complaint of cold (hey, we all tend to kvetch at the trailhead, "Oh my God, it's freezing!"), add a layer of clothing to the complainants and hike a bit more to see if they warm up. If not, return to the trailhead. If you or your day hike buddy is wet and cold and lacks a change of clothing, end the hike and head back to the trailhead via the shortest route.

Never push a hiker with any of the symptoms of hypothermia to "push through it." Strong hikers are often the ones who become subject to hypothermia because they tend to have a no pain-no gain mentality, ignore symptoms and continue hiking.

Who among us hasn't shivered and displayed some impressive goose bumps in chilly weather? Shivering per se doesn't necessarily mean a hiker is developing hypothermia; shivering is part of the body's normal heat-generating response to a cold environment. Look out, though, for prolonged shivering and the other warning signs of hypothermia. Remember that in all stages of hypothermia, the victim might be in total denial of his condition.

Move the person with mild hypothermia into a warm environment as soon as possible. Remove wet clothing and replace it with dry garb—or wrap them in blankets or a sleeping bag. If conscious, give the person warm (not hot) liquids and food.

More severe hypothermia means the person can no longer warm himself. Getting the victim to a hospital should be the highest priority. If this is not possible, standard first aid is the application of warmth (warm water bottles, hand warmers, etc.) under the armpits, to the head and neck, and to the groin area. Treat and move the victim very gently.

Once the victim's temperature rises back to normal, she must hike back to the trailhead or be evacuated. Don't even think about resuming the hike.

Hiking in Hot Weather

Hot and bothered after a mid-day hike? Well, it's no wonder.

Recent studies have shown that optimum temperature for long-distance walks or hikes is in the range of 50 to 55 degrees F. Above this range a hiker's performance degrades as much as two percent for every five-degree increase in temperature. Air quality, wind (or lack of same) and the amount and kind of reflective heat are also environmental factors that affect a hiker's performance.

As temperatures rise, hikers must adjust their routine. Too much sun, too much hiking and too little fluid intake can make even a strong hiker an accident waiting to happen. Heat cramps, heat exhaustion and heat stroke can result.

California hikers, who tend to be a bit blasé about hiking in the heat, were shocked by the death of a twenty-two-year-old hiker who recently died of heat stroke in the Santa Monica Mountains near Los Angeles. The healthy young man perished not five miles as the red-tailed hawk flies from air-conditioned restaurants, shopping malls and suburbs full of swimming pools.

He and his companions started their hike near the hottest part of a day when the temperature climbed to 88 degrees. There was little shade en route on a strenuous hike with a hefty elevation gain.

We can learn at least two major lessons from this kind of tragedy:

- Heat illnesses and deaths are preventable by taking the right precautions.
- A hike near home can be just as deadly as a trek across Death Valley.

The main environmental factors contributing heat-related illnesses are temperatures above 90 degrees F., humidity above 80 percent and sunlight exposure (partial to full).

People can lose up to two percent of their body weight in water before even knowing they are dehydrated," states Dr. Bob Girondola, professor of exercise science at the University of Southern California. Therefore, the often quoted, regularly ignored advice, "Drink before you're thirsty."

Of course, "Wait 'til it cools off" is always the best advice for the hiker contemplating a hike in the heat. If you're determined to hit the trail in the heat, you must take the right precautions.

Tips to Beat the Heat

- Time your hike for the cool of the day—early morning is best, late evening second best. Avoid midday when the sun's rays are directly overhead, and late afternoon when the earth has absorbed the sun's rays but the heat hasn't dissipated at all.
- Wear a hat. A baseball cap will do, but only if you wear it with the bill in the front (hopelessly unhip, but effective). A better bet is an expedition-type hat that has protective flaps to cover the neck. Another style is the wide-brimmed.
- Apply sunblock (minimum SPF 15) on all exposed skin. Read the product directions: some varieties of sunblock need to be put on some time before exposure in order to be effective.
- Wear loose fitting, light-colored, lightweight clothing.
- Carry—and drink—lots of water. You need to consume six to eight ounces for every twenty minutes of exercise on a hot day.

Heat exhaustion can occur when the body is stressed by hot weather and depleted of fluids and salt. Drinking lots of water or a mix of water and an electrolyte replacement drink will help ward off the condition as will moving from the sun to the shade. Eating a salty snack and taking a good rest also help combat heat exhaustion.

More dangerous, heat stroke occurs when temperature increases to the point where the body is unable to cool itself and brain function is affected. Treat this condition by cooling down the victim with cool (not cold) water and cold compresses. Immediate evacuation and medical help is required.

Symptoms of Heat Exhaustion

- Pale skin
- Dizziness
- Agitation
- Nausea
- Headache
- Rapid heartbeat

Symptoms of Heat Stroke

- Rapid pulse and breathing
- Irrational behavior
- Hot, dry skin
- Unconsciousness

Chapter 14 Hiking over Special Terrain

FROM A MUDDY OVERLOOK, I MARVELED AT WAIKOLU (THREE Waters) Falls thundering in the distance, gazed out at precipitous cliffs and what looked like an impenetrable rain forest.

"How can anyone get over terrain like that?" I wondered out loud.

"You just have to know the land and how to hike it," answered Mike, my guide who patrols Kawinkou Preserve on the Hawaiian island of Molokai for its steward, The Nature Conservancy.

The first part of the trail through the preserve is on a narrow wooden boardwalk that leads through Pepeopae Bog, believed to be 10,000 years old. Violets and orchids brighten the primordial ooze.

Then the boardwalk runs out and the fun began. My guide issued me a pair of rubber boots—the same make and model he's wearing—and strode into the bog with what seems to be an effortless gliding motion. I followed and in ten paces came out of my left boot, which seemed super-glued to the muck. Ten more paces and my right boot stayed behind. While Mike skimmed over the surface of the bog, I sank like a stone.

"After a couple of miles, you'll pick up the right technique," my guide advised. "You know, more than 200 plants grow here and nowhere else in the world. They probably wouldn't have survived if just anybody could hike here."

Clearly, different kinds of terrain call for different kinds of preparation and different hiking techniques. You might not ever hike through a bog that looks like a setting for Jurassic Park, but you're likely to encounter a variety of other kinds of terrain, each with its own challenges to the hiker. To prepare yourself for where the trail takes you, learn to safely cross streams, keep your footing on rocks and slippery slopes and remember the safety precautions necessary for a hike at high altitude.

In This Chapter

- Avoiding falls
- Rocks, streams, snow and ice
- High-altitude hiking
- Desert, coast hiking

HIKERS FALL. Some rarely. Some frequently. Softly. Seriously. Falling is by far the most common hiker accident. Fortunately, most falls result in no more than scrapes and bruises, though serious injury and even death can result from falls.

If you hike long enough on a variety of terrain, sooner or later you're going to fall. Canadian park rangers tell hikers bound for Vancouver Island's supremely slippery West Coast Trail that they should expect to fall. Wear gloves to protect your hands, they advise hikers.

Considering the remarkable number of obstacles nature puts in the path of bipedal mammals to trip them up, it's a wonder humans evolved to walk on two feet instead of sticking with the far more secure four-footed locomotion.

Every experienced hiker can rattle off a long list of the types of terrain that seem to conspire to cause us to face-plant or fall on our butts, do the splits or split our heads: muddy paths, scree, earth slumps, algae-covered rocks, roots, logs (wet or dry), rounded boulders, sandy slopes, bogs, and deadfalls. The trail itself can add more hazards: iron stakes, washouts, slippery footbridges, drainage culverts, wooden steps partially buried in mud.

Hikers can also fall prey to other trail users. Hikers get tangled in each other's boots or bump each other off the trail. Be sure to move off the trail during rest stops so you don't crowd another hiker into slipping off the footpath. Mountain bikers and hikers get into some terrible accidents—and usually it's the hiker who takes the hardest fall.

Fall-back Positions

Best advice for backpackers is to fall backwards onto the backpack. (This advice has some application for day hikers who happen to be wearing a well-designed, well-cushioned day pack.) Landing on the pack cushions the impact. Such a fall often momentarily traps the backpacker on his back (turtling, in hiker jargon)—an indignity to be sure, but usually not a serious situation. If you're the hiker doing the turtling, get back to your feet before your trail buddy snaps a silly picture of you,

If you know you're going down, sometimes you have a split-second choice of which body part to land on. The derriere is often a good choice.

Some fall experts (you have to ask yourself how they became experts—by falling?) opine that there's a chance a hiker can get more hurt by Herculean efforts to stay on the feet and prevent a fall. So the idea here is to go with it—fall, but fall down as safely as possible. Drawing your hands and arms into your chest as you fall helps reduce the chance of injury to your arms and helps protect vital organs.

The Rest Step

To ease the strain of hiking up steep terrain, learn the rest step. This special step is a very useful technique when you're tired; it assists weary legs and helps you to slow and regulate your breathing.

As you step forward and down with your foot, pause a second or two while your weight remains on your trailing leg. During the pause (a kind of stop-motion) your hip will take on some of your weight and relieve your lower leg muscles. Next transfer the weight to the front leg, step forward and pause again.

While the rest step isn't exactly a rest, those short pauses between steps adjust your pace to a more comfortable one and sure beat the alternative—climbing 20 steps, gasping, resting, then climbing, gasping and resting again. Because it helps prevent muscle strain, the rest step is a particularly good technique to employ at the start of hiking season when your muscles aren't quite in top form.

Some hikers do a great job of coordinating their breathing with the rest step, which can bring on a kind of meditative state, a Zen-like consciousness.

Rockin' Out: Hiking over Rocks

Constant vigilance is the key to hiking over rocks. Whether picking your way over a shoreline that resembles piles of broken bowling balls or traversing a wide expanse of scree high on the shoulder of a mighty mountain, rock work is hard work, each step different from the last.

"Rock!" In the time-honored tradition of the mountaineer, yell "Rock!" if you dislodge one and send it hurtling down the mountainside.

Wet rock per se doesn't reduce your traction all that much, as long as the angle of the rock is low and your boots have a good sole. However, rock (wet or dry) coated with gravel or slime can easily upend a hiker.

Scree, an accumulation of loose sliding stones found above timberline, can be a challenge to hikers used to firm dirt trails. Ascending scree is two-steps-up-one-step-back kind of hiking. (Sometimes it seems scree-walking is two-steps-up-three steps back!)

One way to climb scree is by kicking steps into it with the toes of your boots. Scree is shallow, so it's easier kicking into solid ground than you might imagine but a tedious way to ascend nevertheless. A better bet is to ascend a scree slope by switchbacking your way upward, gaining elevation a little at a time.

Descending scree is a bit like surfing the curl. Catch that wave of small rocks and ride it, knees bent, skidding down on your boot heels.

Another high mountain challenge for the hiker is talus, rock rubble that ranges in size from boot-sized rocks to SUV-sized boulders. Bigger rocks mean bigger steps, which mean increased demands on your knees, particularly on descents. Ascending this kind of a boulder field requires strength and stamina but is easier than descending.

Hiking downhill on talus requires some nerve and coordination.

Ups and Downs

- Hiking uphill takes energy. Hiking 2 miles an hour up a 10 percent grade requires as much energy as hiking 4 miles an hour on level trail.

- Master the Rest Step (see left). It doesn't look like much, and frankly it looks a little silly, but it does work.

- Use your arms to help your legs. When climbing steeply, as you step upwards, press down on your forward thigh with your hands.

- Slow down. Slow and steady will get you up that steep trail to the summit, and will help prevent injuries on steep descents.

- Use trekking poles for a boost uphill and added stability going downhill.

- Use small steps on steep descents and keep your knees loose.

- Going down too steeply? Don't be embarrassed to sit on your butt and (carefully) slide down the hill. Better to wear out the seat of your pants than blow out a knee or risk a fall.

Those new to the sport tend to hop from one rock to the other, one rock at a time. Talus-experienced trekkers learn to look several steps ahead and, knees bent, dance their way in a side-to-side motion down the slope.

Streams: Crossing to Safety

While most good trails have good crossings (i.e. shallow fords or footbridges), some do not. Wilderness trails sometimes present challenging stream crossings. Rapid snowmelt or a sudden rainstorm can make a tame stream treacherous. Heed the following river-crossing tips:

- River reconnaissance is well worthwhile. A trail might not cross a waterway at the very best place. Survey the scene up and downstream.
- If possible, cross a mountain stream early in the morning when the flow is lowest. (Snow melts slower during the night than during the day.)
- Cross at the widest (usually the most shallow) part of the stream. Look for a flat water section below a wide bend.
- Cross at an angle (downstream is usually best) because heading straight across exposes you to the full force of the current.
- Given a selection, choose a sandy bottom over slippery rocks for your way across.
- Use a hiking stick as a third means of support (third and fourth leg if you're using two trekking poles). If you usually travel without one, search for a suitable makeshift stick along the stream bank.
- Loosen your shoulder straps and unfasten your pack's waist band. You must be able to wriggle out of your pack if you take a tumble; your pack could trap you in—or under—water.
- Step slowly and cautiously. Securely plant your front foot before moving the trailing one.
- Discretion is indeed the better part of valor. If a stream looks too dangerous to cross, it probably is. Retreat and come back another day.
- Whitewater kills; even fairly shallow fast-moving water can knock you down and hold you under.
- Keep your boots on to protect your feet and maximize your footing. Bare feet are okay for crossing wimpy watercourses with sand bottoms.
- If you're hiking a trail with lots of stream crossings, employ alternative footwear such as a sturdy pair of sneakers (I use an old pair of trail-running shoes in this situation) or those amphibious sports sandals popularized by river-rafters.

Hiking on Snow and Ice

Hikers who surmount high mountain passes in the summer, begin hiking in the spring before all the snow is melted or continue hiking into the snow-dusted late autumn months, may encounter the white stuff. The following discussion is not a correspondence course in crampons or a detailed discussion of winter mountaineering, but only a few tips for dealing with snow and ice.

I strongly suggest that hikers take a winter travel lesson (from a climbing or mountaineering school, the Sierra Club or hiking clubs). Look for a one-day introductory class that teaches such basic snow hiking skills as crampon use, self arrest, the plunge step and using an ice axe.

Sometimes on early season (spring in colder climes) outings hikers must negotiate snowbanks that blanket or partially obscure the trail. Unless it's too deep or too steep to cross safely, just walk over it. If for the same reasons, the snowbank looks nonnegotiable, hike around its periphery.

If you're the first hiker—or one of the first hikers—to cross a snowbank, be a good trail citizen by blazing a path across the snow that as nearly as possible follows the route of the path that's hidden underneath. The way the path goes might be obvious or you might need to take an educated guess. When the snow does melt, your pathway through the snow will be right on top of the dirt trail and you won't have created an unsightly, slope-eroding new one.

High Altitude Hiking

From tenderfoot to world-class mountaineer, every hiker can feel the effects of altitude sickness. A strong hiker can be subjected to a trip-ending bout of nausea while a less experienced and less fit hiker might make it up the mountain with little or no effects from high altitude. Even Everest conqueror Sir Edmund Hilary experienced altitude sickness when years after climbing into the record books by being the first to the 29,028-foot summit of the world's highest peak, he hiked at far lower elevation.

Contrary to what seems like common sense, youth and fitness seem to offer no particular advantage to a hiker's susceptibility to altitude sickness. A fit hiker will perform better than a couch potato on the trail, of course, but fitness—or lack of same—is not a predictor of one's sensitivity to altitude sickness.

Every person's response to oxygen deprivation is different. Few feel the effects below a mile high—5,000 to 6,000 feet or so. Headaches and stomachaches are common symptoms of altitude sickness at higher elevations. Many hikers are willing to push through these discomforts in order to experience alpine beauties and/or reach the top of a mountain.

If you're in good shape when you hit the trail at high elevation, you'll certainly breathe easier. A fit hiker loses about two percent of aerobic capacity for each 1,000 feet in elevation gain over 4,000 feet, while someone who's been sedentary down in the flatlands loses double that.

That old bit of mountaineering advice, "Climb High, Sleep Low,"

Altitude Sickness Indicators

- Shortness of breath
- Appetite loss
- Low energy, fatigue
- Headache
- Nausea
- Poor sleep, insomnia

has only limited application for the day hiker. Spending a night—and ideally a day and a night or more—at a high elevation camp or lodge before embarking on an alpine sojourn, will help you acclimatize.

Maintaining a moderate rate of ascent—one thousand feet per day above 7,500 feet—is an ideal, but usually impractical, way to acclimate.

Among the worst acclimatization offenders are West Coast dwellers from San Diego to Seattle, who drive directly from their sea level abodes to very high trailheads. Getting out of the car and beginning a hike at 9,200 feet . . . well, so much for any altitude adjustment plan.

Dehydration contributes to altitude sickness and worsens as the condition progresses. Limit or eliminate coffee, tea or caffeinated beverages because all are diuretics and accelerate fluid loss by prompting increased urination. (The well-hydrated hiker's urine is clear or fairly clear.)

Avoid adult beverages, too, because alcohol is a diuretic. Unfortunately, the symptoms of a hangover are similar to those of altitude sickness, which can be confusing to someone attempting to make a diagnosis, particularly if that someone is the one with fuzzy judgment resulting from a double whammy of altitude sickness and a hangover.

A dose of acetazolamide (more commonly known as Diamox), available only by prescription, has been found to assist one's adaptation to high altitude and alleviate some of the effects of altitude sickness. The drug has been used by hikers and climbers for more than 30 years and many swear by it, though it does have side effects.

Diamox is a diuretic so if you take it you'll have to drink even more fluids than usual. Those of you allergic to sulfa derivatives need to be aware that Diamox is in the sulfa family and produces various other side effects in some people. Consult your physician before use.

In mountainous regions with less oxygen, the hiker's blood thickens making oxygen dispersal to the muscles far less effective than at sea level.

Drink, drink, drink. And drink some more, more than you think you need. While a liter or two of water may get you through a day of hiking along a coastal trail, double that intake might be necessary for a day at high altitude.

Of course when we're hiking hard at elevation, we hikers tend to breathe through our mouths, which dries us out even more.

Even very experienced lowland hikers should not expect to cover as much ground in a day at high elevation as they do at lower elevation. Pace yourself with one of two tried-and-true methods:

- **A slow hiking pace.** Start out slower than you think you can go. Keep it slow and steady. You might think your muscles are capable of a faster pace, and they probably are, but your body needs time to adjust to decreased oxygen levels.
- **Make frequent stops.** Keep a moderately slow, but not very slow pace and stop frequently.

For some hikers, the symptoms start at about 9,000 feet with a headache that won't go away and stomach distress. Many hikers show the signs of altitude sickness the night before when they can't get a "good sleep" or can't sleep at all.

Aspirin can help alleviate a hiker's headache. This particular pain-reliever has the added benefit of helping to thin the blood.

You're unlikely to notice much in the way of effects of altitude at 3,000 feet but already, even at that modest elevation, the body is making adjustments—primarily increasing the rate of respiration. As altitude increases, so does respiration rate.

At sea level, one's capacity for exercise is limited by the heart's ability to supply oxygen to the muscles; at high altitude, one's capacity for exercise is limited by the amount of oxygen that can be gathered by the lungs.

Those hikers planning an extended high altitude expedition, say to the Himalayas, will be pleased to know that the average hiker can get about 80 percent acclimated to high altitude within ten days.

Reduce the odds of getting altitude sickness by drinking lots of water, eating well (even though you might not have much of an appetite) and ascending gradually.

What to do

What goes up must come down is one law of physics that applies to hikers. Descending the mountain is the obvious response to an ascent that makes you sick.

An early morning headache that won't go away and a queasiness in your stomach are more annoyances than serious health threats, and nature's way of reminding you that you need to get acclimated.

Strong hikers often suffer the most from the effects of altitude sickness because they tend to ignore their symptoms and "hike through the pain," particularly if what they consider to be wimpier companions are not similarly stricken. Apparently, an increase in altitude does not bring hikers an increase in humility and a willingness to admit that on some days the mountain just wins.

Ignoring the symptoms of altitude sickness (accurately called Acute Mountain Sickness by the emergency medicine community) can put you in danger. Once a hiker moves from the initial symptoms of headache and nausea to the second set of symptoms—slurred speech, staggering around—it gets really ugly. At this point, a "designated hiker," must escort the sufferer down the mountain right away.

Left untreated, acute mountain sickness can result in a pulmonary or cerebral edema—that is to say, blood plasma gets in the lungs or brain. Add to the above symptoms of altitude sickness a rapid pulse, raspy breathing and increased confusion, even unconsciousness. The victim must immediately be moved to a lower elevation or he/she will die.

When Altitude Sickness Strikes

- Stop the ascent and descend
- Keep drinking fluids
- Rest
- Aspirin

High Altitude Sunlight

Those deep blue skies over the mountains, so inspiring to hikers and to our landscape photography, mean thinner air, which in turn means intense sunlight bearing down upon us. By some accounts, the fair-skinned hiker who starts to sunburn in thirty minutes at sea level can begin burning in just six minutes at high elevation.

Oftentimes high altitude hiking takes place in environmental conditions that include low temperatures or a brisk breeze. When hikers are cool, not hot, they sometimes forget to apply sunscreen. Do remember, because you can get sunburned very badly very quickly at high elevation. After applying sunscreen to your face and neck, remember to dab the back of your hands, too. To avoid painfully chapped lips from the very-dry high altitude air, use a lip balm or ointment.

A hiker's high altitude headache can worsen as the result of the glare of sunlight on the eyes. Ice and snow compound the glare, reflecting the rays right back up at the hiker.

Desert Hiking

Desert Travel Many notable travelers have journeyed through the hot white heart of the Mojave since Father Francisco Garces first passed through in 1776. Other early desert explorers include Jedediah Smith, Kit Carson, and John C. Frémont. They had little idea of what to expect during their desert crossing. Traveling without detailed maps, high-tech equipment, or freeze-dried foods, they still managed to make the overland trek toward the coast.

Today, we enjoy the benefit of all sorts of undreamed-of modern accoutrements, making desert journeys more comfortable than they were in days past. But the most important aids to desert travel remain as simple as they were 200 years ago—common sense, advance planning and packing the right supplies.

Planning Ahead Individuals accustomed to spending their days in air-conditioned comfort are in for a surprise when they venture into the desert. It's a harsh environment that demands adaptation by inhabitants and visitors alike. Daily extremes of hot and cold are the norm; a 100-degree day can become a 50-degree night. It's important to be prepared—not simply for comfort, but for survival.

The unforgiving desert does not allow visitors to make many mistakes. Those ill-prepared may be unable to deal with threatening situations. Desert dangers are real, and using common sense is essential.

Planning ahead is the first rule of desert travel. Study maps and know where you're going. Become informed about weather patterns, and know what temperatures and climatic conditions to expect. Use this information to plan your trip.

As you study your maps, determine where to obtain services— food, water, gas, ice, etc. Anticipate when you'll need to replenish fuel

Trail Wisdom: Walk in the Desert

THE DESERT has proved to be the holiest of lands. From the deserts of the Middle East arose the world's three major monotheistic religions: Judaism, Christianity and Islam.

This land that by outward appearances seems cursed has often been blessed—the scene of great spiritual triumph. Viewed in the right light, with the right spirit, the land rejoices in its austerity. God, speaking through the prophet Isaiah declared: "The desert and the parched land will be glad; the wilderness will rejoice and blossom."

Few want to drive across, much less walk across, the desert. Many travelers drive along the continent's coasts, over its mountains or through its forests and feel inspired by the scenery. A drive through the desert, however, rarely provides similar inspiration. Too flat, too barren, unaccommodating, is the opinion of many motorists.

The desert demands a closer look. To appreciate fully the desert's beauty requires a bit of walking—a stroll on a nature trail, a hike to a palm oasis, a trek to the top of a desert peak. Without a doubt, the desert is most seductive when approached on foot.

Desert hikers and conservationists have helped alter public attitudes about the desert. Land that had previously been considered hideously devoid of life is now celebrated for its rare beauty; places that had once been feared for their harshness are now admired for their uniqueness. Today the desert's desolation seems to attract rather than repel visitors.

Desert monks of the fourth and fifth centuries A.D. renounced city life to seek peace in the deserts of Egypt and Palestine; there they practiced, and wrote about, self control, prayer, patience and pure living in a way that still moves us today.

These ascetics passed along earthy wisdom that is both practical and mystical at the same time. Fr. Gelasius had these words of advice for desert walkers: "He who walks in the desert does not eat bread; if you're weary, eat a few vegetables. He who is in the desert does not lie in a bed, but in the open air; so do the same."

The desert monks were, in some ways, like people at the beginning of the new millennia—seekers in a world with fewer and fewer rules. Somehow the lives of these ancient monks and their wisdom have special meaning for all of us who live in the "desert" of modern secular society.

Despite the outward harshness of the desert, when you walk it, you see it in a different light. As naturalist Joseph Wood Krutch put it: "Hardship looks attractive, scarcity becomes desirable, starkness takes on an unexpected beauty.

In the silence of the desert, far from worldly wants and ambitions, it is easier to regard God with awe and our fellow walkers with increased understanding.

Walk in the desert.

---

and supplies, and purchase them whenever you have the chance, since gas stations and stores are few in the vicinity of most desert parks.

Before you depart on a desert journey, leave a detailed itinerary with a friend or family member. Be sure to indicate when you expect to return; call later if your plans change.

Coast Hiking

Our family members are all enthusiastic beach walkers, so we want to know in advance when it's the opportune time (low tide) to saunter the shore. We'll walk the coast just about anytime but have

Hike-ku
Stand atop the rock
While waves envelope the sand
Archipelago

Hike-ku
Priceless sand dollar
Currency found near the waves
Bank on sandy shore

learned (sometimes the hard way) that it's best to begin a beach hike a few hours before low tide and finish a few hours after.

Before we hit the beach, I always consult a tide book, one of those trading card-sized pamphlets that chart the ocean's rise and fall, sunrise, moonrise and so much more. Where else can you get so much earthly and heavenly knowledge for free?

The times of these high and low tides are predicted and published by the U.S. Hydrographic Office. Newspapers usually publish the times of high and low tides. Local tide booklets are available free from many marine hardware stores, dive shops, and sporting good stores. Having the right tide table in your possession is important because some coast walks are difficult, even impassable, at high tide. Last year's tide table is no more useful than last year's calendar.

The time to go coast walking, tidepool exploring, or seashell collecting is at low tide. We plan our day so that we begin walking a few hours before low tide and finish a few hours after.

So far this year I've picked up three different tide books—from an REI store, a maritime museum and Pt. Reyes National Seashore. The tide book I purchased from REI cost me $1, the one from the private sector was free, and the one from the National Park Service cost only a quarter.

I appreciate those newspapers that publish daily tide tables, but I really prefer holding all 365-days worth of tides in my hand in the form of one of those little tide books. I favor tide books that print out the heights and times of the tides over those that graph the tides like corporate profits in an annual report.

Of course, you have to be sure your tide table is up-to-date. Last year's tide chart is as useless as a Minnesota road map in Massachusetts. And a Maine tide table won't do you much good in North Carolina. Sometimes a hundred miles or so doesn't make that much difference. A San Diego beach hiker could use a Los Angeles tide book and be accurate merely by subtracting ten minutes from L.A.'s tide times.

Responsibility for predicting tides is vested in The National Ocean Survey, a branch of the National Oceanic and Atmospheric Administration of the U.S. Department of Commerce. After the agency calculates the astronomical influences upon our oceans, it factors in such considerations as the shape of the shoreline, the depth of the water and seafloor topography.

Americans who live near the Pacific, Atlantic and Gulf coasts live in rhythm with the tide. About 80 percent of all Californians reside within an hour's drive of the coast. And about 100 percent of Rhode Islanders live within an hour's drive. High percentages of Washingtonians and Floridians live close to the ocean.

(By the way, you residents of the heartland are not altogether removed from tidal forces. To a lesser extent, tides also occur in lakes, the atmosphere and even within the very crust of the earth, acted upon by the same gravitational forces of the moon and the sun that so influence ocean waters.)

Judging from the millions of this handy booklet in print, I'm hardly the only one who thinks tide books, usually bearing such scintillating titles as "Tidal Calendar" or "High and Low Tides," are a great read. My favorite tide books have local lore, wind chill factor charts, grunion run predictions and favorite recipes for clam chowder.

The humble tide book is unlikely to make the best-seller list (most are given away free), but is an indispensable, positively cosmic reference for the beach hiker, seashell collector and tide pool explorer. Take a beach hike. But read a tide book first.

Hike-ku
Mermaid's purse it's called
Place where each shark comes
alive
Such a peaceful start

Chapter 15 Wild Things

ONE OF MY EARLIEST NATURE-WRITING ASSIGNMENTS WAS TO WRITE voice-over narration for a series of (very low budget) wild-life films. Together with the director/cinematographer, I reviewed hours and hours of raw footage of elephant seals, condors, snakes and snow geese and learned how challenging it is to create an entertaining half-hour film that communicates the essence of a particular animal. While the filmmaker had captured some gems—a baby condor's first flight, bull elephant seals fighting for dominance—he also came back from the field with seemingly endless shots of animal butts, as well as creatures eating and just standing around.

In the midst of writing narration for a grizzly bear documentary, trying desperately to craft a half-hour storyline from twenty-five hours of film, I wrote the worst line of my career: "Here comes the big mother now."

My experience in the nature film biz helped me appreciate the extraordinary patience required of those who make wildlife films and the lengths people will go to observe and record animals in their wild kingdom. I learned how difficult it is to capture those "magic moments" when a creature does something we all-too-anthropocentric humans find entertaining.

Making nature documentaries was fun, but I'd rather watch wildlife in the wild instead. Some of my most memorable moments on the trail have been hikes during which I marveled at creatures great and small. That moose in Cape Breton, Nova Scotia, that 'gator in Everglades National Park, that tortoise in the Mojave Desert . . . cherished memories indeed from terrific hikes.

In This Chapter
- Wildlife-watching
- Bird-watching
- Big things that bite
- Little things that bite

A MEMORABLE WILDLIFE SIGHTING can make a good hike great. Learn where the wild things are by consulting a regional guidebook or asking staff at park visitor centers. A little research will tell you that the buffalo roam in South Dakota not South Carolina. Bighorn sheep gambol through the Rockies, not the Berkshires.

Adult wildlife-watchers tend to gravitate toward the larger creatures—a moose with a sky-scraping rack of antlers, for example—while children delight in watching pint-sized critters. Kids will while away half an afternoon playing peek-a-boo with a pocket gopher popping its head above ground.

I've led children on hikes who were hugely fascinated by watching a banana slug move across a trail. Much to my impatience, the kids wouldn't hear of hiking on until the slug crawled sluggishly away.

Some would-be wildlife-watchers hit the trail with such high expectations that they're invariably disappointed. Expecting to see a rare species—whether it's a mountain yellow-legged frog or an *agrimi* (a Greek mountain goat)—is not a good way to start a hike or enjoy wildlife-watching.

All too often hikers setting out to observe wildlife—often narrowly defined as medium-to-large-sized mammals—are disappointed if they "only" see raccoons, a wood rat or a covey of quail. A better attitude to take on the trail is a sense of wonder—be surprised, be delighted by any creatures you see!

Most wildlife checklists obtained from park offices are big on birds, and there are reasons for this. Your basic bird-watcher is a compulsive note-taker, always records sightings, and often reports species seen to the park naturalist. Whether flying or roosting, birds are often easy to spot—at least easier than most quadruped-type animals.

Birds—with the exception of owls, bats and the like—are active during the day while many animals are nocturnal. Unless you're a night owl yourself and equipped with infrared night vision goggles, wildlife-watching at night is unlikely to be fruitful.

Nocturnal animals such as rabbits and skunks, however, are often spotted during the daytime. Best chance for glimpsing nocturnal animals—and many diurnal species as well—is to hit the trail by dawn or still be on the trail at dusk. Obviously the optimal times for wildlife-watching may not coincide with the best time for you to take a hike.

Marvel at how many animals remain unseen, hidden from view of the passing hiker: resting in trees, sleeping underground, feeding in the tall grass, nesting in the undergrowth. We see signs of them in the form of tracks, scat and chewed branches.

Often we hear animals without seeing them—the call of the wild, indeed. We hear their rustlings in the brush—which our imaginations often magnify and lead us to believe come from animals far bigger than the ones really producing the sounds.

Official Watchable Wildlife Areas

Repeated surveys have shown that wildlife associated recreation is hugely popular with Americans, who love observing and photographing wildflowers, wildlife and scenery.

The National Watchable Wildlife Program is a coalition of government agencies and private conservation groups working together to promote wildlife-watching. The underlying premise for the program is the belief that if the public is provided with ample and engaging opportunities to view wildlife, citizens will become better informed about plant and animal species conservation.

A binocular logo designates wildlife-viewing areas. Strategically placed signs with the logo direct motorists from highways and secondary roads to the sites.

Watchable Wildlife Sites are well worth a look and often feature leg-stretcher type trails that lead from parking lots to viewing outposts. Some wildlife-viewing areas feature longer hikes.

Hiking on the Edge Can be a Good Practice

Good wildlife-watching is often found on the edges of habitats. Ecologists say many of the most interesting and dynamic habitats are on the edges: places where the forest meets a meadow, where the land meets the sea, where the city meets the country.

Here plants and animals confront conditions that give rise to increased variety. Studies of bird populations reveal that species are more abundant in places where the chaparral meets the pine forest than in chaparral-only or forest-only environments. Various plants and animals that might be rare in one community or the other may flourish on the edge between them.

Areas of transition between ecological communities are called ecotones: their existence depends on two differing environments, yet also create a world unto themselves. States George Clarke in his classic text, *Elements of Ecology*, "As a rule the ecotone contains more species and often a denser population than either of the neighboring communities, and this is generally known as The Principle of Edges."

Migrations

Whales and Trails Not everyone who loves whale-watching needs to (or wants to) board a boat to sight cetaceans. Each winter Pacific coast hikers, too, welcome the return of the gray whale. One of the great pleasures of hiking the coastal bluffs of California, Oregon and Washington at this time is looking out for a pod of the 50-foot long, 45-ton majestic mammals.

Scientists point out that the creature's migration—from the Arctic to its breeding and birthing waters in Baja and back—is the longest migration of any animal. Gray whales tend to swim close to California's shoreline at Point Reyes, travel through Monterey Bay

TRAILMASTER TALE
Frog Days in the High Sierra

DAVE BRADFORD is becoming a mad scientist, or at least a madder one, as we splosh through this half-frozen High Sierra Meadow. We are up to our gaiters in a viscous mixture of mud and snow, stalking the wild Mountain Yellow-Legged Frog, the highest-dwelling amphibian in the U.S. Our search is along the headwaters of the Kaweah River in Sequoia National Park has so far been in vain.

Bradford is upset because it looks like the previous brutal winter has done-in the entire population of *Rana muscosa*, the subject of his UCLA Ph.D. thesis. We've visited several unnamed lakes and fount them still covered with ice. Bradford is worried about a frog kill, which, like a fish kill, occurs when lakes don't thaw and bacteria and fungi on the bottom consume all the oxygen.

We concentrate our efforts on a number of nameless football-field-sized lakes. (Larger lakes tend to have trout as well as names—the presence of fish being a strong incentive to man's naming proclivity—and trout tend to devour any Yellow Leg tadpoles that have the misfortune to be born in their vicinity.) It is on the banks of one of these unnamed lakes that we discover a grisly sight. Hundreds of yellow frog legs, minus their owners, are scattered about on shore. It looks like an amphibian version of the Donner Party.

"Blackbirds," Bradford mutters. He's seen such carnage before. As the tadpoles changed into froglets and hopped ashore, the birds pounced on them, eating everything but the nice, plump legs. Obviously not gourmets, these blackbirds.

Dispiritedly, we follow the Kaweah and ascend above timberline to a lush basin. Bradford changes into green sneakers, green shirt, green hat, green shades. The frogs must sense a kindred spirit because he immediately finds a Mountain Yellow Leg. It's a large female that he banded the previous summer. Bradford is delighted; after some 150 winter and summer days up here, he's become a bit unscientifically fond of the little buggers.

The captured frog stoically endures the indignities of the tape measure, the scale and the rectal thermometer. Vital statistics: 68 millimeters from snout to rump; weight 27.3 grams; temperature, 22 degrees centigrade (a medium-warm frog). Stoicism, I soon learn, is what the MYL frog is all about.

Bradford goes about collecting tadpoles, leaving me to watch the female Yellow Leg and to guard his instruments from a marauding marmot. The frog moves but once in the next hour to snatch at a fly. She misses.

"Not too entertaining, are they?" teases Bradford, returning just as I'm picking up the frog to make sure it's still alive.

"It smells funny," I note.

"The frog secretes a mucous that doesn't taste good," he confirms. "Blackbirds and garter snakes like them, but they'll eat anything."

and past Big Sur, then fairly close along the Southern California coastline before reaching Mexico.

The spectator sport of whale watching has a full lexicon of terms, as familiar to its fans as the quarterback sneak, sacrifice fly and full court press are to the followers of more traditional sports. When a whale breaches, it comes out of the water and falls over to one side. Spyhopping means the animal rises head first out of the water, seemingly standing on its tail, and comes down slowly.

Where Monarchs Reign Every fall, millions of monarch butterflies migrate south to the damp coastal woodlands of Central and Southern California. The monarch's awe-inspiring migration and for-

After 48 hours of observation, it is clear why no nature film crew has ever gone after the MYL. The lifestyle of this noxious-smelling creature seems deliberately undramatic. It hibernate seven to nine months a year in icebound ponds and is active (if you can call it that) for three to five months. After a night spent resting in the bottom of a lake or stream, it rises well after the sun and swims to shore. Here it makes its major decision of the day: where to bask in the sun. Once it finds a sunny spot, it moves only when the sun changes angle or to swallow flies. The MYL frog is known as a sit and wait predator and seems equally adept at both sitting and waiting. Gulping three flies in twelve hours is a good day's work. If the frog finds an especially nice, sunny spot, it may occupy the same square foot all day. Sometimes a Yellow Leg will join twenty or more of its fellows in a group bask, huddling in a heap, presumably to reduce heat loss.

Except for their communal basks, Yellow Legs are not sociable creatures. They croak only when stepped on, and it is a feeble call, more like a baby wrentit than a bullfrog. Courtship, carried on in the icy water, is a brief and desultory affair, but the sex act itself is prolonged and may go on for several days. The male, somewhat smaller than the female, hops on her back and with his special calloused thumbs, squeezes her behind the armpits. He massages out her eggs and fertilizes them in the water. The jelly-like eggs stick to aquatic vegetation, and the partners swim blithely off in opposite directions.

All in all, the MYL frog wants little more out of life than to stay warm; its ability to survive temperature extremes is what makes it an attractive research subject to Bradford. He implants transmitters in some of the frogs' bellies so that they give off a signal. The result is a series of beeps on an AM radio. So many beeps equal to so many degrees. The temperature readouts are quite accurate until a garter snake swallows the transmitting frog and becomes a transmitting snake. Snakes have completely different temperatures and can really screw up Bradford's data if he's not careful. To retrieve the expensive transmitter, Bradford must track down the snake and induce it to vomit, which comes naturally to the snake (it often vomits to offend predators or to lighten its load for a quick escape) but leaves everyone feeling a bit raw.

The MYL is a survivor. You have to respect this creature, whose chance for long life is as low as its metabolism. No other amphibian and few other life forms can withstand the extreme cold, the high elevation, the ruthless predators. Some of the frogs live to the ripe old age of 25, Bradford believes.

Although he conducts his research in one of the most beautiful alpine meadows on earth, there's little that is romantic or idyllic about his work. A campus flyer he circulated describing the delights of frog research failed to lure any pretty coeds into the Sierra. Bradford's nights are long and lonely. The silence is broken only by the radio, which receives but two transmissions: a rock station from Gilroy, and the endless beeping of his transmitting frogs.

mation of what entomologists call over-wintering colonies are two of nature's most colorful autumn events.

The butterflies seem to have a knack for wintering in some of California's most beautiful coastal locales, including Monterey and Santa Barbara. Many groves are protected within state and local parks and can be reached by some great hiking trails.

Monarchs hang on trees in thick bunches, resembling so many triangular dead brown leaves until, warmed by the sun, they spread their wings and fly around the aptly named butterfly groves. This is fall color, California-style, an autumn spectacle that lingers well into winter and stays in a visitor's heart for a very long time.

About August, great groups of monarchs from Wyoming,

> "What is a butterfly? At best he's but a caterpillar dressed."
> —BENJAMIN FRANKLIN

Wildlife-Watching Tips

- Do it at dawn and dusk. Animals are particularly active at these times.

- Hike slowly, hike quietly. Loud talking—even snapping a twig or dislodging a stone—alerts wildlife to your presence.

- Keep your distance. Approach wildlife in a roundabout way. Never purposely scatter birds to get them to take flight or give chase to an animal.

- Use the right tools. Binoculars or a spotting scope help deliver close-up views. A telephoto lens—400mm or so—on your camera will capture what you see.

- When duck hunting (with a camera, of course), go where the ducks are. Some sites have greater wildlife-spotting potential than others: springs, ponds, perches, ledges and meadows.

- Hide out behind boulders, bushes and tree trunks. Assume as small a profile as possible.

Montana, southern Canada and other locales west of the Rockies begin their long journey to wintering grounds in the Golden State. Arrival and departure times, as well as population sizes, vary from year to year and from locale to locale, but generally speaking the butterflies make it to the California coast in mid-October and may stay until mid-February, or even March.

While monarchs begin life as caterpillars, there's nothing sluggish about their pace. Monarchs have been known to fly as far as 2,000 miles, and as fast as 30 miles an hour at a cruising altitude of 1,000 feet.

How monarchs determine where to go remains a mystery. Do they follow food sources? Scents? Is it all instinct? Do they operate with some kind of celestial navigation? The mystery is all the more baffling because no single monarch completes a round trip.

The female monarch lays her eggs on milkweed plants. A couple days later, caterpillars emerge and feed voraciously for two weeks. Each caterpillar then forms a chrysalis (similar to a cocoon) and attaches itself upside down to a twig. After about two weeks of metamorphosis, the caterpillar is transformed into a butterfly and joins the return northward migration of its parents.

The monarch's evolutionary success lies not only in its unique ability to migrate to warmer climes, but in its mastery of chemical warfare. The butterfly feeds on milkweed—the favored poison of assassins during the Roman Empire. The milkweed diet makes the monarch toxic to birds; after munching a monarch or two and becoming sick, they learn to leave the butterflies alone.

The butterflies advertise their poisonous nature with their conspicuous coloring. They have brownish-red wings with black veins. Outer wing edges are dark brown with white and yellow spots. While one might assume the monarch's startling coloration would make them easy prey for predators, just the opposite is true; bright colors in nature are often a warning that a creature is toxic or distasteful.

Monarchs are excellent field thermometers. When the temperature exceeds 55 degrees F., the monarchs flit about on branches and fly around seeking nectar. However, if it's colder than 55 degrees F., rainy or very damp, the monarchs cluster together in trees for warmth, and for protection from the wind and rain.

While the monarchs' arrival is usually a fairly predictable natural phenomenon—at least in comparison to California's notoriously fickle wildflower displays—call the relevant park or preserve for a monarch update before you make a butterfly pilgrimage.

Bird-watching

How to explain our fascination with the world's winged creatures?

There are bird species aplenty in every ecosystem—resident songsters, waterfowl, migrants from near and far.

Much to the fascination of birders, there are more than 8,000 species. Each winter several billion birds fly south from the temperate zone

Watching birds fills us with wonder. We wonder how birds navigate by the stars. We wonder how fledglings learn their songs from parents and neighbors.

The names of groups of birds are intriguing, even joyous: a host of sparrows, a covey of quail, a flight of doves, an exultation of larks.

Birding is one of the most complementary activities to hiking. (Some enthusiastic bird-watchers might say hiking is complementary to birding while others regard hiking as a necessary evil to reach the best birding spots.)

Hike a variety of landscapes, a variety of different wildlife habitats and reach the best birding spots.

Even subtle shifts in temperature, terrain and food availability results in changes of species and every level.

Basic birding equipment is simple: a field guide, a good pair of binoculars, a notebook.

A good field guide highlights a bird in a drawing or photograph and gives a description (in capsule form or highly detailed). A bird's habitat and range, a bird's voice—its call or song—along with the time of the year it's likely to be sighted in a particular area, are all keys to ID-ing a bird species

Many parks and nature centers offer free or low-cost checklists of birds. A particular species will be easier to identify if you familiarize yourself with the species recorded in an area and review a regional bird guide and checklist.

Birders use a notebook to record observations about birds: where and when observed, appearance, movements and behaviors, call or song.

Big Things that Bite

North American animals that kill humans are few in number and, with some exceptions, roam remote territory. Not so long ago, humans were commonly prey for animals. Nowadays, though, when a human is mauled by an animal it is headline news.

Quite understandably, many hikers want nothing to do with some animals—snakes, bears and mountain lions. When traveling the territory, it's important to learn about the habits and habitat of creatures that bite, use common sense and follow the time-proven rules posted at parks and at trailheads.

Many of the largest predators have very limited ranges. Don't let the fear of certain animals stop you from a wonderful walk in the woods.

Bears and mountain lions are two of the big animals that some hikers would prefer not to encounter—or at least watch only from a safe distance. The wise hiker has a healthy respect—even a little

Bird-watching Tips

- Identify the bird by observing its size compared to other birds, its body shape and its wings, tail, feet and bill, and its distinct colors or markings.

- Note the bird's location: in or near water, in a tree or in flight.

- Listen for the bird's song or call.

- Watch the bird's behavior. Is is perching, pecking, swimming, singing?

- Examine what birds leave behind: foot prints, feathers, droppings and nests to expand your knowledge about them.

- Try to be unobtrusive when watching birds so they're not aware of your presence. Keep your distance, move slowly and quietly.

- Stay on established trails and resist the urge to trample fragile vegetation in order to get a closer look.

- Never touch eggs and young birds or get too close to a nest. You could frighten parents into abandoning it.

Pink Birds at the Edge of the World

INAGUA, in the Bahamas, is full of salty water, an attraction for the Morton Salt Company, which operates the world's second largest solar evaporation saltworks here. The salt, "Inagua snow," accumulates in rinds along the edge of vast reservoirs, piles into drifts, sting the face when the trade winds kicks up.

A hellish landscape it is for humans, yet a perfect habitat for the long-legged, long-necked pink flamingo.

In 1963, the Bahamas National Trust convinced the government to set aside 287 square miles in the interior of the island as a preserve for the birds. Inagua Park encompasses 12-mile-long Windsor Lake and numerous mucky Salinas lined with mangroves—all of the flamingo's customary feeding and nesting grounds.

At dawn I join Game Warden Jimmy Nixon for a trek across the saltscape to the Upper Lakes region, the brackish habitat favored by the formerly almost extinct flamingo.

"Forty thousand boids live here," relates warden Nixon. "I got no authority to speak for the fillymingos, but they do seem to like Inagua."

The spry 68-year-old Inaguan has been protecting the flamingos for more than four decades, first as an Audubon warden and now as an employee of the Bahamas National Trust. Nixon's uniform is a khaki shirt with a patch on the left sleeve depicting two flying flamingos.

"In the old days they used to hunt fillymingos. A terrible thing. 'Course, they stopped when they were almost—extinct."

On Inagua, Nixon recalls flamingo roundups—men, women children and dogs chasing after the flightless young. Now Nixon guards against local poachers with a taste for "Inagua steak."

As we hike along the salt flats, Nixon and I talk of another island creature that's special to us—the green turtle. The future remains uncertain for this ancient creature whose unalterable nesting behavior brings it into fatal contact with humans.

Green turtles are making a comeback on Inagua thanks to the release of thousands of newly hatched turtles into Inaguan water. Conservationists hope that these young hardshells will grow to maturity and return to nest on Inagua's protected beaches.

Nixon's affection for turtles was strained a bit recently when he was cajoled into helping an American graduate student with her turtle studies. The student concentrated on collecting turtle feces, which required affixing plastic bags to the posteriors of the sometimes recalcitrant research subjects, a process that left everyone—student, Nixon and the turtles—feeling a little testy.

"God to be my judge, I don't understand what she planned to do with a thousand bags full of tuttle chit," Nixon puzzles. "But we got that gal her Ph.D."

Nixon scans the salt flats. "You know, the truth is I prefer working with the fillymingos."

The Audubon Society established Long Cay camp as a flamingo research station. Spartan accommodations: a tent, water tank, a picnic table, a privy. Some visitors swear this place was the inspiration for one of James Bond's adventures. Agent 007's creator, Ian Fleming, was an avid birdwatcher and filched the name of his superhero from the real-life ornithologist James Bond, author of a West Indies bird guide. In the Bond thriller, Dr. No, the action takes place at an Audubon camp on a remote island suspiciously like Inagua. Fortunately, there's no real-life Dr. No, a nasty fellow who barbecues birds and game wardens with a flamethrower.

While Nixon builds a cooking fire, I watch flamingos through field glasses. A few hundred of them feed nearby, sending a raucous chorus echoing across the water. I'm transfixed, oblivious even to the attentions of the well-named ferocious sandfly. Nothing stands between me and the edge of the world but pink birds, forty thousand of them.

fear—of big animals that bite. Nevertheless, don't stay away from the trail because of fear of wild animals. Do, however, learn about their habits and habitat, use common sense, and heed the time-proven rules posted at park and forest offices and at trailheads.

No sense worrying about grizzly bears while hiking in the redwoods; alas, ol' griz has been extinct in California for more than a century—though Californians keep the grizzly on the state flag and as the official state animal. While hiking in the Hawaiian rain forest, don't worry about a snake slithering through some vines to bite you because no poisonous serpents are to be found on the islands. Paradise, indeed.

Little Things that Bite

Late spring and summer are excellent times of the year for hiking. The air is mild, streams are flowing, birds are chirping and, unfortunately, bugs are biting. Blood-loving insects are out in full force when the weather is warm—and they sure know how to spoil a good time.

In North America, hikers' most prevalent buggy foes are mosquitoes, black flies, and ticks. The good thing is that bites from these insects are very rarely life threatening and at least somewhat preventable.

Best ways to avoid bites

- Wear long pants and a long-sleeved shirt with elasticized , buttoned or Velcro-tabbed cuffs. With the exception of gigantic biting flies, bugs can't reach you through your clothing. If the weather is really warm, pants and long sleeves may not sound like a great idea, but some of the newer, more breathable hiking fabrics may change your mind, however. Retailers now carry lots of lightweight, long sleeved clothing that can help keep you dry, cool, and bug free.
- Tuck in your shirt! Bugs can easily fly or crawl up your back if you aren't careful.
- Wear bug repellent that contains DEET. Regardless of any misgivings you may have about slathering chemicals on your skin, there is no denying that DEET keeps bugs away. Reapply on exposed skin throughout the day as directed.
- Stay on the trail. Bushwhacking through heavily forested areas or grassy fields will increase your chances of picking up ticks.
- Don't take long rests near swamps or marshes. Mosquitoes love standing water, and will assault any human visitors who linger nearby.
- As silly as it might look, mosquito netting can actually be a real blessing in buggy conditions. Netted hats, pants and shirts can be found at hiking or travel stores and online.

More Wildlife-Watching Tips

- Consult park wildlife checklists and field guides to determine which animals are likely to be spotted where.
- Stay on maintained trails. Not only is sticking to the trail an environmentally sound practice, it can actually help you see more wildlife as well. Animals often take the easiest and most direct path through the woods—just like hikers.
- Look for signs: tracks, scat, bedding sites, burrows, mounds, cavities.
- Patience, please. Don't expect to spot a moose around the first bend along the trail to Moose Bog.
- Don't feed wildlife. Nature provides adequately without supplemental feeding from human handouts. Such foodstuffs can hurt an animal's digestive system, even kill it.
- Wear natural-colored clothing and lotions and deodorant without fragrances.

A few dos and don'ts for getting rid of ticks

DO—

- Dab rubbing alcohol on the skin around the tick and on the tick itself. It sterilizes the area and some experts argue that it causes the tick to loosen its grip, making it easier to pull out.
- Firmly grab the tick with a pair of sharp-pointed tweezers right where the head meets your skin.
- Slowly pull the tick straight out.
- If Lyme disease is a problem in your area, save the tick in a plastic bag or jar for later testing.

DON'T—

- Smother the tick with petroleum jelly or butter. Some people believe that this will suffocate the tick and cause it to pull out on its own. To my knowledge, this method does little more than create a greasy mess.
- Use the heat from a match or cigarette to remove the tick. Like the petroleum jelly idea, it was once thought that ticks will pull themselves out to escape the intense heat. Instead, it is more likely that they will burrow even deeper into the skin.
- Try to pull on the tick with your fingers.
- Twist the tick as you pull it out. This may increase the chance of leaving the head behind.

Ticks

Ticks are small arachnids (like spiders) that feed on the blood of mammals, birds and even reptiles. They frequently attach to human hosts in warm areas where they will likely go undisturbed—behind the ears or knees, armpits, and in the scalp. If left undetected, ticks will feed up to five days before moving on to another host.

Ticks are usually most prominent in wooded areas with lots of leaf litter and dense underbrush, or in overgrown grassy areas. Ticks often wait for passing animals under leaves or the tips of grasses.

Not only are they ugly, and insidiously vampire-like, ticks are liable to carry nasty diseases. In North America, the most common tick-borne illness is Lyme disease, a bacterial infection that can be very serious if left untreated.

Preventing tick problems Some places are more likely to harbor ticks than others. Thick, wooded areas, for example, are often laden with these nasty bugs.

- Before you head home from a hike, check your fellow hikers (and have them check you!) for ticks. Brush off your clothes before you climb into the car.
- Did you bring your dog with you? He or she needs to undergo a thorough inspection as well. As you probably know, dogs spend a lot more time "hiking" in the surrounding shrubbery and running through grassy fields than sticking to the trail.
- In a post-hike shower, scan your body one more time—your hair, behind your ears, your lower legs, etc.
- Make sure to wash your hiking clothes soon after you get home.

Removing a tick Removing a tick can be tricky. While it's tempting to pull it out quickly, be careful—it's easy to leave the tick's head behind.

Pay attention to what happens afterwards! I once ignored a tick bite on my abdomen until my wife pointed out what appeared to be a rapidly growing red bulls-eye on my stomach. A quick trip to my doctor, a prescription for antibiotics and a little time-off the trail tamed my encounter with the tick.

If the tick's head does stay in the skin, you can remove it yourself or with the help of a friend:

- First: With your thumb and forefinger, pinch the skin with the embedded tick head.
- Second: Carefully scrape the area containing the head and mouth with a sterilized razor blade. If the head is too deep, use a sterilized needle to break the skin and gently pull it out.
- Third: Clean area with rubbing alcohol or other antiseptic.

Lyme disease Hikers in the Northeast, Mid-Atlantic and the Northern Midwest are more likely to contract Lyme disease (a tick-borne illness) than hikers in other parts of the country. In fact, the disease was named for Lyme, Connecticut, in the 1970s.

So, how do you know if you have it?

Symptoms of Lyme disease generally show up within four weeks of being bitten. One nearly universal symptom is the development of a circular rash at the tick site that looks a little like a bullseye—red with a pale center.

A smaller number of Lyme disease sufferers also exhibit flu-like symptoms, including headaches, fatigue, swollen lymph nodes, chills and fever. Lyme disease is a bacterial infection, and can be successfully treated with a three-week course of amoxicillin, doxycycline, or other antibiotic drugs.

Mosquitoes

Mosquitoes are the most universally well-known—and deeply hated—insects around. Both historians and biologists believe that they've plagued human civilization since its inception.

Like ticks, mosquitoes feed on the blood of animal hosts. But unlike ticks, only the females bite. They lay eggs in standing water, in anything from large swamps to tiny puddles, which makes it nearly impossible to avoid them on a summertime hike.

Not only do mosquitoes leave behind irritating, itchy bumps after feeding, they sometimes carry—and spread—deadly diseases like the West Nile virus, malaria, and the occasionally fatal Dengue fever.

It is extremely unlikely that hikers in northern climes will contract these diseases, no matter how often they are bitten. However, a handful of West Nile virus and Dengue fever cases are reported ever year in the U.S. Despite the low risk, it is important take appropriate precautions.

Black Flies

Black flies are small, annoying, and almost everywhere. They feed on the blood of humans and other mammals, and occasionally birds. Like mosquitoes, only the females bite. But unlike mosquitoes, black flies can breed in moving water.

The good news is, there are no known diseases carried by North American black flies. The pain and itch of a bite is about as bad as it gets.

DEET is hard to beat

DEET, or N,N-diethyl-m-toluamide, was developed by the USDA in the mid-1940s for American soldiers, and its effectiveness against biting insects was striking. It became commercially available in the 1950s, and has been used ever since in most over-the-counter insect repellents.

Like other insect repellent agents, DEET overpowers the scent

Hike-ku
Mosquito drilling
Through arm skin effortlessly
Energy Transfer

"God in His wisdom
made the fly.
And then forgot
to tell us why."
—OGDEN NASH

DEET Guidelines for Children

- Children under the age of 12 should not be allowed to apply DEET themselves.

- Apply DEET only one time per day.

- Wash off DEET daily.

- DEET should not be used in a product that combines the repellent with a sunscreen. Sunscreens often are applied repeatedly because they wash off and DEET is not water-soluble. Repeated application of DEET may increase its potential toxic effects.

- Apply DEET before applying sunscreen.

- Up to 30 percent DEET is safe if used properly, with the duration of need determining the appropriate percentage, e.g. use a lower percentage if you're going out for a short period of time.

- Ten percent DEET will provide up to two hours of protection.

—St. Louis
Children's Hospital

that mosquitoes normally pick up from humans. What is different about DEET, however, is that it lasts much longer than repellents that contain citronella, eucalyptus, soybean oil, and other natural ingredients known for their anti-bug properties.

The New England Journal of Medicine published a study in 2002, that listed the results of a study that compared "first bite" times of eleven commercial insect repellents. Study participants coated their arm with one of these substances, and inserted it into a cage containing ten mosquitoes. Researchers noted the time it took until the first mosquito bit with each repellent.

Sure enough, the products that contain high concentrations of DEET fended off mosquitoes far longer than DEET-free or low-DEET repellents. The time to the first bite with OFF! Deep Woods (with a 23.8 percent concentration of DEET) was the longest, 301.5 minutes, whereas OFF! Skintastic (with 6.65 percent concentration of DEET) lasted 112.4 minutes, and Skin-So-Soft Bug Guard (with a 0.1 concentration of Citronella) lasted a mere 10.3 minutes.

DEET is powerful stuff, however. It can damage some plastics, spandex, leather, and rayon. Parents need to exercise caution when applying DEET products to children.

Some Things about Stings

Bees, yellowjackets and wasps can be major problems as well, but they are unlikely to seek out hikers. Leave them alone, and they'll likely leave you alone.

Most of us experience slight swelling, itching, and redness from a bee sting. But there are many people who have severe allergic reactions that can include:

- Extreme swelling in areas other than the sting site
- Tightness in the chest
- Dizziness or sharp drop in blood pressure
- Unconsciousness or cardiac arrest

Most adults who have allergic reactions are aware of their allergy already. If you are one of these people, we strongly encourage you to bring along an epinephrine kit wherever you go, especially on extended trips in the out-of-doors. If you are unsure whether you have bee sting allergies, please consult with your doctor.

Tips for staying sting-free

Don't wear bright clothing, or scented lotions or perfumes (yes, I've been on hikes with women wearing designer scents you could smell a hundred yards away). Bright colors and sweet smells attract bees and can fool them into thinking you're a delicious-smelling flower.

Never swat at stinging insects. Waving your hands in front of your face may shoo away a mosquito, but it will likely provoke bees, wasps and yellowjackets. As hard as it may be, let them linger awhile, and eventually they'll take off.

Removing a stinger

To remove a stinger, don't pull it straight out. A bee stinger has tiny barbs that cling to your skin, making it difficult to remove. Rather, scrape the stinger and surrounding area with a credit card or fingernail to gently work it out of the skin.

Oddly enough, a bee stinger continues to pump venom into the body for up to twenty minutes after the bee has stung. So, it is wise to be expedient when removing the stinger.

While bees only sting once, wasps and yellowjackets may sting repeatedly. Calmly remove wasp and yellowjacket stingers in the same manner you would those of a bee.

Poison Ivy and Poison Oak

About 85 percent of Americans are susceptible to poison ivy and poison oak; only about 15 percent are resistant and won't develop a rash. Some people appear to be immune because they don't get a rash after repeated exposures; sometimes, though, the apparently immune are affected by repeated, heavy contacts.

Poison ivy was discovered early in American history. Captain John Smith named it in the early 1600s. Poison oak was discovered on Vancouver Island by famed early nineteenth-century botanist David Douglas. Fortunately for his revered place in floral history, he is remembered by the Douglas fir, not the "Poison Douglas Oak."

Poison ivy often grows as a vine, creeping over the ground or climbing tree trunks. It can also be a self-supporting bush. The infamous leaflets three are red in early spring, changing to a shiny green. Autumn leaves are red, yellow and orange hues. The plant displays small greenish flowers and clusters of poisonous berry-like white drupes.

Poison oak grows abundantly throughout western mountains up to an elevation of 5,000 feet. It's a sneaky devil. It may lurk under other shrubs or take the form of a vine and climb up an oak tree. The leaves are one to four inches long and glossy, as if waxed.

Urushiol (you-ROO-shee-ol), an oil similar to carbolic acid, is the "poison" in poison ivy and poison oak. It's potent stuff! Only one nanogram (billionth of a gram) is needed to cause a rash. Just one-quarter of an ounce of urushiol could cause a rash to erupt on every person on earth.

All parts of these plants at all times of the year contain poisonous sap that can severely blister skin and mucous membranes. Its sap is most toxic during spring and summer. In fall, poison oak is particularly conspicuous; its leaves turn to flaming crimson or orange. However, its color change is more a response to heat and dryness than season; its "fall color" can occur anytime in Southern California. Leaves on some plants can be turning yellow or red while plants in most spots are putting out green leaves. In winter, poison oak is naked, its stalks blending into the dull hue of the forest.

> "The wild requires that we learn the terrain, nod to all the plants and animals and birds, ford the streams and cross the ridges, and tell a story when we get back home."
> —GARY SNYDER

Contrary to popular belief, you can't catch poison oak/ivy from someone else's rash, nor from oozing blisters, but petting an animal or handling a piece of clothing that carries it can make you a victim. You can even catch it from dead plants; urushiol can stay active on any surface for as long as five years.

A long-sleeved shirt, long plants and gloves comprise a helpful barrier, but not an impenetrable one. Various skin creams are also helpful, but not failsafe, barriers.

Rash outbreak can occur as quickly as six to twelve hours after exposure, but is usually in the 24- to 48-hour range, and may start as late as a week after exposure. The rash may emerge at different times over different parts of the body, depending on the concentration of urushiol and the severity of the exposure.

There are a multitude of remedies. Perhaps most common is the regular application of calamine lotion or cortisone cream. If you're particularly sensitive to poison oak, always wash down thoroughly immediately after a hike with cold water and a basic soap such as laundry detergent. Launder your hiking clothing separately as soon as possible. A dip in the ocean can help; a few tablespoons of baking soda added to a tub of lukewarm water calms the itchies as well. You organic types will probably want to pick some mugwort, an effective panacea. Its fresh juice applied directly to the pained area relieves itching.

Hay Fever

Some 35 million Americans suffer from seasonal allergies, otherwise known as hay fever.

Unfortunately, hikers are not immune to the uncomfortable symptoms—the itchy eyes, runny nose, sneezing fits and utter exhaustion—that accompany a sensitivity to pollen. Hay fever tends to be worse in the spring, but can hit anytime, anyplace, particularly when unfamiliar weeds and grasses are in bloom.

My wife, for example, experienced one of her worst-ever attacks on an idyllic, flower-bedecked trail near Telluride, Colorado. Thankfully, she had an allergy medicine in her day pack and, after taking it, we were able to complete a hike far from home. Another time, we had to visit the local chemist in a tiny shop in the English countryside when she endured what the locals call "pollen nose".

Allergy-prone hikers have a couple of strategies to deal with the discomfort: avoidance and treatment.

Avoidance

- Hike early in the morning when pollen counts are low.
- Learn to identify which pollens trigger your allergies and avoid particular blooming plants.
- Substitute one hike for another. For example, avoid allergy-prompting mountain meadows by hiking near a lakeshore or seashore.

Treatment of Symptoms

- Consider trying one of the new low-side effect allergy treatments.
- Consider taking a natural or an herbal approach.
- Some allergy-prone individuals undergo desensitization treatment with varying degrees of success.

Safety Tips for Hiking in Bear Country

You can encounter a bear even on a short hike in a popular national park. Wildlife biologists remind us that bears are individuals and each can behave in a different manner in different circumstances. Unfortunately, for many hikers, black bears and grizzly bears can be difficult to tell apart. Size and color are not distinguishing characteristics.

Rangers in bear country are enforcing ever more stringent rules in regard to food handling and storage. Food and food-related supplies must not be left in vehicles parked overnight at trailheads because bears are liable to break-in for as little as a candy bar or an empty soda can. Vehicles containing food overnight may be impounded or cited by Yosemite rangers. Storage boxes for departing backpackers are available at many trailheads.

No absolute and precise rules exist to tell you what to do if you encounter a bear, but there are generally effective procedures to follow. The tips below come from national park staffs of North Cascades and Yosemite, two parks with long experience in human-bear encounters.

- Always stay alert to your surroundings. Be especially wary in places where there is food favored by bears; for example, berries or carcasses of large animals. If you smell a dead animal, do not investigate! Leave the area and inform a ranger.
- Avoid startling a bear. Where sight distance is limited or flowing water muffles sounds, make noise by talking, singing, shouting, or clapping your hands. Do not make shrill or high-pitched noises, as these may attract bears. Some hikers use bells for noise, but talking carries better, and bells may arouse a bear's curiosity.
- Be especially alert if hiking around dawn or dusk. Bears can be active at any time of the day or night but are more often encountered at those times.
- It is best to not hike alone. Bears are less likely to approach several people.
- If you are hiking with children, make sure they stay with you at all times.
- If dogs are permitted where you are hiking, keep yours on a leash and under your control. Loose dogs disturb wildlife and may lead a bear back to you.
- Be watchful when traveling off trail. Bears rest and sleep in day beds; for example, next to a log, in dense brush, the depression of a fallen tree, or out in a grassy meadow.

Safety Tips for Hiking in Mountain Lion Country

Mountain lions, usually shy and elusive, are rarely sighted by hikers; still, many recent reports of lion-human encounters have experts concerned that these majestic creatures are losing their fear of humans. The California Department of Fish and Game recommends that you take the following actions in cougar country:

Do not hike alone. Make plenty of noise to reduce your chances of surprising a lion. Go in groups, with adults supervising children. A sturdy walking stick is a good idea: you can use it to ward off a lion.

Keep children close to you. Observations of captured lions reveal that the animals seem especially drawn to children. Keep children within your sight at all times.

Do not run from a lion. Back away from it slowly, but only if you can do so safely. Running may stimulate a lion's instinct to chase and attack. Face the lion and stand upright. Make eye contact. If you have small children with you, pick them up so they won't panic and run. Although it may seem awkward, pick them up without bending over or turning away from the lion.

More Safety Tips for Hiking in Mountain Lion Country

Do not bend or crouch over. In fact, do all you can do to appear larger. A person squatting or bending over looks a lot like a four-legged prey animal. Raise your arms. Open your jacket, if you're wearing one. Throw stones, branches, or whatever you can grab without crouching down or turning your back. Wave your arms slowly and speak firmly in a loud voice.

Do not approach a mountain lion, especially one that is feeding or with kittens. Most mountain lions will try to avoid confrontation. Give them a way to escape.

Fight back if attacked. Try to stay on your feet if a lion attacks you. Lions have been driven off by prey that fights back. Some hikers have fought back successfully with sticks, caps, jackets, garden tools, and their bare hands. Since lions usually try to bite the head or neck, try to remain standing and face the attacking animal.

- Do not approach a bear to take a photograph or for any other reason. If the bear has not seen you, calmly leave the area while talking aloud to make it aware you are there and are moving away. Most bears will leave when they see or hear you.
- If you cannot change your route to avoid a bear, try shaking leafy branches (don't break them off trees or shrubs), snapping small downed limbs with your feet, and talking in a loud but low tone. Bears often communicate their discomfort at being too close to one another by snapping small branches. You may need to do these things repeatedly before they have any effect.
- Do not come between a bear and her cubs. Bears are very protective of their offspring.
- A bear stands up to better identify what you are, not to threaten you.
- If a bear approaches you, do not scream or run or make sudden motions. You cannot outrun a bear, and screaming may increase the danger of the situation.
- Bear repellents (such as pepper spray), even when effective, only work at such close range that depending on them could endanger you. Horns are unproven in their effectiveness. High-pitched noises can arouse curiosity or anger in bears.
- Bears are curious and may want to "check you out." Try to avoid direct eye contact, which a bear may see as a threat. Generally, if you just stand your ground, the bear will soon leave. Wild bears rarely attack unless threatened or provoked. Talking in low, soothing tones may help keep you calm. Do not panic.
- If a bear approaches you very quickly, drop a hat or bandana (but not your pack or anything else associated with food) and move away without running. The bear may stop to examine what you have dropped, distracting it from you.
- Offensive attacks by bears are very rare. It is difficult to generalize accurately about the reasons for attacks or what to do when they occur. Most attacks thought to have been predation involved black bears, while most attacks by grizzly bears have been defensive, especially by females with cubs. Every instance is different, and what works best cannot be known with certainty in advance.
- If a black bear attacks you, fight back with rocks, sticks, equipment, or your bare hands if nothing else is available. Aim for the bear's eyes or nose.
- A grizzly bear with young or protecting a food source may want to make sure you are not a threat. People have weathered grizzly attacks by dropping into a "cannonball position" with neck and face between the knees. If the bear takes you out of this position, try to resume it. Usually, the bear will see that you are not a threat and will leave you alone. Do not take the offensive against a bear with cubs.

PART FIVE
Hiking Near and Far

Chapter 16 America's Long-Distance Trails

AMERICA'S LONG-DISTANCE TRAILS ARE AS BIG, AS BEAUTIFUL and diverse as America itself. Spectacular scenery, well-engineered, well-maintained (mostly), they're the pride of the nation.

I've admired many hundreds of miles of their beauty and even got something more from them. Like good friends, they've always been there for me. As a Boy Scout, a trek on the Pacific Crest Trail helped me earn my hiking merit badge. During my college days, I joined my eastern friends for backpacking trips along the Appalachian Trail and Long Trail.

As my adult responsibilities increased, my long-distance trail time decreased: weeks on the trail became weekends, weekend excursions became day hikes. Next came two children and all of a sudden I was toting a child carrier, not a backpack. But how quickly children grow, and our family samplings of America's best trails are getting more extensive with each passing year.

Still, no matter how my life changes, I'm glad that America's marquee trails will always be there for me, for all of us looking for a nature hike or a grand adventure.

In 1968, the U.S. Congress approved legislation creating the National Scenic Trails System and placed the Appalachian Trail and the Pacific Crest Trail under the stewardship of the U.S. Department of the Interior. Congress also authorized a system of shorter foot-paths with a regional emphasis called National Recreation Trails. To date, America has eight National Scenic Trails and more than 800 National Recreation Trails.

Each year brings the heartwarming story of someone who hikes one of America's national scenic trails in its entirety to raise awareness of a disease, overcome a personal tragedy, celebrate retirement, or just because it's there.

Most hikers, however, are not end-to-enders but day hikers, weekenders or week-long excursionists, These enthusiastic, but

In This Chapter

- All about the National Scenic Trails system
- The eight great National Scenic Trails
- Four more Trailmaster favorites

America's National Scenic Trails

- Appalachian National Scenic Trail (1968)
- Pacific Crest National Scenic Trail (1968)
- Continental Divide National Scenic Trail (1978)
- North Country National Scenic Trail (1980)
- Ice Age National Scenic Trail (1980)
- Natchez Trace National Scenic Trail (1983)
- Florida National Scenic Trail (1983)
- Potomac Heritage National Scenic Trail (1983)

often pressed-for-time hikers seek out samplings of the great trails to enjoy for themselves, friends and families. "Hike your own hike," is the oft-repeated mantra on the Appalachian Trail.

DURING THE 1920s, hikers on both coasts envisioned long distance trails that would extend north-south across the major mountain ranges of the east and west. On the east coast, Benton MacKaye envisioned a trail along the spine of the Appalachian Mountains while Clinton Clarke and Warren Rogers imagined a footpath that traced the crests of the High Sierra and Cascades.

While Rogers trail-blazed the Pacific Crest, the older trail philosopher Clarke offered the "vision thing" in the form of "Trails for America," which later became the basis for the National Trail System Act of 1968.

America's a big country and these trails are big in scope. These trails are standout national examples; just as the crown-jewel national parks such as Olympic, Yellowstone, and Zion so, too, are the national trails. And they're very long, hundreds of miles long, thousands of miles long.

The paths are scenic jewels, crossing great tracts of national forest wilderness, national parks and state parks. They connect the dots on the map between parks, preserves and special places. The scenery by the trail is protected by stricter-than-usual regulations on timber cutting, livestock grazing and development of all kinds. A buffer zone along the trail is mandated to further protect the integrity of the trail.

National Scenic Trails give the hiker a slow-motion look at the wonders of nature and something more: an inner peace, a quiet confidence, a desire to live more with less. What an idea! Take a hike across a whole state, a whole region or the whole darn country.

Chances are, if you've hiked for any length of time, you've sampled—deliberately or inadvertently—one of the national scenic trails. Those in the northeast and southeast have experienced the Appalachian Trail, those in the east and upper Midwest the North Country Trail, and those on the west coast the Pacific Crest Trail.

The two most renowned trails—the Appalachian Trail and the Pacific Crest—are kind of linear national parks and have distinct hiker cultures that evolved with the two trails. Read their newsletters and website community forums.

Appalachian National Scenic Trail

Length:	2,172 miles
Completion:	100 percent
Terrain:	forests, mountains
Highlights:	the best of the eastern U.S.

Even the name sounds 2,000 miles long. The Appalachian Trail stretches through more than a dozen states, from Springer Mountain, Georgia, to Mt. Katahdin, Maine. From its southernmost point, just outside Atlanta, the trail passes through the Great Smoky Mountains in Tennessee, along the Appalachians and the Blue Ridge ranges, and through Shenandoah National Park, Bear Mountain State Park and Green Mountain National Forest.

The trail is situated near the populous cities of Knoxville, Baltimore, Harrisburg, Allentown, New York and Albany. It's easily accessed from Washington, D.C., Boston, and Philadelphia, making it popular with city-bound day hikers. More than 150 million Americans live within a day's drive from some portion of the Appalachian Trail.

In Connecticut, the AT ascends into the rugged Taconic Mountains to the top of Bear Mountain (2,136 feet), the state's highest summit. Eighty-five miles of AT travel the western edge of Massachusetts, touring the Taconic Mountains and the Berkshires. The AT winds 157 miles through the heart of the White Mountains, offering some of the most dramatic views in all of New England. A glorious and rugged final stretch of the AT extends 274 miles across Maine to trail's end on mighty Mt. Katahdin.

Many of the New England segments of the Appalachian Trail offer great day hikes. Feeder trails leading from well-signed trailheads connect to the AT and offer hikers the opportunity to tailor outings to time and abilities.

The terrain ranges from bare mountains to heavily forested valleys; foliage from delicate wildflowers to stands of spruce and fir, poplars, and hemlocks. Hikers step back in time along this "footpath through the wilderness" across a land called Chattachoochee, Nantahala, Manassas and by many other Indian names.

Because it extends along the ridgeline of a number of mountain ranges, the hiking can be slow-going on the steepest ascents and descents. Nevertheless, the AT is well traveled. Few hike it from end to end, but many dream of the challenge.

More than 200 shelters, ranging from simple lean-tos to beautifully built wooden structures welcome hikers. These accommodations are available on a first-come, first-served basis. Hostels are located in some of the towns along the trail.

Hiking the Appalachian Trail—and writing about it—has spawned a small industry all its own. There are a few dozen reminiscences of hikers who have hiked solo or on their honeymoon, to

> "... the Appalachian Trail, a ridiculous footpath 2,000 miles long, running the length of the Appalachian Mountains, up and down a thousand peaks, in and out of a thousand valleys, across a thousand meadows, through a thousand forest glades ... the idea—the idea!—of some year actually getting into harness and walking the entire Trail has always haunted me at the back of my mind. It's one of those outdoor dream adventures we all dream and very few have the nerve to realize."
>
> —EDWARD ABBEY

detailed trail guides. Bill Bryson's *A Walk in the Woods*, a hilarious account of the author's travels on the AT was a bestseller.

At the dawn of the twentieth century, New England hikers were already dreaming of a long distance trail over the Appalachian crest. Massachusetts hiker Benton MacKaye, a planner by trade, formalized the idea of an Appalachian Trail as the centerpiece of a vast greenbelt, a sanctuary from hectic Eastern urban life, such as it was in 1921.

Hiking clubs and volunteer groups were quick to embrace MacKaye's plan, and pro-trail forces soon coalesced with the founding of the Appalachian Trail Conference in 1925. The politically savvy group secured the cooperation of the Forest Service and National Park Service from the beginning. Thanks to tremendous efforts at route finding and trail-building during the 1920s and 1930s, and a mighty assist from Depression-era Civilian Conservation Corps crews, a continuous trail opened in the summer of 1937.

Alas, assorted natural disasters, a road-building fervor and the considerable distraction of World War II and its aftermath put a damper on hiking the AT and it was not until the 1950s that hikers made widespread use of a now signed and realigned route.

The Appalachian Trail follows the ridge crests and traverses the major valleys of the Appalachian Mountains from Springer Mountain in north Georgia to Mount Katahdin in Maine. The trail winds its way through Georgia, North Carolina, Tennessee, Virginia, West Virginia, Maryland, Pennsylvania, New Jersey, New York, Connecticut, Massachusetts, Vermont, New Hampshire and Maine.

Pacific Crest National Scenic Trail

Length:	2,655 miles
Completion:	100 percent
Terrain:	the High Sierra, the Cascades and much more
Highlights:	many claim it's the finest stretch of scenery in the U.S.

The western counterpart to the Appalachian Trail extends over 2,600 miles from the Mexican border near San Diego, California to the Canadian border in Washington state. Although it extends the length of only three states, it passes through extremes of temperature and terrain. Like its eastern cousin, the path skirts a number of population centers, including San Diego, Los Angeles, Sacramento, San Francisco, Portland and Seattle.

The Pacific Crest Trail was the brainchild of Clinton Clarke, a Pasadena hiking enthusiast and then chairman of the Mountain League of Los Angeles County. Clarke coordinated representatives of youth groups and hiking/mountaineering organizations with the Pacific Crest Trail System Conference and served as its President for many years.

From its southern end in the California desert, the Pacific Crest

"To maintain and defend for the benefit and enjoyment of nature lovers the Pacific Crest Trailway as a primitive wilderness pathway in an environment of solitude, free from the sights and sounds of a mechanically disturbed nature."

—CLINTON CLARKE

Trail crosses the Mojave desert, travels the surprisingly high and wild San Gabriel Mountains and San Bernardino Mountains of Southern California, then winds north to the High Sierra, through Kings Canyon, Sequoia and Yosemite national parks, past Lake Tahoe, Lassen Volcanic National Park and Mount Shasta.

Passing into Oregon, the trail enters Crater Lake National Park and Mount Hood, and dips into the spectacular Columbia River Gorge. Rising out of the Gorge into Washington, PCT passes through Mount Rainier and North Cascades national parks, and finally to the Canadian border.

The diversity of the terrain, the landforms, and the biotic zones the trail passes through make traveling on it a lesson in geography, botany and biology. Ranging from the searing heat and expansive sandscape of the California desert to the heavily wooded forest of Cascade National Park, the trail offers an environment for every preference.

The Pacific Crest Trail Association is the non-profit organization that works to protect, preserve and maintain the PCT. Although the PCT was officially completed in 1993, there are still many miles remaining on private land. The PCTA is working to permanently protect all 2,655 miles of the PCT.

Continental Divide National Scenic Trail

Length:	3,100 miles
Completion:	more than 70 percent
Terrain:	high desert, crest of the Rockies
Highlights:	the Rocky Mountains west in all its glory

Along with the Pacific Crest Trail and Appalachian Trail, the Continental Divide Trail is the third member of the hiker's "Triple Crown." Considered the most rugged of America's National Scenic Trails, the 3,100-mile footpath traverses the crest of the Rocky Mountains from Mexico to Canada.

The path travels through five Western States—New Mexico, Colorado, Wyoming, Idaho and Montana—and through five ecological zones from the high desert to alpine peaks. CDT tours some two dozen national forests, twenty wilderness areas, three national parks and eight, sprawling Bureau of Land Management wildlands.

From its southern trailhead at the U.S.-Mexican border near Antelope Wells, New Mexico, CDT crosses the desert and heads north through the Gila National Forest and Aldo Leopold Wilderness. Part of the route overlaps a trail of the ancients—a thousand years old, Zuní-Acoma trade route. After traveling through a trio of national forests—Cibolá, Carson and Santa Fe—CDT enters Colorado and ascends to rugged mountain wilderness. The trail zigzags across the Continental Divide and proceeds in tandem with the Colorado Trail for more than 100 miles. CDT continues its high country adventure through Colorado by way of eight more national forests and that gem

Hike-ku
Brush up against sage
Scent of Old West releases
Into the warm breeze

of the Rockies—Rocky Mountains National Park.

Wyoming highlights include the Bridger-Teton National Forest, some mighty remote wilderness areas and famed Yellowstone National Park. After exploring a bit of Idaho in the Targhee National Forest, the path enters Montana and visits a half-dozen national forests and wilderness areas, including the remote and beautiful Bob Marshall Wilderness. After a grand finale in Glacier National Park, CDT reaches its northern terminus at the U.S.-Canada border.

The Continental Divide Trail alliance aims to complete the national scenic trail by 2008, the path's thirtieth anniversary. (Many of the miles of yet-to-be-completed CDT are on BLM lands in New Mexico and Wyoming.) Part of the alliance's ambitious goal is a commitment to make the Continental Divide Trail a "silent trail"—that is to say, a path fully removed from roads and motorized trails.

North Country National Scenic Trail

Length:	4,000 miles
Completion:	45 percent
Terrain:	woods, wilderness and rural communities
Highlights:	when completed, the longest hiking trail in the U.S.

From New York's Adirondack Mountains to North Dakota's tall grass prairies, North Country Trail offers a grand seven-state tour across the northern U.S. From its eastern trailhead at Crown Point State Historic Park on the Vermont-New York border, the path extends westward through Pennsylvania's hardwood forests and the quiet Ohio countryside, traces the shores of the Great Lakes, explores the lakes and forests of northern Michigan, Wisconsin, and Minnesota, and finally the plains of North Dakota.

Hikers like the diversity of landscapes en route—the great north woods, bogs, lakes, sand dunes and tall-grass prairies. NCT also offers an array of historical and cultural experiences including Revolutionary War forts, nineteenth-century rail lines and canals.

In New York, North Country Trail proceeds in tandem with Finger Lakes Trail across the state into Pennsylvania. The Finger Lakes Trail crosses fields and forests, gorges and mountains and, of course, visits plenty of streams and lakes.

In Ohio, much of the NCT hitchhikes along with the pride-of-the-state Buckeye Trail. One of the longest continuous trails in a single state, it passes through major urban centers as well as isolated rural areas. The northern half of the state features mostly flat terrain and rolling hills, while the south offers thick forests and mountainous land. One 50-mile segment follows the Miami & Erie Canal.

Michigan boasts nearly 600 miles of completed NCT, more than any other state. Upper Peninsula highlights include Porcupine Mountains Wilderness State Park and Hiawatha National Forest.

Many North Country Trail hikers consider the 43-mile segment through Pictured Rocks National Lakeshore to be the most scenic part of the National Scenic Trail. NCT crosses the beaches and towering sandstone bluffs on the shore of Lake Superior, offering grand vistas across—and into—its deep waters.

Wisconsin and Minnesota offer modest segments of completed trail, as well as the opportunity to fish in a generous number of lakes and streams. Two lengths of the trail across North Dakota are particularly memorable. Hikers observe great flocks of ducks, geese and sandhill cranes as they cross the Sheyenne National Grassland and the Lone Tree Wildlife Management Area. The path traverses the lonely prairie, home to the sharptail grouse and the prairie chicken, and to not very many humans, to its western terminus at Lake Sacajawea State Park in west-central North Dakota, where it joins the route of the Lewis and Clark National Historic Trail.

The North Country Trail Association, in partnership with the National Park Service, is dedicated to championing, developing and maintaining the North Country National Scenic Trail. NCT national headquarters, is located in Lowell, Michigan, which just happens to be near the exact geographic center of the trail; the organization's office is but a block's walk to the trail, where it meanders along with the Flat River.

Ice Age National Scenic Trail

Length:	1,000 miles
Completion:	more than 50 percent
Terrain:	Wisconsin's glacial landscape of moraines, prairies, bogs, lakes, and the great north woods
Highlights:	the planet's most notable and scenic collection of glacial evidence

"The Land Time Forgot" will be long remembered by walkers who roam Wisconsin's glacial landscape on the Ice Age Trail.

From sand prairies festooned with wildflowers in southern Wisconsin to the old hemlock and fragrant balsam in the north woods, and from the rushing waters of the St. Croix River to the shores of Lake Michigan, the Ice Age Trail links the continents best and most scenic examples of glaciation in a series of parks, preserves and forests.

Ice Age Trail is intended to be a recognition—indeed, a celebration—of America's glacial heritage. Hiking the trail gives you a close-up look at the ice-carved landscapes left behind when the glaciers retreated. The trail follows the edge of the terminal line of the last glaciation, which occurred some 10,000 years ago. If Wisconsin has more than a passing resemblance to Scandinavia, it's because "America's Dairyland" and Northern Europe were glaciated at the same time.

The thick sheets of ice that once completely covered what is now Wisconsin carved the state's most distinctive features. The rolling hills and vast plains were cut by advancing glaciers; the lakes, bogs and marshes formed as they melted.

To walk the trail is to be immersed in a kind of Ice-Speak, a language of eskers and moraines, drumlin fields and kettle lakes, erratics and striations. The geological story behind the scenery is almost as fascinating as the scenery itself.

From the path you can spot loons picking their way among boulders dragged from Canada by colossal sheets of ice. Hike the beds of ancient glacial lakes and rivers and listen for the lonely call of the wolf.

Balsam-fir forests and oak woodlands, open prairie and clear glacial lakes are other Northern European-like features of the trail, which can be accessed easily by walkers heading out from Green Bay, Madison, and Milwaukee.

Communities along the trail add a foreign accent to the landscape. Mischicot and New Clarus are two villages founded by Swiss immigrants, Erin by the Irish, Scandinavia by you guessed it. Poles, Finns and Norwegians predominate in other towns near the trail.

From its eastern end at Potowatomi State Park on Green Bay, the trail follows the present and former shorelines of Lake Michigan, the crests of eskers, and the edges of bogs. It passes through state forest lands and the famed Kettle Moraine.

The longest lengths of trail are in the forested Wisconsin counties to the north and west. Amid spruce, fir, maple and birch of the northern forest, the trail enters a region full of lakes and bogs formed by the melting of glaciers. It's wet walking through a rough and swampy land; the trail crosses many beaver dams. In the lake-sprinkled Harrison Hills is the highpoint of the trail, 1,875-foot Lookout Mountain. While walking through Chequamon National Forests, walkers get a hint of what was once a vast white pine and hemlock forest—timber that built the cities of the Midwest.

Much of the trail is way-marked by signs with the Ice Age Trail logo—a map of Wisconsin depicting sheets of ice and two sets of hikers' footprints. Paint blazes (usually yellow) and wooden directional signs also help out. Surely America's cutest trail symbol is the mastodon used by the Ice Age Park and Trail Foundation.

Florida National Scenic Trail

Length:	1,300 miles
Completion:	85 percent
Terrain:	swamps, prairies, palmetto groves, hardwood forests
Highlights:	the wild side of the Sunshine State, a sojourn through the subtropics; America's flattest footpath; great wintertime adventure

Few hikers think of Florida when they contemplate their next journey afoot. But the Sunshine State has a little-known 1,300-mile long trail that extends from the Everglades to Big Cypress National Preserve, and north to the Panhandle.

This trail is the Florida Trail, which visits practically every remaining natural area in the state from way down upon the Suwannee River to the banks of Lake Okeechobee.

The flat terrain, semi-tropical climate and miles of beach walking along the Gulf of Mexico combine to make the Florida Trail an enticing winter adventure. America's only wintertime-walkable long distance trail leads to places whose very names sound intriguing: Withlacoochee State Forest and Apalachiola National Forest, Green Swamp and Orange Hammock, Memery Island and Fodderstack Slough.

Unlike the nation's other long distance trails, such as the Appalachian Trail and Pacific Crest Trail, which are best hiked during the warmer months, the best and most popular time to trek the Florida Trail is wintertime. During winter, temperatures are mild, insect populations lower and less bloodthirsty and the footpath is fairly dry. From April to October, rains are frequent and it's mighty hot, humid and buggy.

Fans of the Florida Trail object to the common view of hikers from other states who think of Florida as nothing but swamp. Boosters admit that in Big Cypress Preserve there are 30 miles of trail; hikers will probably get their feet wet, but it's one of the few places on the Florida Trail where that happens. Still, bring your best water-proof footwear and quality raingear to Florida, and try to arrange your hiking trip during the drier, cooler months.

While the Florida Trail is probably the flattest footpath on earth ("high" point en route is a mere 90 feet above sea level), even the tiniest change in elevation brings a change in vegetation. Various plant communities have differing water requirements and tolerances; pine forests, for example, thrive in higher, well-drained areas while cypress and mangrove groves are water-lovers.

Volunteers from the nonprofit Florida Trail Association maintain the path and are working to complete it. More than 1,100 miles of the 1,300-mile trail is way-marked and walkable. National Scenic Trail status has helped publicize the trail and helped the FTA promote Florida as "The Winter Hiking Capital of the United States."

The FTA publishes a guidebook that gives an overview of the trail and suggested day hikes. The guide is an indispensable trip planner. Flat and relatively unforgiving the Florida Trail may be, but it's no walk in the park. Advice from the guide includes: "If you swim in unknown waters, you run the risk of an alligator encounter." And "Don't handle crippled, sluggish or 'dead' snakes."

My favorite part of the Florida Trail is through the primeval swampland of Big Cypress National Preserve, located on the north edge of Everglades National Park. Thirty-one miles of Florida Trail led me through a wet world of giant ferns, cabbage palms and sus-pended bromeliads (air plants). By the way, Big Cypress is named for its great expanse (900 square miles of subtropical terrain) not for the size of its predominant tree—the dwarf pond cypress.

Another Florida Trail best bet is a 75-mile stretch along the Suwannee River, where the trail winds through savannahs and pine forests. Orchids bloom in the spring and there's great riverside camping.

Natchez Trace National Scenic Trail

Length:	440 miles
Completion:	15 percent, 63 miles or so of footpath
Terrain:	piney woods, hardwood forests, rolling hills
Highlights:	the lush rural South, hikes into history

Natchez Trace, the trail, (occasionally) shadows Natchez Trace Parkway, which extends some 450 miles from Natchez, Misssisippi to Nashville, Tennessee. History buffs will likely enjoy the trail far more than purist hikers.

First a Native American footpath, the Trace was later used by let-ter-carriers, boatmen returning from down-the-Mississippi River and the military. In the pre-motorized boat era, farmers constructed flat-boats and floated their produce down the Mississippi River to mar-ket. They hiked home on the trail.

Road-walking the parkway isn't quite as awful as it sounds; it resembles a quiet Southern country road, not the New Jersey Turn-pike. Still, the hiking opportunities aren't going to compel anyone to drive far from home to hit the trail along the trace.

At the far south end of the trail, a hiker can observe a portion of the path where tens of thousands of early trampers of the trace wore a 12-foot deep groove in the trail.

It's unlikely Natchez Trace Trail will ever become a renowned long-distance footpath mentioned in the same breath as the other hiker-oriented National Scenic Trails. Think of the Natchez Trace as a splendid parkway, An All American Road, a fine auto tour with a few leg-stretcher day hikes along the way.

Potomac Heritage National Scenic Trail

Length:	700 miles
Completion:	about 40 percent
Highlights:	canal towpath, Mt. Vernon Trail, many historic towns and sites

The Potomac, the famed river that flows by America's capital, is considered a "corridor"—that is to say, a general route rather than a signed hiking trail that links the many natural and historical sites along the river from the Allegheny Highlands to Chesapeake Bay.

The corridor crosses Pennsylvania, the District of Columbia, Virginia and Maryland.

For a long while after its 1983 promotion to National Scenic Trail status, Potomac Heritage Trail languished—more a paper trail than a proper pathway—but in recent years a consortium of trail savvy citizens groups and regional governmental agencies began helping the PHT to realize its considerable potential. Imagine a nature walk amongst beech, poplar and sycamore, right across the river from the Capitol, tranquil relief from the stresses of modern life. PHT can become a gem of a greenway/blueway.

Hikers can enjoy four lengthy walks along the Potomac Heritage Trail. The longest PHT excursion is the 184.5-mile walk through Chesapeake and Ohio Canal National Historical Park along the old towpath between Georgetown (in the District of Columbia) and Cumberland, Maryland.

The trail's other highlights include the 17-mile Mt. Vernon Trail in Virginia and two Pennsylvania paths—the 70-mile Laurel Highlands Trail and the 150-mile Great Allegheny Passage.

> "I hiked with enthusiasm and vigor, buoyed by fresh air and splendor."
>
> —BILL BRYSON
> A Walk in the Woods

Cult of the Thru-Hiker

The gutty few who hike a long distance trail in its entirety at one time are known as thru-hikers or end-to-enders. These individuals comprise a unique hiker culture, one that has done much to celebrate the wisdom of creating America's great trail system.

Obviously, every hiker who's trekked 2,172 miles from Georgia to Maine on the Appalachian Trail or hoofed it 2,650 miles from Mexico to Canada on the Pacific Crest Trail can be proud of what is undoubtedly an athletic accomplishment. And yet such a journey is much more, often a profound emotional, even spiritual, experience.

The thru-hiker must conquer seemingly infinite ups and downs, battle the elements, and struggle with whatever inner conflicts he or she brings to the trail. Every end-to-ender comes back from the trail a changed person.

Few of us in this modern age and economy can afford to essentially put one's life on hold and take six months off. (I'd argue that our employers should grant *all* of us a six-month mental health leave at some point during our working life.) The thru-hiker must be able to leave job and family commitments for half a year and be willing to spend an additional six months prior to hitting the trail in planning and training for the big hike. Would-be thru-hikers use trip calculators to determine the cost and timing of their hikes.

The typical thru-hiker might spend five to six thousand dollars for trail food and equipment worn or carried. To this sum must be added restaurant meals, grocery store indulgences, fast-food binges, motels and replacement boots, clothing and gear. Some hikers are quite frugal, and consider it a matter of pride to travel as cheaply as possible, while others figure it's a once-in-a-lifetime experience and indulge themselves

> *"How can a book describe the psychological factors a person must prepare for . . . the despair, the alienation, the anxiety and especially the pain, both physical and mental, which slices to the very heart of the hiker's volition, which are the real things that must be planned for? No words can transmit those factors, which are more a part of planning than the elementary rituals of food, money, and equipment, and how to get them."*
>
> —CHUCK LONG,
> *Pacific Crest Trail Hike Planning Guide*

(a quart of chocolate ice cream, a double cheeseburger, a cold beer) a bit in the outposts of civilization, such as they are, along the way.

Backpack weight is another matter of endless debate among thru-hikers. All hikers want to carry as little weight as possible and look at each item toted on an ounce-by-ounce basis. Some of the more weight-obsessive long distance hikers have actually reduced the weight of their loads to ten pounds (exclusive of food and water).

Although today's thru-hikers need as much pluck and stamina as the previous generation of long-distance trekkers, the lighter weight and improved performance of backpacking gear greatly assists the hikers of today. Footwear in particular has greatly evolved: while you might suppose a serious trekker would opt for heavy leather boots, these days growing numbers of hikers wear lightweight hiking boots or running shoes. Staying in touch with home and family is lots easier these days, too, what with cell phones and pocket e-mail devices.

Success rates for completion of a long distance trail have risen rapidly over the years and are higher than you might guess. On the Pacific Crest Trail, for example, some 300 hikers a year begin with end-to-end ambitions and more than 50 percent make it all the way through. This success rate is much better than the estimated 10 percent completion rate of thru-hikers of the 1970s.

Such is the personal transformation of a thru-hiker that many select "trail names" that are different from their real names. Maybe Wily Coyote, Sagebrush Philosopher and Chicago Kate get to be who they really are on a long, long hike—yet another reason to celebrate the joy of the trail and the call of the wild.

Four More Favorite Long-Distance Trails

(Not nationally recognized by federal designation, but gems nonetheless.)

Vermont's Long Trail

Length:	270 miles through Vermont, from Massachusetts border to Canadian border; many fine days hikes as well
Terrain:	ridgeline of Green Mountains, hardwood and conifer forests
Highlights:	nation's oldest long-distance trail through exceptional setting; ideal hut-to-hut hiking

Vermont's Green Mountains are the impressive setting for the famous Long Trail. The 270-mile path visits the highest mountains and wildest scenery in the state as it traverses the ridgeline of the Green Mountains.

The Long Trail, conceived in 1910 as a "footpath in the wilderness," is the nation's oldest long-distance footpath, and remains one of America's best. The trail was built with the support of the Green

Mountain Club, the organization that maintains the trail today.

GMC also maintains 175 miles of side trail and five-dozen rustic cabins. The club publishes an indispensable guide to the Long Trail, as well as maps and other useful publications. GMC's conservation activities include efforts to preserve threatened lands and trails in Northern Vermont.

Long Trail highlights are many, particularly in Green Mountain National Forest in southern and central Vermont, which encompasses the state's most beautifully wooded areas. Bread Loaf Wilderness, Lye Brook Wilderness and four smaller wilderness areas protect spruce, fir and hardwood forests, steep peaks and plateaus, lakes, brooks and waterfalls. About half the Long Trail is included within the boundaries of the national forest.

Another highlight—and the state's high point—is mighty Mt. Mansfield, whose rocky summit offers Vermont's finest views. On Mansfield's broad shoulder is a botanically rare area of arctic-alpine tundra that attracts researchers from around the world.

One more gem is Camel's Hump, the rare Vermont promontory untouched by a ski lift or any other development. Up top is an austere landscape of green lichen, gray rock, and alpine plants that have survived since the last Ice Age.

Although a few stretches of Long Trail are walk-in-the-park easy, most lengths are moderate to strenuous. Adding to its difficulty for hikers is the trail's very design; hikers will find few of the gentle contours or switchbacks typical of newer trails. In this respect, the Long Trail is as stubborn and straight-forward as Vermonters themselves. Even the Green Mountain Club huts are more spartan than those along the Appalachian Trail and other long-distance trails. Hikers must pack in just about everything—food, fuel and sleeping gear.

In southern Vermont, the first hundred miles of the Long Trail coincide with the Appalachian Trail. Proud Vermont walkers sometimes joke that the upstart AT, constructed a few years after the Long Trail, is but a side trail to the Long Trail.

Favorite all-day or weekend walks along the Long Trail include the path between Lincoln Gap and the Appalachian Gap; it's one of the most scenic ridge walks in Vermont, with views of New York's Adirondack Mountains and New Hampshire's White Mountains. The 11-mile hike leads over six mountain summits, three of which are over 4,000 feet. The Long Trail from Lincoln Gap to the Winooksi River is called Monroe Skyline, after Professor Will S. Monroe who located the trail along this ridgeline.

The Long Trail between Little Rock Pond and Clarendon Gorge crosses a valley,, mountains and a dramatic gorge on a suspension bridge. A number of trail shelters en route on the 14.5-mile route suggest an overnight stay.

A must-visit via the Long Trail is Mount Mansfield, elevation 4,393 feet, highest Vermont peak and a National Natural Landmark.

> "... It's time to turn on the old trail, our own trail, the out trail, pull out, pull out, on the Long Trail—the trail that is always new!"
>
> —RUDYARD KIPLING, *The Long Trail*

The summit ridge supports a rare and beautiful arctic-alpine plant community, flora remnants of an era when ice sheets covered northern New England. Nine trails climb the mountain, but the choice of many is the 9.5-mile ascent up the Long Trail and descent via Haselton Trail.

Oregon Coast Trail

Length:	360 miles
Terrain:	sandy beaches, bold headlands, dunes
Highlights:	deserted beaches, spectacular sea views, intriguing towns and historical sites

The names alone are almost irrestistable: North Spit and South Beach, Yachats and Yaquina Head, Devils Punchbowl, Dragons Teeth, House Rock and Hug Point.

This coast with the unusual names is California's neighbor-to-the-north—Oregon, where 400 miles of sandy beaches and bold headlands await the adventurous hiker. From the Columbia River at Astoria to Brookings near the California border, Oregon's oceanside attractions are visited by the Oregon Coast Trail, a network of blufftop footpaths and beach trails.

True, a drive along U.S. 101, the Oregon Coast Highway, puts most of the beach within reach, but to truly savor the shore, take a hike. The trail can be joined from many roadside turnouts and from some fifty Oregon state parks, as well as from the famed Oregon Dunes National Recreation Area, administered by the U.S. Forest Service.

The trail is signed in many places with mileage numbers and with the distinctive Oregon Coast Trail logo, which bears a distinct resemblance to a 1960s peace symbol. Signage is good at state park trailheads and along woodsy headland trails.

"The trail is a chance to experience the Oregon coast in all its diversity," explains Pete Bond, Ocean Shore & Recreational Trails Coordinator for the state parks system. "On the wild side, the hiker can walk grass-balled headlands, around bays and estuaries, through old-growth fir forests, and along empty beaches. The trail also gives walkers the chance to explore some wonderful small towns, sample the local cuisine and hospitality."

The most exciting, and longest-uninterrupted stretch of trail, explains Bond, is the well-signed, 60-mile coast path between the Columbia River at the Washington border south to Tillamook Bay. Many a B&B has sprung up along this length of coast, which appeals to those hikers looking for a good meal, a hot shower and a comfortable bed at the end of a long day of coastal hiking. The trail plus the nearby amenities adds up to a terrific Euro-style inn-to-inn adventure, Bond suggests.

For the more casual day tripper, some of the best places to

explore via Oregon Coast Trail are, from south to north:

- **Samuel H. Boardman Park,** with some 15 miles of trail, is a great sampling of the southern Oregon coast. Highlights include Indian Sands, a series of sand dunes and rows of jagged rock "teeth," including famed Dragons Teeth.
- **Sunset Bay Park,** on the outskirts of Coos Bay has a terrific four-mile trail that alternates between fog-wrapped forest and open headland. Watch for the many boisterous sea lions in residence on the offshore rocks.
- **Oregon Dunes National Recreation Area,** a 40-mile stretch of sand dunes between North Bend and Florence is a must-see and must-hike. Oregon Dunes Overlook, in the middle of the dunes, provides access to picnic sites, observation platforms and hiking trails.
- **Oswald West Park** is the trailhead for the couple mile trek to the top of 2,500-foot Neahkahnie Mountain. Panoramic views from the peak include both the coast and forested mountains.
- **Ecola Park** has an excellent two-mile trail that explores "the Big Sur of Oregon." The rugged Tillamook Head offers grand vistas toward Astoria and the mouth of the Columbia River.

Wonderland Trail

Length:	93-mile loop around Mt. Rainier
Terrain:	forests, majestic meadows, glaciers
Highlights:	waterfalls, great day hiking or backpacking experience

In the pantheon of long-distance pathways, Wonderland Trail occupies an exalted place. Many experienced backpackers call it the Pacific Northwest's greatest hike.

It's an old trail as national park trails go, constructed at the turn of the century just after Mt. Rainier National Park was established. Long before the park was ringed by paved highways, rangers used the Wonderland Trail to patrol Rainier on horseback. During the 1930s, Civilian Conservation Corps' efforts made the trail into the nationally recognized recreation trail it is today.

Long ago, "Wonderland" was a park promoter's phrase; in this instance, the name did not overstate the region's allure. Wonderland Trail tours a grand assemblage of alpine meadows, thick forests, awesome glaciers, dramatic creeks and rivers. With every turn there is a different view up at the many faces of Mt. Rainier.

The prudent hiker will allow ten to fourteen days for a full circumnavigation of the mountain, but encounters with bad weather can considerably slow progress. In decent conditions, an average of seven to ten miles a day is about it, veteran hikers advise, as the trail has lots of ups and downs. Several hiking days climb 3,500 feet or so; the whole route requires gains in excess of 20,000 feet.

Some hikers figure hiking the Wonderland is a terrific summer vacation and complete the whole mountain-encircling route at one time. Others tramp the trail in sections, savoring the Wonderland a few days at a time.

Logistics are a bit complicated. The eighteen Wonderland Trail camps are situated three to seven miles apart, and reservations are required. National Park Service policy has been to limit the number and capacity of campsites. Critics say this unduly limits backpacking, while other praise the policy and suggest it provides a superior wilderness experience for both day hikers and backpackers.

Required backcountry permits are issued at the Hiker Information Centers in Longmire and White River. As part of the permit process, you must commit to a particular trailside camp; exercise a little flexibility here because your first choice might be full.

Other camping options for experienced hikers are "cross country zones," where backpackers find their own places to camp. Such camps are required to be located at least a quarter-mile from roads and trails, and a minimum of 100 feet from any water source.

You certainly won't want to carry two weeks or even ten day's worth of food on your Wonderland walk. Take advantage of the National Park Service's Food Cache Program and store a food cache or two or three. The park has detailed instruction for the right waterproof and rodent-proof containers, how to ship them (UPS) and the five stations—Paradise, Sunrise, White River, Ohanapecosh and Longmire where you may stash your cache. By all means try to convince friends or family to meet you with a fresh food supply; you'll enjoy the company and they'll enjoy a day on the Wonderland.

The Wonderland can be day hiked from a dozen or so trailheads around the mountain.

The 30-mile route from Paradise to Sunrise is noted for its watery scenery: lakes, waterfalls and a dramatic river canyon. On the 16-mile jaunt from Sunrise to Carbon River, hikers get up-close views of Winthrop and Carbon glaciers. The 39-mile section from Carbon River to Longmire passes beautiful lakes, including Mowich Lake and Golden Lakes, as well as such wildflower-strewn meadows as Sunset Park, Klapatche Park and Indian Henry's Hunting Grounds. A last 6.5 miles (a good one-way day hike) travels from Longmire to Paradise via Carter, Madcap and Narada falls.

Mid-July through September is the best period for hiking, as the snow has melted to reveal the trail. However, even during these months, rain, fog and poor visibility are often problems, and map and compass navigation may be required. Even during the ten-week "safe travel" window, no one will laugh at you if you carry an ice ax.

Ozark Highlands Trail, the Pride of Arkansas

Length: 187 miles
Terrain: wooded valleys, lakes
Highlights: waterfalls, spring and fall colors, the
                 pride of Arkansas

Arkansas is one of America's most outdoorsy states, and it works hard to promote itself as a destination for canoeing, camping, fishing and hiking. "The Natural State," as it calls itself, has varied topography: hardwood forests, cypress-draped bayous, prairies, misty lakes, a thousand and one named and unnamed creeks.

But for all of Arkansas' splendid diversity, it's the Ozarks that may be the most fascinating destination to travelers. Visitors can listen to Ozark music and observe the fashioning of rag rugs, oak rockers or other Ozark crafts.

For the hiker, a great way to explore the Ozarks is on the Ozark Highlands Trail, often rated one of the top ten trails in America by hiking experts. White Rock Mountain, Little Mulberry Creek, Haw Creek Falls, Ozone Camp, Salt Fork and Potato Knob are some of the intriguing places on the route. Most of the trail meanders through the one-million-acre Ozark National Forest, created by President Theodore Roosevelt in 1908.

"The Ozarks are largely undiscovered by tourists, and the Ozark Highland Trail is virtually unknown to hikers," says Tim Ernst, president of the Ozark Highland Trail Association and author of a guidebook to the trail.

The trail has been a longtime labor of love for the Fayetteville-based nature photographer. During the 1970s, while employed by the National Forest Service, Ernst championed the cause of a trans-Ozarks trail. The Forest Service began cutting the trail, but when it faltered in 1981, Ernst founded the Ozark Highland Trail Association to oversee the trail's completion. He has organized trail-building crews, lobbied in Washington, D.C., and rallied conservationists in his native state.

The Ozarks Highlands Trail is very well-marked. Thanks to Ernst and his trail association, there is a milepost for every mile of trail. Innumerable two-by-six-inch paint blazes mark the way: white for the main trail, blue for all side and spur trails.

Not every step of the way is pretty, Ernst points out. Ozark National Forest is very much a working forest—that is to say, hikers may hear the sounds of bulldozers cutting roads and chain saws cutting trees. And one more sound, too: gunfire. Ernst cautions hikers, particularly those from out of state, that Arkansas has a huge population of hunters—and one animal or another, it seems, is "in season" from September to June.

For most of America's long-distance trails—the Appalachian, Continental Divide, Pacific Crest, etc.—summer is the season to sojourn. Not so, however, on the Ozark Highlands Trail, when summer brings intense heat and humidity, dangerous lightning storms and more ticks, chiggers and bloodthirsty bugs than you can shake a walking stick at.

Winter months are good hiking months. The woods are in a state of what Arkansans call "leaf out"; that is to say, they are barren of foliage, allowing good views. Daytime temperatures are in the 30s to 50s—good hiking weather if you're warmly attired. Nights are long and cold, with temperatures in the teens or lower.

Springtime, when the azaleas and dogwood bloom, is another terrific time to be on the trail, and October is a grand month to gambol through the Ozarks. Daytime temperatures are in the 70s, with nighttime lows in the 40s and 50s. The fall color display (one of the state's best-kept secrets) rivals that of Colorado and New England.

A great place to begin exploring the Ozarks is at the beginning of the Ozark Highlands Trail in Lake Fort Smith State Park. Tucked away in an Ozark Mountain valley, this park offers a splendid sampling of the Ozarks and a taste of the trail that might just whet your appetite for hiking the entire 187 miles to its end at the Buffalo River, near the Missouri border.

Chapter 17 Hiking Europe

B Y A COMBINATION OF LUCK AND DESIGN, BUSINESS AND PLEASURE, I've been fortunate to be able to hike in a number of European countries. Most Americans will discover, as I did, that Europe in general and Britain in particular, offers a superb first out-of-the-country hiking experience.

(By singing the praises of Euro-hiking, I do not mean to suggest that there aren't many compelling hikes awaiting the traveler in the three A's—Asia, Africa and Australia—as well as South America and around the Pacific Rim. New Zealand's Milford Track and Patagonia are two hiking destinations on my personal wish list.)

Certain aspects of hiking in Europe will be familiar to Americans. For one thing, most European countries have a long tradition of hiking. It's a popular form of outdoor recreation, not something they have to do because they can't afford a car.

Hiking Europe is very different from hiking America; that is to say more civilized, but not necessarily less wild. A day on the trail may mean a trek through a dark forest, a ramble across a wildflower-strewn meadow, a glimpse of a fleet footed ibex; in short, a day in the wild by any mountaineer's measure.

Ah, but the nights; that's where the civilization comes in. In Europe, an extensive network of refuges (*hutten, chalets, rifugi,* etc.) offer shelter ranging from a bed in a dormitory to a plush room in a country hotel listed with stars next to its name in the guidebooks. Meals are readily available—varying from a bowl of soup to a full course dinner complete with a bottle of fine local wine.

Crisscrossing the mountains and forests of Europe are a thousand tempting trails. They are well-traveled by Europeans, for whom walking has always been a part of life.

Some of these footpaths are well-mapped and documented, others are not. Some are known only to nearby residents or a handful of mountaineers, others are renowned worldwide.

Increasingly, Euro-hiking is becoming part of the American way of life, too. England is the favorite destination for American hikers who hit the trail abroad, followed by France. Each year, the Matterhorn and Mt. Olympus, the Dolomites and Dordogne attract more and more Americans. American tour companies lead hikes in most European countries.

Yet for all this "civilization" the pathways of Europe remain wild, powerful, alluring.

MOST OF EUROPE'S BEST HIKES take vacation time—a few days or a week or more—but they are adaptable to both a hurried or unhurried schedule. Long or short, one of these great walks provides a lot more for the traveler's budget, and lots more insight into a region than the usual eat-too-much, see-too-much, sit-on-the-bus-too-much tour.

Hiking Europe is much more than taking a hike. It's hiking through history, through the most delightful of geography lessons, through a diversity of cultures, and through the lives of warm, welcoming, intriguing people. Hiking offers an intimacy with the Old World that's simply not possible traveling any other way. Hiking Europe is as much living a story as following a footpath.

All of Europe's great hikes have at least one moment of splendid revelation. It might be the sight of a Greek monk in black cassock ringing a church bell; the view of the Matterhorn from an alpine pass; the silhouette of a medieval village when you round the bend of a field in Luxembourg.

But hiking through Europe is much more than a single sight or photo opportunity, it's the smells, sounds, and tastes of the land one step at a time.

Europeans are passionate about their paths. The British have a well-marked system of long-distance footpaths, the French have their Grande Randonées, the Dutch their Grote Routepad. France alone, with 35,000 miles of well-marked, well maintained footpaths, has a much more extensive system of national trails than does the U.S.

Trails that cross national borders are administered by the European Rambler's Association, which also promotes protection of the environment and greater understanding among Europeans—at least among ramblers anyway.

A walk through Europe can be timeless: a pilgrimage following the Way of St. James on Spain's Camino de Santiago. A walk through Europe can be *delizioso:* the focaccia, panforte di Siena and the chianti in Italy's Tuscany region. A walk through Europe can be panoramic: the shimmering glaciers, alpine lakes and emerald valleys of Switzerland's Alps.

The continent's trails bring a wealth of European culture and terrain to life for hikers of all abilities. There's no better way to fully experience the countries of Europe, the wonders of the Old World, than on foot.

Great European Trails: Ten to Remember

Spain: Make a Pilgrimage on Camino de Santiago

Sunlight streaming through the stained glass windows of a cathedral, a black kite soaring overhead, a cross beckoning from a distant peak, aromatic sage perfuming the way . . . there are times when, and places where, the modern-day hiker shares the same vistas and sensations experienced by pilgrims travelling this way in the Middle Ages.

The Way of St. James, as pilgrims call it, is lots more than a long trail between churches. For immersion in a splendid landscape, close-up views of architectural treasures, a challenge to the body and a call to the spirit, as well as the opportunity to participate in a thousand-year old tradition, this is your hike.

A well-marked, well-designed route of 457 miles crosses northern Spain from Roncesvalles on the border with France to Santiago de Compostella. A walk along the Camino offers a rich mixture of history and nature: Gothic spires and wind-sculpted pines, medieval monasteries and mountainsides carpeted with red poppies.

Provence: Pathways of the Impressionists

"No nature is more beautiful," said the great Renaissance poet Petrarch about Provence. This lovely landscape of olive groves, vineyards, river-sculpted gorges and unspoiled villages has long inspired writers, musicians, and painters such as van Gogh and Cézanne.

For the walker, Provence stirs the senses with its color, light and scent. The same light that inspired the palette of the Impressionists seems to brighten the green hills, the yellow sunflowers, the fields of lavender and the impossibly blue sky, while breezes carry the fragrances of rosemary, thyme and sage.

Wander past towering medieval châteaux, through cherry orchards and deep green valleys, through deep gorges and past sparkling rivers, past craggy stone walls and almond trees and enjoy the cuisine that has inspired generations of cooks, cookbooks and food lovers from around the world.

The Loire: Go with the Flow

The Loire, France's longest river, springs to life high in the Cevennes Mountains and flows north to Orléans, then west to the Atlantic Ocean. It meanders through lush green countryside, past ancient villages, vineyards and imposing châteaux.

Meandering with the Loire is the GR3, a 675-km long footpath as smooth, as classic, as mellow as the Loire Valley wine. And, oh, what wines! Each village has its specialty—light white wines, muscadet and champagne. As in all areas of Europe where vines are cultivated, the people are friendlier and more welcoming than usual.

A particular favorite of hikers is the route leading to and from

Spanish Vocabulary

arroyo	stream, creek
agua potable	drinking water
barranco	ravine
camino	footpath, trail
cascada	waterfall
costa	coast
cuesta	hillside
garganta	gorge
guia	guide
lago	lake
mapa	map
parque nacionál	national park
pico	peak
pista	trail
playa	beach
río	river
sendero	footpath
sierra	mountain range
torrente	mountain stream
valle	valley

French Vocabulary

allee (f)	path
balise (f)	way-marker
belvedere (m)	viewpoint
cascade (f)	waterfall
chemin (m)	path
col (m)	path
côte (f)	coast
eau potable (f)	water
emplacement (m)	tent site
fleuve (m)	river
forêt (f)	forest
grande randonnée (f)	long-distance hiking route
île (f)	island
maison du parc (f)	park information center
parc national (m)	national park
pic (m)	peak
plage (f)	beach
randonnée (f)	walk; also walking
sentier (m)	trail
vallée (m)	valley

Tours. Because of the fertility of its valleys, the Touraine has long been described as "the garden of France."

The middle of the GR3, the middle of the Loire Valley is the most inspiring part of the hike. It was here a young man named Jean Jacques Rousseau let his mind wander as he walked and started writing his "Reveries of a Solitary Walker." And one of the castles here is said to be the inspiration for Sleeping Beauty's castle.

The trail is a mostly fairly level river path and the well-conditioned hiker can pile up the kilometers—20, 25, 30 in a day. A mellow, moist (but not too humid) climate aids the walker's pace, too.

But if there was ever a place to idle, it is the Loire Valley. Step off the path and explore Chambord, the prettiest of villages, seemingly suspended in the sky; pay homage to Joan of Arc, heroine of Orléans; sip a glass of Vouvray in Vouvray. "Each glass gladdens the heart," villagers say.

Above all else, is the River Loire itself, flowing between fertile fields and white sandbanks, the river of painters, poets and philosophers, builders of churches, cathedrals and châteaux.

Little Luxembourg: Big on Hiking

Luxembourg is not such a small country when you hike across it. True, the country is only 82 kilometers long, but the GR5 takes 200 kilometers to cross it. A week on foot in the Grand Duchy gives a close-up look at misty forests and meandering rivers, as well as castles and towns that look like backdrops for a grand opera.

Luxembourg's highly educated citizens are big-time hikers. With 5,000 kilometers of marked trails, Luxembourg claims to have the densest trail network of any country.

The nation's premier trail is the GR5, a path along three rivers—the Our, which forms the border with Germany; the Sure which flows east and empties into the Moselle, also the border with Germany. In Luxembourg, the GR5 is way-marked with yellow discs.

For the hiker, the wooded hills along the Our River are no picnic. Relentless ups and downs. Such exertions are quickly forgotten, however, when you spot Vianden Castle. Turrets and gables looming out of the forest gloom, the castle is a fairytale come to life. Inside is a Grand Hall said to accommodate five hundred soldiers, and a scary dungeon.

The hike along the Sure is a walk on the wild side—challenging trails through deep and dark forest. River's end is its confluence with the great Moselle. Walking the Moselle is a stately and serene promenade through beech forests, vineyards and villages that look like Walt Disney film sets. GR5 gourmets sample famed Moselle Valley wines—white, dry, fruity—and the local catch of pike and trout.

The spa town of Mondorf-les-Bains, where you soak your sore limbs in hot mineral baths, is a good place to conclude the hike.

Czech Republic: Check it Out

With a long tradition of hiking, a network of well-tended footpaths and great natural beauty, the Czech Republic is an ideal location for a hiking vacation. An amazing trove of architectural treasures—fairy-tale castles, glittering châteaux and well-preserved old towns—thankfully escaped damage from centuries of invaders, and today these jewels delight the visitor afoot.

To hike the Czech Republic is to experience the highlights of a very old culture and a very new country. Whether you join an organized hiking tour or decide to meander on your own you'll discover lovely traditional towns, rolling farmland and nature reserves. There are hiking highlights in the country's two regions—Bohemia to the west and Moravia to the east.

Czech beer is among the best in the world, and thirsty hikers will appreciate a brewing tradition dating back to the thirteenth century. Along with engaging sights-to-see, comfortable lodging, and the hospitable Czech people, there is a spirit of freedom in the air that makes hiking here extra special.

Switzerland: Alpine Treasures and Pleasures

Nowhere on earth does a winter wonderland famous for its skiing transform so quickly or so well into a summer mountain majesty renowned for its hiking. Swiss resort culture doesn't disappear with the melting snow, as it does in many ski centers elsewhere, but takes on a life of its own, one oriented around hiking and the country's considerable alpine treasures and pleasures.

Switzerland's allure to the hiker is a happy combination of the alpine beauties of the Alps and a classic mountain resort culture that's long been the world's standard. The extraordinary amount of transport at the service of hikers—ski lifts, funiculars, trains and even boats across lakes—means wonderful one-way walking, as well as the option of customizing a day's hike to suit one's fancy.

Swiss hospitality is particularly accommodating to walkers, who are often surprised and delighted at the warm welcome they receive from fine hotels when they stride into the lobby in their hiking boots.

Some of the most intriguing hikes are those in the Bernese Oberland, the classic Switzerland of green valleys, glacial lakes and high mountains. Above, at more than 13,000 feet, towers that famed triple-peaked ridge of Eiger, Monch and Jungfrau.

Each town in its own way seems more quintessentially Swiss than the last: from Rougemont, a historic village of traditional broad-eaved wooden chalets, to Kanderstag, laid-back and idyllically located. Nestled below the craggy summits of the Wetterhorn, Mettenberg and Eiger, lovely Grindelwald, too, boasts a hiker-friendly network of cable cars ascending to the start of some glorious footpaths.

Italian Vocabulary

alta via	high-level hiking route
becco	mountain peak
bosco	woodland
canalone	large rocky alpine gorge
cascata	waterfall
cresta	mountain ridge
discesa	descent, downhill hike
escursione	walk, hike
inseriemento	connector trail
montagna	mountain
passo	pass
pineta	pine forest
rifugio	mountain refuge, bunkhouse style
scarpone	hiking boots
sentiero	footpath
tempo di percorrenza	time needed to complete a hike
torrente	small river
valle	valley
vetta	mountain peak
zaino	backpack

Bella Tuscany: A Distinctive Way of Life

Tuscany may just have the best of everything: art, architecture, food, wine and hiking. Here where the Renaissance was born, the countryside itself seems a work of art—a montage of farms, forest, vineyards and olive groves—accessible to the walker by cypress-lined trails and byways that have been in use since the days of the Roman Empire.

Footpaths lead across the very landscapes that inspired Renaissance masters and through Montalcino and Montepulciano, two of Italy's most noted wine regions. Wander over rolling hills that change color from violet to green to gold with the seasons to reach churches full of magnificent frescos as well as enchanting towns and villages. Some of Tuscany's well-marked trails, some of which are actually Etruscan paths, loop through ancient forests and tranquil pastureland and lead to splendid hill towns with gardens, piazzas and a usually warm welcome from the locals.

Hiking Tuscany is in every way a feast for the senses.

The region's cuisine is one of Europe's most distinctive: polenta, focaccia, rich bean soup and wild boar, plus a splendid array of local cheeses. You'll need to hike a lot of miles over those hills to work off the amazing food served up just off the trail.

Cinque Terre: Five Enchanted Lands

Perched above the dramatic coastline east of Genoa, the fabled villages of the Cinque Terre are powerful attractions for the hiker inspired by dramatic coastal scenery and elegant, old-world towns. Explore these shores of uncommon beauty by way of some engaging footpaths, including the famed Sentiero Azzuro (Blue Trail) named for its close proximity to the Ligurian Sea.

Fun alternative transportation—a ferry, train and cable car—help the hiker reach a remote monastery, distant forest, and lovely villages. Descend verdant hillsides to Portofino and Santa Margarita Ligure, where the wealthiest of Europeans anchor their yachts.

Hike across hillsides that have been cultivated for centuries, past terraced vineyards and olive groves, meadows and woodland. At many a turn in the trail, you'll pause to enjoy breathtaking views of colorful fishing boats bobbing in tiny harbors, beaches backed by spectacular bluffs, and villages that seem to cascade like waterfalls down steep ravines to the turquoise sea.

Crete: Greek for Great Hiking

I love hiking in Crete, Europe's southernmost island; it's a great place to view Greece at its wildest and most beautiful. Happily for we hikers, Crete's rugged White Mountains, which for centuries helped the Cretans repel invaders, have been preserved and protected from development.

Samaria Gorge, Europe's deepest and longest gorge, is a great gash in the White Mountains of Crete. The rim of the gorge, where a very long, one-way, all-day hike begins, is 4,000 feet above the village of Ayia Roumeli on the Libyan Sea, where the hike ends.

The massive walls of the gorge and the towering pines and bold cypresses are the most dramatic features of Samaria National Park, but there are other, more subtle beauties. A sturdy, chaparral-like ecosystem of juniper, myrtle and thyme thrives in the White Mountains. White cyclamen, pink rock rose and golden dandelions splash color on the mountainsides. I was lucky enough to glimpse an elusive *agrimi*, the Cretan ibex, an agile, goat-like creature with large, bow-like horns

The trail reaches the famous Sideroportes, "Iron gates," where the gorge is at its narrowest (about nine feet across). This narrow passage, where the Tarraios River becomes a raging torrent in winter, is the main reason why Samaria Gorge is closed during the rainy season.

The path emerges on a sandy plain at the mouth of the gorge, where food and refreshment await, as does a ferry to return hikers to civilization. This hike whets the appetite for more adventures in the White Mountains—fabulous scenery, thousands of years of history and legendary Greek hospitality.

Cyprus: You'll Love Hiking on Aphrodite's Isle

On most Mediterranean islands, you go to the beach to get away from it all; not on Cyprus, however, where the wise traveler heads for the hills to beat the heat and crowds. The hills in this case are the Troodos Mountains, whose forested slopes offer superb picnicking, camping and hiking. Exploring on foot is the best way to get to know Aphrodite's isle.

A vast, green natural park towering in the center of Cyprus, the mountains are laced with footpaths. The woodsy scene also includes some extraordinary Byzantine churches, remote monasteries with striking wall paintings, and Greek-style al fresco dining.

Trails climb, sometimes gently, sometimes steeply, through a mixed conifer forest of Aleppo pine, Corsican pine and cedar. Lucky hikers may get a glimpse of the *moufflon*, the Cypriot mountain sheep, a regal creature with a pale brown coat and curled, ram-like horns.

One favorite walk is to the top of Mt. Olympus (6,401 feet) the highest peak on the island. During winter months, (January-March) skiing, not hiking, is the most popular pastime on the slopes of Mt. Olympus.

Perhaps the most popular hike is along the nature trail beginning at Troodos Square and ending at Chromion Camp. At six miles in length, with 61 numbered stops, it's surely one of the world's longest interpreted nature trails. Besides offering an island ecology lesson, the trail offers breathtaking views of distant villages and monasteries.

Away from the popular beach resorts, a profound tranquility reigns. The Mediterranean laps against castellated rocks, pine resin perfumes the mountain air, grasshopper *chir-rup* around the ruins of ancient temples, and the warm sum wraps the island in a peaceful forgetfulness.

English 101 for Hikers

Those hikers and writers (admittedly there are only about five of us worldwide) fascinated with the history of walking for recreation credit Wordsworth, Samuel Taylor Coleridge, and fellow poets for "inventing" and popularizing the sport. After visiting their homes and haunts in the Lake District, and following in their footsteps on the fabulous footpaths that weave through Lakeland, it's easy to understand why these Lake Poets walked fifteen, twenty, even twenty-five miles a day, and what inspired some of the greatest poetry in the English language.

In renowned hiking areas such as the Lake District or Exmoor National Park, the visiting hiker can get the impression that just about every person, place and pathway seems oriented to the traveler afoot. Information center staff and locals know the pathways well and cheerfully assist you to find the perfect walk for your interests, abilities, time frame, mood and the ever-changing weather. This expert advice is supplemented by a wide array of inexpensive pamphlets, maps and guidebooks to hiking areas.

Speaking of guidebooks—it was the great bard himself, William Wordsworth, who first floated the notion of preserving the Lake District as a national park in the 1835 edition of his *Guide to the Lakes*. Wordsworth warned of the impact that land-scarring industries and uncaring landowners were having on the region and suggested that "persons of pure taste throughout the island" should support the protection of the Lake District in a "national property". Wordsworth's vision finally became a reality in 1951 when England established Lake District National Park.

The British are passionate about their pathways—from their world-famous long-distance trails to short paths that tour nature preserves and historical sites. Families and hikers of all ages take to the trail in droves on the weekends and often vacation in hiker-friendly locales.

British trails are well-maintained, but they've gone to the dogs, too. A high percentage of hikers are canine-accompanied. Dogs scamper along the trail and sometimes may sit with their masters in mutt-friendly pubs. Dog-walkers have even installed doggy gates (contraptions resembling vertical trap-doors) to enable their canine companions to pass through stiles designed for their two-legged owners.

England, Scotland, Ireland and Wales have plenty of wild backcountry, but the best of hiking-oriented civilization is often close-at-hand. The hiker can relax with a delicious cream tea in a café or tea room or enjoy a hearty local ale at a historic pubs—often in establishments located within park boundaries or seemingly in the middle of nowhere. Plenty of accommodation (ranging from the most basic B&Bs to modest inns to pricey hotels) are located just steps from the coastal path.

With judicious use of maps and guidebooks, and by tapping the wisdom of local tourists boards and footpath organizations such as the Offa's Dyke Association, travelers can plan a superb week (or more) of walking in the British Isles. Particularly useful are the itinerary suggestions, comprehensive lists of lodging along the trails, and contacts to arrange transportation and the transport of your luggage from inn to inn.

Ten Great Hikes in the British Isles

Cornwall: Britain's Best Climate and Coastal Trail

The Cornwall Coast Path, as it's officially known, leads walkers past sandy coves and cobbled shores, across unforgettably high Atlantic-facing cliffs and along spines of rock thrusting out to sea.

If you yearn for an English hiking holiday, the Cornwall Coast is a good choice. The 162-mile long coast path is one of the best-maintained trails in the country. I particularly recommend the 30 miles or so of hiking from Falmouth, south to Lizard Point and north to Nare Head.

The Cornwall Coast Path never drifts far from the cry of the gull, the wail of the foghorn and the crash of the sea against the cliffs.

British English for Hikers

American English and British English are not always the same language. Here is some English English that might just baffle Americans enjoying the pleasure of hiking the British Isles.

aye	yes (Scotland, northern England)	*ladder stile*	Over walls and fences via two ladders, back to back
beck	stream	*moor*	high, open, treeless area
ben	mountain (Scotland)	*Ordnance Survey (OS)*	the British mapping agency
biscuit	cookie		
brae	hill (Scotland)	*pen*	peak (Wales)
burn	stream (Scotland)	*pike*	peak (northern England)
downs	rolling, grassy hills	*ramble*	a short to medium length hike
drove road	ancient route used to bring livestock to market	*sack*	backpack
glen	valley (Scotland)	*squeeze gate*	narrow gap in wall allows people, not animals, through
glyn	valley (Wales)	*tarn*	small mountain lake
jumper	sweater	*twitchers*	avid bird-watchers
kissing gate	swinging gate that allows passage of hikers (but not animals)	*way*	a long distance trail

Thanks to waters warmed by the Gulf Stream, Cornwall is blessed with a temperate climate—about the best in the British Isles. The coast path can be hiked from late winter to mid-to-late autumn.

While the path does have its ups and downs, the well-organized hiker can see to it that there aren't too many "arounds." Judicious use of ferries from harbor to harbor reduce both driving and walking time for the coastal trail hiker. A short ferry across the Helford River saved me an hour's drive from one headland to another. I opened a big yellow disk to signal the ferryman on the opposite bank and within minutes he was motoring across the water to meet me.

Fortified by Cornish pasties (meat and vegetable pies) I rambled through the forested estates of Lord Falmouth and along the mysterious Frenchman's Creek, immortalized by Daphne du Maurier. I watched gray seals haul-out onto the rocks, toured St. Mawes Castle, built by Henry VIII, and visited churches built in the twelfth century. Any hiker looking for a memorable shoreline sojourn in the United Kingdom-by-the-Sea will find it on the coast of Cornwall.

Exmoor: It Delivers More

Exmoor might be England's smallest national park, but it packs a grand variety of natural attractions within its borders, from magnificent coastal bluffs to lush woodland watered by tumbling streams. While Exmoor has long been a favorite walking locale for British ramblers in the know, the region has almost completely escaped the attention of American hikers.

I enjoyed rambles through an ancient oak woodland, and through a lovely "cleave," a steep-sided valley sculpted by a river on its way to the sea. Those wily survivors from the last Ice Age, the rare Exmoor ponies, roam the moors. The agile, shaggy-haired creatures are often spotted in close proximity to large numbers of red deer.

Exmoor offers more because both its coastline and countryside are so intriguing. The country is a mosaic of beech-hedged pasture with scattered stands of ancient oaks. Some of these antiquarian oaks are protected in nature reserves. Exmoor's moors extend from the hilltops to the sea and are thickly carpeted with bell-heather, bracken, ling, gorse and a purple moor grass known in this corner of England as flying bent.

The diverse hiking includes bluff-top paths tracing the edge of the North Devon and Somerset coastlines. One of my favorites led through the Valley of Rocks and across a landscape of oddly shaped tors (peaks) populated by wild goats.

Exmoor National Park is extremely hiker-friendly. The park boasts five visitor centers and offers plenty of information about pathways, public transport and local lodging, plus a variety of guided hikes such as "In the Footsteps of Coleridge" and "Butterflies at Ashton Cleave."

The Cotswold Way: Through the Heart of England

"High wild hills and rough uneven ways" is how Shakespeare in Richard II characterized the Cotswolds. Some of the rough ways have been smoothed out since Shakespeare's day.

In fact, Britain's Cotswold Way is often described as a model long-distance path, a 100-mile long trail with a range of natural and historical attractions. Often called "the heart of England," the Cotswold region is a series of almost unimaginably green wolds (rolling meadows) topped by the occasional stone escarpment. Only the bleating of sheep breaks the silence of the countryside. This is the England of stone cottages with thatched roofs, drowsy villages and friendly pubs.

The names on the land are as colorful as the Cotswolds themselves: Fish Hill and Folly Farm, Burton-on-the-Water and Stow-on-the-Wold, Chipping Campden, Lower Swell and Upper Slaughter, Great Witcombe and Little Washbourne.

Most walkers agree that the southern half of the Cotswold Way from Bath (the second most-visited place in England after London) to Cheltenham is pleasant enough, but doesn't have the beauty or historical interest of the fifty-mile stretch from Cheltenham to Chipping Campden.

Unlike the roller-coaster paths of Cornwall or the steep paths of Scottish highlands, the Way offers mellow walking—an excursion into the countryside rather than a trek through "high wild hills."

The Peak District: A Peak Experience

Peak District National Park, Britain's first, and one of the country's largest national parks, beckons hikers with a microcosm of the English landscape: moors, meadows, rivers, woods, peaks and dales. Particularly engaging are the Derbyshire Dales, Ice Age-sculpted river valleys endowed with a rich diversity of flora and wildlife.

Derbyshire has long been recognized as something special by generations of walkers and more than a few poets.

Follow in the footsteps of that memorable Victorian character, Jane Eyre, a not-very-fictionalized creation of novelist Charlotte Bronte. Meander the banks of the River Dove and along other rivers fished by the legendary seventeenth-century angler and author Izaak Walton, whose *The Compleat Angler*, is still regarded as the greatest book ever about fishing.

In medieval times, a large section of the Peak was proclaimed The Royal Forest and severe penalties imposed against commoners who trespassed or poached deer. This was the era and setting for the legendary Robin Hood, whose exploits take on new meaning for hikers who tramp these storied woods that adjoin Sherwood Forest.

Lake District: Romantic Reservoirs of Calm

Welcome to Lakeland, a kind of hiker's Nirvana: lovely lakes surrounded by England's most rugged mountains and the country's largest national park. Add to the scenery that inspired generations of romantic poets a transportation system that makes it easy to get around without a car, lodging and meals in every price range, plus a superb network of footpaths, and you have a pretty near perfect part of the world for a hiking vacation.

Ice Age glaciers scooped out locations for the lakes, which are known in this part of England as "waters" or "meres." Windermere, England's largest lake, can be enjoyed by taking a steamboat ride as well as a shoreline saunter.

One of the best ways to enjoy a memorable hiking holiday in the Lake District is to headquarter in one of the walker-friendly towns in the heart of Lakeland, such as Grasmere, Windermere, Keswick or Ambleside. Step out the door of your lodging and take what British hikers call a "circular walk" or plan a one-way adventure with a return to home base with the help of a bus or taxi.

Lakes aren't the only attraction of the Lake District. Jagged peaks of volcanic rock thrust skyward from behind the lakes and from lush deep valleys. While obviously known for it namesake lakes, the district also boasts England's finest mountain scenery with more than 100 summits, called fells exceeding 2,000 feet in elevation. The heart-stirring views from the summits take in mountain tarns (little lakes among the crags), dense woods, tumbling streams, drowsy hamlets and even the Atlantic Ocean.

Count me as one hiker who can't resist the call of peaks named Cat Bells, Hay Stacks or the Old Man of Coniston. Scafell Peak, at 3,210 feet the high point of England, is irresistible to hikers. Reportedly the peak is so popular that on some busy days climbers must endure the country's least favorite sport (queuing) in order to stand on the summit.

Coast to Coast: Across England from Sea to Sea

In a nation that admires, even reveres, its walkers, Alfred Wainwright was one of Britain's most beloved twentieth-century ramblers. The famed fell-walker (as the British like to put it) began his "walking writer" career in the 1930s with adventures in the fells (hills) of Cumbria and the Penines.

After many years of research and field work, Wainwright designed a route across England from the Irish Sea to the North Sea. Bold, brilliant and imaginative, the path explores England's finest landscapes: the wilds of the Lake District, the bucolic villages and valleys of the Yorkshire Dales, the haunting North Yorkshire Moors.

His masterwork, both as a book and as a walking route, Wainwright called *A Coast to Coast Route.* It's hard to imagine a better immersion into Britain's natural wonders, history and geography than this two-week-long hike.

A Coast-to-Coast Walk includes generous samplings of the three national parks en route—Lake District, Yorkshire Dales and North Yorkshire Dales. While soul-stirring, and first in the hearts of British countrymen and walkers from around the world, a Coast to Coast is not an official (capital N, please) National Trail and not particularly well way-marked. It definitely helps to have a good guidebook or an experienced Brit showing the way at many critical junctions.

Many walkers call this splendid sea-to-sea sojourn "The Coast-to-Coast," but Wainwright himself called it "A Coast-to-Coast," implying that his creation was one of the many possible ways of marching across England. Whether you follow Wainwright's route exactly or improvise a bit, the hike presents ever-changing environments and landscapes as well as the constant hospitality of rural England.

Wales: Wye Valley Wanderings

Bibliophiles make a beeline for the village of Hay-on-Wye, where more than two-dozen bookstores offer thousands of used books—many of them very old, rare and collectible.

While Hay-on-Wye may have put the area on the map, most of the map is a lovely montage of hills, dales, woods, fields, castle ruins and drowsy villages situated on the border between Wales and England.

Two long-distance trails explore the region. One path, the Wye Valley Walk, follows the Wye River Valley from South Wales to Mid-Wales, crisscrossing the border between England and Wales. The 112-mile route visits dramatic limestone gorges, rolling green hills and historic market towns. The Walk's southernmost sections lead through what the British call ancient woodland—trees that have not been cut since the Middle Ages.

Offa's Dyke Path offers not only a walk through history, but a walk on top of it as well. Ruthless King Offa of Mercia (now the English Midlands) ordered his eighth-century subjects to construct a long earthworks to keep out the Welsh to the west.

The path sticks more rather than less to the dyke, with frequent detours across the quiet Wye Valley and onto higher ground that offers grand vistas of the Welsh-English border. Nine crossings of the Wales-England border occur en route. End-to-end hikers usually allow about twelve days to walk the 177-mile path. A leaping salmon logo guides hikers on the Wye Valley Walk while Offa's Dyke Path is way-marked with acorns.

No doubt the Wye Valley will continue to be better known for its bookstores than its footpaths, but the traveler seeking an enchanted walk in Wales would do well to heed the words of a Welsh monk, who lived in the region's famed Tintern Abbey, and wrote: "You will find among the woods something you never found in books."

Scotland: Hikers Reach for the Misty Isle of Skye

Rugged mountains, forested glens and a magnificent coastline draw hikers to Skye, one of Scotland's most scenic and storied islands. The isle contains one of the greatest concentrations of tall peaks in Britain, and offers an array of outings for enthusiastic hikers.

Skye's skyline is dominated by the jagged Cuillins, granite ramparts that rise 3,000 feet above the nearby sea. The peaks are often hidden in the clouds—one reason why Skye is nicknamed "The Misty Island."

Unaccountably called "hills" when they're most definitely mountains, the Cuillins rise like fists from the sea. The range includes the heaps of lava forming the Trotternish hills in the northern part of the island and the Black and Red Cuillins in the south.

Well-built trails ascend even the highest and wildest of the hills, including island highpoint, 3,257-foot Sgurr Alasdair. Another excellent trail visits Loch Coruisk, one of Scotland's most dramatic lochs.

The island's coastline is dramatic, too. Deep inlets (sea lochs as they're called in Scotland) penetrate the land and form several long peninsulas. These peninsulas are sometimes described as crab claws; in fact, the island itself looks like a giant crab. So deep are the sea lochs that even though Skye is good-sized (measuring 60 miles long and 40 miles wide), no place on the island is more than five miles from the sea. Keen-eyed coast walkers may spot whales, dolphins, seals, sea otters and flocks of sea birds.

Shetland Islands: Undiscovered Coastal Trails

Vintage Shetland it was. Over the treeless, peat-patterned headlands I tramped, my boots making squishing noises on the wide grassy platforms shorn by a multitude of sheep. Offshore was the most Gothic of spectacles—arches, pinnacles and grotesquely sculptured spikes of ancient red sandstone called The Drongs.

"As a hiking destination, Shetland has to rank as one of the most undiscovered spots in Europe," affirms nature guidebook author and Shetlander Peter Guy.

Guy has written four guidebooks in a series called "Walking the Coastline of Shetland:" *The Island of Yell*, *The Island of Unst*, *The Island of Fetlar*, and *The Island of Northmavine*. Guy gives a mile-by-mile account of a coastal walk around each isle: Yell (100 miles), Unst (60 miles), Fetlar (31 miles) and Northmavine (120 miles). The author breaks the coastline into day trips of six to sixteen miles, and also describes a number of what Americans call "loop trails" and the Shetlanders and British ramblers call "circular walks."

As I hiked the coastal trials I passed many a croft (family farm) and Shetland sheep. Most of the breed is white-faced and white-wooled and produces a soft and hardy fleece that's transformed into sweaters (highly recommended for hikers) by island knitters, who rework traditional patterns. I walked Shetland's tattered coastline past brave little Shetland ponies and neatly patterned fields, in good weather and bad.

During summer, at this latitude (only six degrees south of the Arctic Circle), there's a lot of day in which to day hike: nearly nineteen hours of light. I spent a wonderful week wandering the isles—with time enough for two long hikes every day.

Ireland's Ring of Kerry

"I have spread my dreams under your feet," wrote William Butler Yeats. A hike around the remote Ring of Kerry is indeed a dream of emerald hills, deep blue lakes and idyllic seascapes.

Visit Killarney National Park and meander through woodlands thick with mosses, ferns and rhododendrons, marvel at a waterfall that inspired the poet Tennyson, and inhale great draughts of air fresh with the scents of damp woods and heather moors. Trails lead to ancient Celtic churches, Iron-age forts and the curious Ogham Stones. While hiking the coast, watch dolphins frolic offshore and seabirds nesting atop the dramatic bluffs.

You could spend a pleasant week walking The Ring of Kerry. Saunter through the blissfully quiet and undiscovered countryside of the Beara Peninsula to isolated villages, savor idyllic sea views over Kenmare Bay to the Atlantic Ocean, pause to examine the ancient Celtic writings on the curious Ogham Stones, follow an old track beside a stream to Dingle Bay with sweeping sea views to the distant Mt. Eagle, hike the Kerry Way over the gorse- and heather-covered hills above Caragh Lake Blackstone Bridge, where salmon fishermen gather.

Even more memorable than the splendid scenery are the innately friendly Irish people, who share their legends, lore, and boundless hospitality.

Chapter 18   Hiking Holidays

S OMEDAY I MIGHT WRITE "CONFESSIONS OF A TOUR GUIDE," A witty look at what it's like to lead guests on hiking holidays. In the meantime, I wanted to share my insider's look at walking/hiking vacations, the fastest growing segment of the active vacation biz.

I've served as a consultant to a walking vacation company, reported on a number of hiking holidays conducted by various companies, and even led quite a few week-long tours myself. While I lack the patient temperament to be a full-time hiking guide, I really enjoy leading a few tours a year, showing hikers from across the nation and around the world the beauty of California's coastal trails, guiding them through vineyards to winery tasting rooms, and helping them work up an appetite for some great California cuisine.

All these experiences have led me to some very strong opinions about what makes a really memorable hiking vacation and what doesn't, as well as the difference between an active vacation company that delivers a great hiking experience and one that just goes through the motions.

Who hasn't spent plenty of time and money on a trip far from home, and then returned with the sad, dawning realization that you didn't get a full sense of the place you visited? Even though visiting one museum after another gave you great insights into the history and culture, you didn't get to know any of the people, didn't spend enough time outdoors, and you probably gained a few pounds because you gave up your fitness program while you were traveling.

If you want to return fitter, not fatter, and get in better tune with the people and the land, abandon the auto, say goodbye to the tour bus, turn in your train ticket and your boarding pass. And take a hike.

YOU MAY NOT THINK of hiking as a form of transportation—especially not one that will take you on the vacation of your dreams—but it may be the best way to get to know a place and its people. Smell the fresh air, listen to the local political discussions, watch the farmers at work, taste a fresh-picked fig. Hiking tours encourage intimate contact with the local people. You're using the same mode of transportation that they are.

Walking-hiking vacations have been rapidly increasing in popularity. More than 100 tour companies offer such vacations in places near and far. Your choices range from a literary tour of England to adventure hiking in Hawaii, and from an overland trek in Nepal or the wilds of Peru to the back roads and trails of Vermont.

You can go on a walking vacation on your own or join an organized tour group. Each has its pluses and minuses.

On Your Own

When you plan your own trip, you enjoy a flexibility in your schedule that's virtually impossible to have on an organized tour. If you find yourself in a place where you simply must spend more time, you're free to adjust your itinerary accordingly. Similarly, if you happen upon a place that has absolutely no appeal for you, despite your careful research, then you can press on. You don't have to worry about the needs of a group.

You can also save money by planning your own trip, but planning takes time, talent, and energy. You'll need to hit the internet hard and often, hunt down the best maps, guidebook and tourist information on your destination, as well as make arrangements for accommodations, then book your own arrangements one by one or at least work well with a travel agent.

Working out the travel arrangements on your own at your destination can sometimes be exasperating. Traveling alone in some countries is not a vacation, it's a job. Making flight-reservations, and transport arrangements can be very difficult.

Without a doubt, the internet has made it possible to secure information almost instantly. Using that information, evaluating that information and translating it into a memorable hiking vacation on the ground is another story.

Another negative to consider is that when you take a self-planned hiking holiday, the transport of your gear becomes a daily concern. Your options are usually limited to carrying your bags with you each day, storing them in a safe place (airport and train station lockers are no longer much of an option, given heightened security concerns) or making short day-trips from your hotel while you leave them there for the day. (Tour groups usually transport your bags from point to point each day.)

If for you, however, the positives of designing your vacation outweigh the negatives, then your first step is to plan your trip—a stage that many travelers love to delve into.

First zip around the internet and request brochures from the places you want to visit. Buy and study maps; examine guidebooks, travel books and photographic essays of the places you'd like to visit. Be sure to get a sense of the weather you can expect when you go; also determine whether there are any special events occurring near the time when you would like to take your trip.

By the way, keep in mind that you'll need to rely on more than maps and guidebooks (which are sometimes poorly written) on your hiking holiday. You need to have a certain trail sense, and be willing to check in with locals for the best information.

The more research you do, the more information you uncover, and the more you know about the people and places you'll be visiting, the richer your travel experience will be.

Self-Guided Tours

Halfway between going it on your own and joining a guided tour are self-guided hiking tours. On a self-guided walking vacation (independent trails, as they're sometimes called in the active vacation biz) you hike a suggested route without a guide and stay somewhere different every night. The tour company arranges your lodging along the trail (a linear or circular walk route), provides you with maps, detailed trail notes, and transports your luggage to the next night's accommodation. Typically, these walking tours are crafted for five or seven nights.

You set your own pace on a self-guided walking tour and need not be constrained by other members of a tour group. Certainly you are able to improvise and customize, add mileage or subtract, in a way that works best for you.

The British have refined the inn-to-inn independent walking vacation. The way the British like to travel, the country's marvelous system of pathways, and abundant close-to-the-trail accommodation, add up to some superb weeks of walking. Numerous quality British companies offer self-guided tours. Other European locales that self-guided hikers seem to enjoy include The Dordogne and Corsica in France, Andalucia in Spain, the isle of Crete in Greece, the Amalfi Coast in Italy, and the Black Forest in Germany. The Swiss Alps are a wonderland for self-guided hikers, who delight in the classic Haute Route, Bernese Oberland, the pathways of Mont Blanc and many more locales.

Breakfast is provided by the inn. Packed lunches are often available from your accommodation, though most hikers prefer to stop for lunch at an inn or café along the trail. Evening meals may be offered at your accommodation or at another inn or restaurant nearby.

Typically, a self-guided walking vacation includes:
- Lodging in hotels, inns, guesthouses and farmhouses
- A hearty breakfast
- Luggage transfer between overnight stops

- Maps, detailed itinerary and route description
- Information pack with instructions on how to get navigate to the walk's start point, lodging details.
- Emergency assistance

Single Inn Walks

A variation on the self-guided inn-to-inn walking concept is the Single Center tour; that is staying put in one place for several days or a week and heading out each day for a different walk. This hiking holiday appeals to people who want to walk independently, and like the idea of a company arranging all the logistics, but do not want the hassle of repacking and moving on each day.

Organized Tours

If you have fewer budgetary considerations, if you prefer somewhat more luxurious accommodations and restaurant fare, and if you appreciate the convenience of having your entire trip planned and arranged, an organized tour might just be the ticket for you.

An organized hiking holiday offers almost total safety. It allows you to feel quite pampered while you get plenty of fresh air and exercise. It helps you get in touch with the culture and history.

Naturally, a group tour requires that you travel, hike, dine and rest with several strangers—a fact that those who prefer to travel solo or choose their travel-mates should be aware of. Actually, many women—and men, too—appreciate the companionship, camaraderie, and sharing of insight that emerges in the group dynamic; it's not uncommon to strike up lifelong friendships with fellow tour group members.

The first step in arranging a walking vacation is to e-mail, write or call several organizations and request their catalogs. Many of these catalogs, incidentally, with glorious photographs and tour descriptions, will make you want to leave tomorrow. That possibility might not be too outrageous, actually, as many tours are offered more than one time during the year and a last minute great deal on an airfare from the internet could send you on your way.

When reading the brochures and catalogs, pay careful attention to the wording. Be aware of key words such as "challenging," "breathtaking," and "reasonably good condition." A tour operator's notion of breathtaking might literally leave you breathless—and exhausted—at the top of a towering peak. If the words raise red flags in your mind, get them defined before you commit yourself to a tour. Even if you want "challenging," get the term defined anyway just to be sure it means what you think it does.

Is a Walking Vacation for You?

You like to walk and you like to travel. You know the healthful benefits of walking, and the notion of taking a walking vacation is

TRAILMASTER TALE
A Honeymoon Hike in the Heart of England

WHEN I announced to my bride-to-be a few weeks before our wedding that I signed us up for a honeymoon hiking vacation, she nearly told me to take a hike.

"A group tour?" Cheri puzzled. "You mean spend our whole honeymoon with complete strangers?"

"Not with strangers, you'll be with me."

Still, she was dubious.

"This walking company provides all the lodging, meals, and guide service. We don't have to arrange transportation, ask directions—"

"Not that you would ever ask for directions."

"All we have to do is hike eight or ten miles a day through the Cotswolds—very romantic, they assured me."

"I hope so. We're only going on one honeymoon, you know."

Cheri said little more about the group aspect of our upcoming hiking tour before the wedding or during our flight to England but I could tell she still had major reservations. And frankly, I began to wonder if I had made the right decision myself.

Our doubts vanished within minutes of joining our group and being shown to our room, decorated with antique furnishings that included an exquisite 400-year-old bed. Soon afterward we met our fellow walkers, a convivial group convinced we'd made a brilliant decision to take a hiking honeymoon. "Wish hiking vacations were around when we got married," one older couple told us.

The countryside itself proved to be wonderfully romantic. We hiked hand in hand through the heart of England.

With much satisfaction (and relief) I watched my new bride shed her considerable plan-the-wedding stresses and slip into the gentle rhythm of a long day's walk. We and eight other hikers assembled every morning after one of those awesome English breakfasts and our leader marched us over hill and dale.

We stopped for a picnic or at a pub for lunch, walked during the afternoon past field and stream, with stops at gardens, castles, bucolic villages and, of course, for tea, arriving in the late afternoon at our evening's accommodation—usually a historic inn or a friendly B&B. There we found our luggage waiting for us. After a hot bath and—well, it was our honeymoon—we were ready for a delicious dinner.

As we passed from one pasture to another, we learned about "kissing gates," designed to allow one cow through at a time. The name comes from the fact that the gates resemble wooden revolving doors that offer cheek-to-cheek passage for hikers in love. Naturally the newlyweds, as our companions referred to us, were encouraged to smooch for the camera at every gate.

During our week of hiking we enjoyed the pleasure of each other's company, as well as that of our fellow hikers. Occasionally we hikers divided up by gender: when we walked into one English theme-park-perfect town, the women enthusiastically browsed the shoppes for mementos, while we guys retreated to the local pub for a pint.

Our fellow hikers couldn't have been better companions, particularly a couple celebrating their 30th anniversary. Always take the time to walk together, it's really good for the marriage, they advised. A recent divorcee concurred.

One morning Cheri and I climbed to the top of Cleeve Hill, highest point in the Cotswolds, gulped the clear, clover-scented air and looked down at an England frozen in time, at woods, pastures and a crumbling castle wrapped in the mist. When she leaned over to whisper how much she was enjoying our honeymoon afoot, I knew I made the right decision. About her. About starting off our life together with a long hike.

"The course of true love never did run smooth," wrote Shakespeare. Unless of course you're on a smoothly run hiking vacation, a great way for a couple to start a marriage off on the right foot.

enticing. Everybody seems to be walking everywhere these days. But you have a few questions before you sign up for a memorable walking vacation of your own.

Both for the casual walker and the experienced rambler who loves to travel, a walking vacation might just be the very best way to go. But walking vacations, per se, are a relatively new kind of holiday and the wise traveler, quite naturally, will have questions about this whole notion of taking a guided walking trip: Where will I stay? Who is the leader? Who goes on these trips? How many miles a day do we walk?

This section is designed to answer the important questions and address the understandable concerns common to walkers who are considering a walking vacation. For those who love to walk but aren't quite sure about taking a walking vacation, this section offers an introduction to a very special travel experience. You'll learn how to choose a walk for your interests and abilities, what to expect from a week of walking with a group, how to choose a quality walking company, and how to pack and prepare for your adventure.

What is a Walking Vacation?

A walking vacation by my definition is an escorted, guided holiday with an emphasis on walking as the way to experience the countryside, a region of a country, or even an entire country. Usually about five to seven days in length, a walking vacation includes meals, accommodation, transportation and the services of a guide.

High Sierra backpacking trips, Himalayas expeditions, and African safaris are fine ways to travel but not, by definition, walking vacations. Neither are those grand cultural tours organized by museums that happen to have a little walking or those city explorations organized by cruise lines in ports of call.

Choosing your vacation destination

A walking company's catalog, with its gorgeous photos and captivating descriptions, can seem like a book of dreams with each walk seeming more tempting than the last. But before you sign up, there are still a few considerations.

No doubt a choice of destination is often influenced by what one is looking for in a holiday. Some walkers are looking for an escape from the ordinary, wildlife watching, immersion in a foreign culture, a healthy holiday or a week-long hike that's a vacation from driving. Many hope for all of the above from a sojourn afoot.

Once you've narrowed your selection to a few destinations, take a close look at the walk's itinerary. Most walks blend natural, cultural and historical attractions. A walk's emphasis can vary widely from region to region and from company to company. Look for the emphasis that's right for you. If your idea of a great walk is fifteen miles a day over rough terrain and you hope to lose ten pounds on your vacation, don't sign up for a gourmet trip that has a lot of eating and very little walking. On the other hand, if you prefer fairly gentle saunters through quaint villages, don't join a walk featuring all-day treks over a rugged mountain range. Average number of miles per day walked, climate, altitude and seasonal considerations can also influence your choice of walking destinations.

A Hiking Holiday One Day at a Time

Whatever your choice of destinations, you're sure to experience a very special vacation, and one that is a step beyond all other kinds of holidays, when you sign up for a walking trip. While no two days are exactly alike, and each day brings new challenges and unique adventures, a good day of walking with a quality company has a rhythm and time-tested pattern that makes for a very special holiday.

• **Morning** The day begins with breakfast, usually served between 7:30 and 8:30 A.M. Usually the leader is present to go over the day's schedule. Walkers depart the inn at about 9 A.M. either on foot or with a short van shuttle to the start of the route. Morning goals gained might include a stunning hilltop viewpoint, a spring bubbling amidst an ancient forest or a sixteenth-century abbey that can only be reached on foot. Along with major sights, walkers stop to savor the little things along the footpath: a deer and fawn browsing a meadow, a hawk riding the thermals, a rare variety of wildflower.

• **Afternoon** Often the group walks together (though at different paces) in the morning until the noon lunch break. The lunch stop might be a pub, a village café or a picnic among the pines. In the afternoon, walkers may be offered a choice of destinations and walks of varying distances. At anytime during the day, walkers might be joined by local experts eager to share their observations and regional pride: a gallery owner talking about local landscape painting or a winemaker explaining his art and offering a taste. Often these colorful characters offer quotes to remember such as the owner of the 54-room castle who complained to me "It's so hard to keep up a place like this!" or the profound observation of a farmer: "Pigs are smarter than some people, you know."

• **Evening** By late afternoon the group returns to the inn from where the walk started, or to accommodations farther along the trail. Here the walkers retire to their cozy rooms where they find their luggage awaiting them. It's time to relax, take a hot bath, read, write postcards home or stroll into the village to shop. Rested and refreshed, walkers meet for dinner about 7 or 7:30 P.M. After an invigorating day outdoors, appetites are hearty. It's time to savor the local cuisine and replace the calories burned during the day's journey. Give into the temptation of that fabulous dessert; you'll walk it off tomorrow when you explore another beautiful part of the country. It's also a time to enjoy the convivial nature of the group, a chance to toast your accomplishments and anticipate the challenges that lie ahead.

Seven Steps to a Wonderful Walking Vacation

1. Leave your work at home. A great walk often depends on what walkers bring along with them. No, I'm not referring to a day pack stuffed with the Ten Essentials and more, but to the point-of-view a hiker brings to a hiking holiday. Try to leave those deadlines and stresses behind. You know very well that your work will be there when you get back. Walking has the effect of clearing your head, but if you get started clearing it before you go, you'll have an even better time. Feel free, however, to pack your cell phone and even your laptop if you must, and catch up in the evenings after you've taken your walk. (Remember, though, there are few things more obnoxious to a walk leader or fellow guests, than someone taking or making a cell phone call from the trail.)

2. Plan a relaxed day just before the walk begins. Arrive at your destination a day early and take in the local sights. Sure, in this day of global travel it's possible to literally get halfway around the world and arrive a half-hour before the group assembles for its welcome dinner, but you'll enjoy your holiday far more if you have a day to relax and recover from jet lag before you meet your fellow walkers. In high-altitude destinations, you'll want to schedule a couple of days to acclimate before the trip begins. Use the opportunity to leisurely explore the area or take advantage of company "extras" that may be available.

3. Appreciate the unique qualities of your group. Each walking group comes together in its own way, depending on many variables. Weather, terrain, time of year, and, of course, the individuals involved all combine to create a one-time-only assembly. Expect to join in lively conversation reflecting both similar and different points of view from the well-educated and world-wise travelers who share the walk with you. And enjoy the opportunity to hike together in companionable silence, sometimes while lost in your own thoughts.

4. Address any difficulties right away. Should a problem arise that requires immediate attention, speak one-on-one with the tour leader or manager as soon as possible. If it's a more generalized concern be sure to make your feelings known with a call or letter to the walking company office and by carefully filling out the walking company evaluation forms (good companies appreciate honest feedback!). Remember that some complaints about the weather, trail conditions, etc. are beyond the control of the tour company.

5. Satisfy your curiosity. Read up on a region before you go. Ask the walking company office for a reading list for the region you plan to visit. Ask questions. Ask lots of them: about the countryside, the regional cuisine, the history, and traditions.

6. Be yourself. Joining a walking vacation indicates your willingness to become part of group for a given time; it does not mean giving up your individuality or all your valued routines. Take time for morning stretches or a little prayer, meditation or yoga. Get enough sleep. Your spirit will be nourished if you get the amount of "alone time" that you need, whether that's a little solo hiking within the group or just a little time to contemplate the sunset alone and write postcards to friends back home.

7. Show your appreciation. Customarily, the walk leader and the manager both are tipped by guests. Oftentimes each guest will contribute (an amount collectively agreed upon by group members) to a pool for the two walking company representatives.

Getting Ready

A walking vacation gives you the chance to do what comes naturally: lace up your boots and take a walk. Individuals are sometimes concerned about whether or not they're in shape for a journey afoot. Most likely you are—unless, of course, you're a confirmed couch potato. If you lead a busy, reasonably active life, you're probably looking forward to the chance to get a little more exercise than usual while you're away from home. You'll probably enjoy your trip even more if you give yourself a chance to take a few nice walks before you go.

Must-haves and optional items

On a guided walk, you certainly don't have to be as concerned about self-sufficiency on the trail as you would on a solo trek into the wilderness. Your leader and manager will offer water and snacks and carry a first-aid kit. Most walkers pack only some, not all of the items on the lists following. Modify these to suit individual needs.

Two necessities

Good boots Top-quality hiking boots or sturdy walking shoes are the most important investment the walking adventurer can make. Don't compromise at all on how boots fit your feet. Make sure the boots have plenty of toe room for downhill hiking, and sufficient width for comfort. And break them in before you embark on your walking holiday.

Good day pack Padded shoulder pads are an essential feature for a day pack. The better packs have a padded hip band or waist belt for support. Buy a high-quality one with ample storage, rugged, covered zippers and easy access to pouches. Be sure the pack you choose comfortably carries water bottles.

Packing it in

Soft sided-luggage is definitely easier for transport on a walking vacation. Don't over-pack, but do take sufficient clothing. Don't forget quality rainwear. Hikers know how to dress in layers to control body temperature—and how to pack accordingly. In addition to your hiking garb, you'll want to bring "classy casual" clothing and shoes to wear to dinner in certain American and Euro tours.

Who takes a hiking holiday?

Walking vacations appeal to people of varied interests and backgrounds who all share a love for walking and an appreciation for travel. The diverse personalities of those who enjoy walking vacations defy categorization, but these unique individuals do possess certain traits in common, including a:

- **Spirit of adventure.** What lies around the next bend in the trail? What went on behind those castle walls? What's the secret ingredient in this recipe?

- **Natural curiosity** about people and places far from home.

- **Love of nature,** an appreciation for the green world.

- **Sense of humor** and ability to take every curve in the road in stride.

- **Desire to stay active,** and healthy while participating in activities that challenge body and mind.

- **High regard for fine food,** graceful accommodation, art, history and expanding one's knowledge of the world.

- **Sense of camaraderie** and conviviality with fellow travelers.

- **Young-at-heart spirit** common to active people of all ages and stages of life.

Along with the Ten Essentials, consider these items:

1. Sunscreen is a must, particularly along the coast or at high altitude.
2. Hat keeps body heat in, solar heat out.
3. Camera, film, extra battery. (Consider adding one of those pre-loaded little panoramic cameras, too.)
4. Walking stick, the collapsible, telescoping variety.
5. Small binoculars for wildlife-watching.
6. Notepad or journal for writing down contacts, interesting sights, details of photos you took.
7. Bandana soaked in water and wrapped around neck is refreshing. Plus 100 more uses.
8. Microcassette tape recorder to records thoughts, talks, sounds to remember.
9. Heart-rate monitor worn on wrist to track target heart rate.
10. A good book, classic or modern work set in hiking locale (check with walking company for specific titles).

Who takes a walking vacation? People who have reason to celebrate or people who have no particular reason at all; they simply want to enjoy a wonderful week of walking. They may include: couples celebrating a special anniversary, even a honeymoon or individuals marking a special passage in life: a birthday, a recent retirement, a big promotion. While some people sign up to meet new friends, others join to rediscover each other and even themselves. Friends with common interests may sign up for the same trip—imagine your book discussion group, various club members, or a few neighbors enjoying a walking vacation together!

Adding It All Up

It's difficult to enjoy a day's walk when you're worried about where to eat dinner, where you'll stay or how you'll get back from your walk to your rental car. One of the greatest benefits of taking a walking vacation is that the experts take care of every detail while you just enjoy yourself. By all means compare the cost between signing up for a walking vacation and making all the arrangements yourself. You might save a little money traveling solo in some regions or you might not.

However, first, list the required arrangements: Research a far-off region, plot a walking route on the map, find accommodations, negotiate with hotels, make reservations, look for good restaurants, arrange transport or rent a car from one walking destination to another, hire the services of a local guide . . . well, you get the idea. In a world where time is the most precious commodity, do you want to make all those arrangements? What price do you put on all the intangibles that a walking company can provide?

A local guide knows the area's most engaging footpath, most stunning scenic vista, and the shadiest spot for a picnic. The experienced behind-the-scenes planning and first-hand knowledge about a special place provided by a top-notch walking company elevates a guided walk beyond the pedestrian to a trip of a lifetime. Add it all up and you're likely to conclude a walking vacation is a great value in terms of both time and money.

Ten questions to help you evaluate a walking-hiking vacation company

1. **How physically fit do I have to be for a walking vacation?** A walking vacation is a pleasure if you're in overall good health, enjoy the outdoors, and are able to walk 6 to 8 miles a day over rolling terrain. If this description fits you, then you'll enjoy a walking vacation and be able to select a walk from a wide variety that match your pace and comfort level. In my experience, very often walkers underestimate their abilities and then pleasantly surprise themselves by their accomplishments!

2. **How many people do you usually have on a trip?** To ensure personal attention and a quality experience, go with a company that averages twelve walkers or so per trip and limits participants to a maximum of sixteen. Groups exceeding twenty are unwieldy; they often fail to coalesce as a team, and can lack the camaraderie that develops naturally in a smaller group.

3. **As a solo hiker, will I be out of place?** "Absolutely not," should be the answer. Singles should be welcome on all walking vacations. On many walking vacations the ratio of couples to singles is about fifty-fifty. On a well-run trip, solo travelers and couples generally mix and charges and whether there is an option to share accommodations.

4. **Who is leading my trip?** Good leaders don't simply walk you from place to place, but offer an insider's view of a region. Ask about the leader's experience and qualifications. Some companies are content to use college students on summer break for leaders while the more quality-conscious look for mature, convivial individuals who are experts in such fields as botany, history or wildlife biology.

5. **What kind of support is provided while walking?** A top-notch walking company offers a leader who's with you just about every step of the way and a manager who handles meal arrangements and a thousand and one other details so that you, the walker are able to simply enjoy your time on- and off-the trail. A support vehicle should be at the ready should you choose to hike a little more—or a little less— than the day's planned itinerary.

6. **Where will we stay?** What will we eat? Lodging should be comfortable, have all the desired amenities, and possess

something of the character of the countryside. Meals should be fresh, delicious and, when appropriate, embrace the best of regional cuisine. A guest's special dietary restrictions should be cheerfully accommodated.

7. **What are my individual options?** A well-crafted walk is not a group tour, but a shared adventure that allows for some individual preferences. Frequently, walkers may be offered afternoon options of a walk or other planned activity—a visit to a gallery, botanic garden, or historic castle, for example. If you wish to miss a meal, a museum tour or a mountaintop climb with the group in order to have some free time to shop, snooze or simply explore on your own, the company should oblige.

8. **What if it rains?** "A little rain never hurt anyone," should be the optimistic reply. As long as it's safe to do so, a walk in the rain is a memorable experience. Wrapped in the mist, a landscape seems altogether different, beautiful in a special way. And oh those rainbows! Alternative recreation or a cultural activity should be offered in the case of truly inclement weather.

9. **How do I get to the starting point?** Some companies pick you up at the airport or nearest rail station. Walk away from any company that states, "It's your responsibility to get to the starting point on your own" and offers little or no information on how to do this. Detailed instructions should be sent to you immediately after booking a trip. Your walking company should also provide pre- and post-walk lodging and touring tips. A quality company will recommend the most efficient and low-cost flights and ground transportation to the start of your walk or direct you to a travel agent or proven on-line source to help you book.

10. **What exactly is included in the cost?** Make sure any additional costs such as buying lunches, wine with dinner, museum admissions, etc. are spelled out. Better yet, look for a walking vacation that has a fixed price, everything included. If a walking trip's cost is described as all-inclusive, make sure the company really delivers.

Chapter 19 Paths Less Taken

OH, THOSE DEMANDING EDITORS. AS THE *LOS ANGELES TIMES* hiking columnist, I wrote about my favorite subject every week for 18 years. A typical column detailed a hike, the majority of the time in California, as well as enticing destinations in other states and even in other countries.

Was that enough?

Nooooooo.

This was a *news*paper, my editors reminded me. Give us something new. What's new about hiking?

With these directives, I began searching out special-interest trails and hiking experiences that might be new to my readers—or at least add another dimension to already-popular sport.

Some readers responded by saying they were perfectly happy hiking the same kind of trail in the same way time after time—just tell us what's so great about this hike and give us directions to the trailhead. Other readers were pleased to hear about something new.

I always got plenty of reader feedback about my stories detailing new twists on the hiking experience so it wasn't hard to determine what worked and what didn't. Stories about snowshoeing ("that's not hiking") and multi-sport adventures ("If I want to hike, I'll hike, if I want to bike, I'll bike; it's ridiculous to try to do both.") turned out to be two ways to go that did not resonate at all with my readers. Other kinds of hiking adventures proved considerably more popular and I share them with you here.

Trails are where you find them. Most of us look for trails in all the right places—national parks and renowned hiking locales, plus the best of what our home town's and home mountains have to offer.

More hiking opportunities are available beyond the obvious. With a little sleuthing, the sojourner afoot can locate some out-of-the-way trails to hike. Here are some ways to discover new trails.

Join a Trail Work Party

I don't know why they call them parties—at least during the day when you're working on a trail. At night around the campfire, it might be a different story. The Sierra Club and other conservation

TRAILMASTER TALE
Heli-hiking in the Bugaboos

THE HELICOPTER that dropped we eight hikers and our guide into the wilderness of Bugaboo Provincial Park speeds out of earshot in 30 seconds and vanishes from sight in a minute. In complete silence, my fellow adventurers and I savor a mesmerizing panorama of a many-spired granite cathedral surrounded by glaciers, ice fields and vast fir forests.

Hiking along Grizzly Ridge, the vistas get even better and we behold the Bugaboos in all their glory: rocky escarpments, lush green meadows, creeks cascading in braids off the shoulders of mountains down to cobalt blue alpine lakes rimmed by fire weed.

We inhale great draughts of alpine air and count our blessings. By my watch, flying time to this rocky mountain high was only three minutes and 40 seconds. A hearty hiker would need two days to cover that distance on the ground.

My fellow adventurers on this Canadian Mountain Holidays trip range in age from 30s to 70s, from novice to experienced in hiking ability, and there are at least as many, if not more, women than men.

Here's the drill. The guide radios the copter pilot and gives a quickie description of our location, wind conditions and the terrain. As the helicopter approaches, guide and guests get into a heli-huddle, that is to say, we form a circle around piled-up day packs and hiking poles, get down on

our knees, duck our heads and in less than a minute the copter lands right next to us. OK, maybe not right next to us, but less than free-throw distance away. (This close proximity to the craft keeps hikers out of the prop-wash and away from the gale-force winds generated by the propeller, which can whip cinders into eyes and even blow the skinnier hikers among us off a ridgetop. Keeping us close to the copter also helps extend the company's 25-year-old 100 percent perfect safety record and guarantees that every hiking holidaymaker returns with his/her head.)

The guide waves us into our seats and stows our gear. We fasten our seatbelts and almost instantly the Bell 212 is high in the air. The twin-engine jet copter leaves terra firma rapidly behind and zooms over a vast mountain kingdom devoid of roads, trails or humanity. After three to eight minutes of flying, the copter drops like a rock from the sky, hurtling toward a knife edge ridge. You brace yourself, anticipating the biggest bump of your life and…the helicopter lands with all the thud of a butterfly alighting on a twig.

Damn, those pilots are good.

The copter zooms away, and you and your guide start hiking. (At this latitude, summer days are very long—meaning heli-hiking days can be long, too, if you're in the mood for it.) The day's sojourn might include crossing an alpine meadow while identifying a dozen different wildflowers,

organizations sponsor low-cost and no-cost weekend and week-long trail work activities.

For example, you might join a backpack into the Rocky Mountains, work on a remote length of trail or clean up and restore a long abandoned camp. The sponsoring organizations want to make sure volunteers have some fun, so they usually plan hikes to secret spots, talks by naturalists, special meals and more.

Peak-bagging is Great Sport

Hiking to the summit of every named peak in a park or every peak over a certain elevation in a mountain range is a tangible accomplishment

eating lunch by a bubbling stream, hiking through a forest and popping out on a promontory for a fabulous view. At day's end, the helicopter picks you up and returns you to the lodge for a hot bath, dinner, and drinks around the fire with your new friends.

Guests are divided into groups by hiking experience and the amount of energy and effort they'd like to expend on their holiday. I was placed in the A-group, categorized as "a person who is very active and enjoys strenuous, fast-paced hiking." In practice, our group did cover a good bit of ground, but we didn't try to break any speed records. And the other groups who took it easier, hikers who were merely meandering or perhaps more interested in learning about the local wonders of nature than reaching the top of a peak, had an equally terrific time.

Weather in the Bugaboos is constantly changing and the CMH crew is always getting the latest radio and internet updates. In just three days, I experienced rain, hail, wind, calm and bright sunshine. And the weather can change several times in the course of a day, too. We wore wind pants and parkas, shorts and short-sleeves and everything in between, a kind of hiking textbook demonstration of the principle of layering.

Bugaoo hikes range from 6,000 to 9,000 feet in elevation, which means thin air, but not so high to leave your breathing challenged. Compared to other ranges such as the Rockies or High Sierra, the Bugaboos are lower in elevation, but because they're at high latitude, the range features the kind of glacier sculpted scenery found in loftier areas. I liked that the hiking was mostly off-trail, which definitely contributed to a deeper appreciation of the mountains and to a greater sense of adventure.

While hiking the Bugaboos, I puzzled over the issue of the environmental impacts of helicopters used anywhere in the wild, and pressed all the guides on the issue. My thoughts: Copters are undoubtedly an intrusion in the wilderness, but thankfully a very brief one. Short of beaming up the mountain like a Star Trek character, I don't know how a hiker could travel from ridge to ridge any faster. As long as they're used as trailhead machines to hop from one area to another in the most concisely routed manner possible and not used as touring machines, as long as required environmental restrictions (such as no over-flying mountain goat habitat) are observed, the craft get a qualified OK from me.

My hiking group begins our final hike with a saunter through an alpine garden bedecked in western anemone, buttercup, columbine and yellow glacier lily. After a short helicopter lift, we hike to a ridgetop, where no heli-hikers had been in several seasons by the name of… No, I'm not going to tell you, because this is a land of a hundred knife-edge ridges and a thousand fabulous vistas awaiting your discovery.

Near the end of the day our guide radios Bugaboo Lodge with a request: "Let's reschedule Alice's 5 o'clock massage for later in the evening. And hold the copter. We're having too much fun out here to come in right now."

and an ideal way to go for the goal-oriented individual. Some are critical of such individuals who are "working on" checking peaks off a list and say this compulsion is anathema to the pure joy of hiking.

Some of my best friends are compulsive peak-baggers, afflicted by incurable summit fever. If hiking by a list helps people hit the trail, I'm all for it. There isn't just one school of hiking philosophy; whether you choose walks in the woods or a compilation of peaks is okay by me.

Colorado's collection of 54 "Fourteeners" (summits over 14,000 feet in elevation) are America's most famous peaks to bag, while Switzerland's list of Alps over 4,000 meters high is the goal for European hikers. In Scotland, ambitious hikers try to climb all 284 peaks in the Munros on the Scottish Mountaineering Club's list.

American hikers can pursue lesser-known, even obscure, peak lists from coast to coast. The AMC's New Hampshire 4,000-Footer List includes 48 peaks to bag. In Southern California, Sierra Club members can join the Hundred Peaks Section by scaling 100 of the 278 Southland summits higher than 5,000 feet. If that's too much, hikers can choose from a Lower Peaks list.

Get a lift from a Ski Lift

American ski resorts have been very slow to learn from the Swiss, who transform their winter wonderland into a hiker's paradise by operating all the country's gondolas and funiculars during the summer months. However, some resorts, from world-class to funky, are getting the message. Whistler, often ranked as the number one ski resort in North America, encourages summer hikers to ride the Blackcomb or Whistler Mountain ski lifts to several trailheads.

Ski resorts that operate lifts during the summer (usually on a limited basis) can give the hiker a great head-start into the mountains and make possible some excellent one-way (sometimes all-downhill) hiking adventures or give nearly instant access to backcountry that would ordinarily require a half-day or a day to reach.

Rails to Trails: Take a Hike on the Reading!

An abandoned rail line has big-time trail potential: an already existing right-of-way, a usually very well engineered route, a de-facto conservation corridor. Add the advantages of cultural and historical preservation and the contribution to physical fitness a rail converted to a trail makes, and the future seems bright for thousands of miles of disused railway to be put to good use.

Founded in 1986, The Rails-to-Trails Conservancy (RTC) aims to enrich America's communities and countryside with the conversion of abandoned private rail lines into public recreation trails. The Washington D.C.-based group envisions a nationwide network of public trails from former rail lines.

As The Rails-to-Trails Conservancy tells it, the rail-trail movement began in the Midwest during the 1960s as railroad companies, big and small, in response to competition from the trucking industry, began pulling up tracks. Curious history buffs and the odd recreational walker began exploring these abandoned lines.

A lot of people began asking the same question at the same time: Why not convert these rail lines to recreation paths? Some of these railway corridors were paved for walkways/bicycle paths while others were graded and left with a natural surface.

Every time I walk a rail-trail I enjoy it and I wonder why someone didn't think of the notion earlier. With some exceptions, I've found many of the trails are best suited for bicycling, though walkers in urban areas certainly make good use of them.

I like to integrate a rail-trail into my travel plans. The 25-mile long Cape Cod Rail Trail is an excellent connection to the beaches and resort towns of the Cape and the 18-mile long Mt. Vernon Trail that extends along the Potomac River to George Washington's estate offers a healthful way to absorb American history.

Thanks to the leadership of the Rails-to-Trails Conservancy and countless local governments and park agencies that know a good thing when they see it, America's trail system boasts more than 12,000 miles of rail-trail used by more than 100 million happy hikers, walkers and cyclists per year.

Hike a Millennium Legacy Trail

At the turn of the twenty-first century, the governors of each of the fifty states, nominated a Millennium Legacy Trail, one that reflected the essence and spirit of their particular state. Millennium Legacy Trails are representative of the diversity of trails: rail-trails, greenways, historic trails, cultural interpretation routes, recreation paths, and many other types of trails.

As First Lady Hillary Rodham Clinton said when she announced these trails in 1999, "Each of them stitch a design in our landscape and together help to create a picture of America."

America's Millennium Legacy Trails

Alabama:	Pinhoti National Recreation Trail
Alaska:	Chilkoot Trail
Arizona:	Arizona Trail
Arkansas:	Trail of Tears Routes
California:	California Coastal Trail
Colorado:	America the Beautiful Trail
Connecticut:	Connecticut Impressionist Art Trail
Delaware:	The Coastal Heritage Greenway
District of Columbia:	Metropolitan Branch Trail
Florida:	Florida National Scenic Trail
Georgia:	Coastal Georgia Greenway
Hawaii:	The Hana Highway
Idaho:	North Idaho Centennial Trail

Illinois:	I&M Canal Trail
Indiana:	Monon Rail-Trail Corridor
Iowa:	American Discovery Trail: Iowa Route
Kansas:	Kanopolis State Park Multi-use Trails
Kentucky:	Pine Mountain Trail
Louisiana:	The Tammany Trace
Maine:	Acadia National Park Trail
Maryland:	BWI Trail/Baltimore & Annapolis Trail/ Colonial Annapolis Maritime Trail
Massachusetts:	Norwottuck Network
Michigan:	Southeast Michigan Greenways Trail
Minnesota:	Willard Munger State Trail
Mississippi:	Mississippi Delta Blues Trail
Missouri:	The Katy Trail
Montana:	Route of the Hiawatha Rail-Trail
Nebraska:	The Cowboy Recreation and Nature Trail
Nevada:	Tahoe Rim Trail
New Hampshire:	Franconia Notch State Park Recreation Trail
New Jersey:	Highlands Trail
New Mexico:	El Camino Real de Tierra Adentro (The Royal Road of the Interior)
North Carolina:	Blue Ridge Heritage Trail
North Dakota:	Bismarck/Mandan Missouri Valley Trail
Ohio:	The Buckeye Trail
Oklahoma:	Standing Bear Native American Memorial Park & Trail
Oregon:	Historic Columbia River Highway State Trail
Pennsylvania:	Pittsburgh to Harrisburg Greenway
Rhode Island:	Rhode Island Statewide Greenway System
South Carolina:	The Palmetto Trail
South Dakota:	George S. Mickelson Trail
Tennessee:	Cumberland Trail State Park
Utah:	Bonneville Shoreline Trail
Vermont:	Lake Champlain Bikeways
Virginia:	New River Trail State Park
Washington:	John Wayne Pioneer Trail
West Virginia:	Greenbrier River Trail
Wisconsin:	Hank Aaron State Trail
Wyoming:	Wyoming Continental Divide Snowmobile Trail

•

Puerto Rico:	The Rio Camuy Cave Park
Virgin Islands:	St. Croix Heritage Trail

Pioneering a Millennium Trail

Years ago, I helped pioneer what turned out to be California's official Millennium Trail, the California Coastal Trail. I wrote a book about my experience entitled, *A Walk Along Land's End, Discovering the Living California Coast.* Here are my thoughts on the day I began my long hike up the California Coast from the Mexican border to Oregon.

The California Coastline is mountains and rivers and deltas and estuaries, rocky shore and sandy beach, coral bottom and mud bottom, blue, green and red tides, plankton and gray whales, clear waters and muddy waters, pillars and stacks and blowholes, pickleweed and salt grass, palms and redwoods, all the different kinds of trees and shrubs and all the kinds of cockles and mussels and limpets that people have named and not yet named on its ever-changing shore, a thousand different yet interconnected things at the end of one continent and the beginning of another.

And I've got a job to do on this coastline—at least that's what I'm thinking about during the predawn hours of my first day on the trail. It's my job to pioneer a trail along land's end, to connect California's remaining coastal wildlands to each other and those walkers willing to make an effort to visit them. I must select the best combination of cow trails, horse trails and people trails, ranch roads, fire roads, logging roads and mining roads. I must avoid, as much as possible, towns, cities, military bases, nuclear power plants, and marijuana growers who shoot at hikers. I must figure out a route for the new California Coastal Trail so that hikers less experienced than I can follow in my footsteps.

National Millennium Trails

In 1999, sixteen National Millennium Trails were designated that reflect defining aspects America's history and culture. The selected trails are intended to tell the story of the nation's past, as well as create a positive vision of the future.

National Millennium Trails include: The North Country National Scenic Trail, The Unicoi Turnpike, American Discovery Trail, Appalachian National Scenic Trail, Civil War Discovery Trail, Hatfield-McCoy Recreation Area, Iditarod National Historic Trail, The Cascadia Marine Trail, The East Coast Greenway, The Freedom Trail, The Great Western Trail, The International Express, The Juan Bautista de Anza National Historic Trail, The Lewis And Clark National Historic Trail, The Mississippi River Trail and The Underground Railroad.

Ten Most Popular National Parks

These parks don't always score in the same order, but are perennially the most popular

1. Great Smoky
2. Grand Canyon
3. Olympic
4. Yosemite
5. Rocky Mountain
6. Yellowstone
7. Acadia
8. Grand Teton
9. Zion
10. Mammoth Caves

Ten Less-Visited National Parks

1. Big Bend
2. Canyonlands
3. Capitol Reef
4. Channel Islands
5. Great Basin
6. Isle Royale
7. Lassen Volcanic
8. Mojave
9. Redwood
10. Shenandoah

National Park Trails

In my judgment, the state of the nation's national park trail system is quite good. Trailhead parking, interpretive panels and displays, as well as signage are generally excellent. Backcountry junctions are usually signed and trail conditions generally range from good to excellent.

Of course parks are not static ecosystems and are subject to natural and not-so-natural disasters that may affect trails. In recent years, wildfires have scorched Yellowstone, floods inundated Yosemite Valley, and record snowfalls buried Lassen. Such natural phenomena inevitably damage trails.

The various trail systems evolved on a park-by-park basis and it's difficult to speak in generalities about their respective origins. A good deal of Yosemite's trail system was in place before the early horseless carriages chugged into the park. Newer parks, such as Channel Islands National Park, will be building trails well into the twenty-first century.

Many national parks were aided greatly by the Depression-era Civilian Conservation Corps of the 1930s. Older parks have hand-built trails that are true gems, highlighted by stonework and bridges that would no doubt be prohibitively expensive to construct today. Today volunteer groups help park staff build and maintain trails.

The trail system in national parklands shares many characteristics in common with pathways overseen by other governmental bodies. Often a hiker will notice no profound differences in pathways when, for example, traveling from a national park into a national forest or into a state or regional park.

While sharing similarities with trails in other jurisdictions, national parkland trails nevertheless have unique qualities, too, that distinguish them from pathways elsewhere. One major difference between national parks and, for example, many state parks, is the amount of land preserved as wilderness. Denali, Gates of the Arctic, Glacier Bay and Wrangell St. Elias National Parks encompass some 21 million acres of designated wilderness in Alaska. A majority of such desert national parks as Death Valley and Joshua Tree are wilderness. Wilderness comprises some 94 percent of Yosemite National Park.

On national park maps you'll find such wilderness areas delineated as simply "Wilderness." Unlike the Forest Service, the Bureau of Land Management and other wilderness stewards, the National Park Service does not name its wilderness areas.

Wilderness designation is more than a name for a wild or pristine area. By law, a wilderness is restricted to non-motorized entry—that is to say, equestrian and foot travel. Hikers do not have to share the trails with snowmobiles or mountain bikes in national park wilderness.

Other national park service wilderness regulations are designed to protect resources and ensure visitor safety. Review these wilderness regulations before hitting the trail.

The hikers you meet on a national park trail may be different from the company you keep on trails near home. National parks attract visitors from across the nation and around the world. I've hiked with Japanese visitors across Death Valley's sand dunes, with German visitors in the Olympic rain forest, with New Zealanders in the Rockies, with a French couple to the top of Lassen Peak, with Brazilians in the Everglades. Once I counted ten different languages on a popular nature trail in Muir Woods National Monument. Not surprisingly, the park service has printed selected brochures in French, German, Spanish, Japanese and Chinese.

Because of the park's attraction to visitors worldwide, the park service uses lots of international symbols on its signage, and the metric system as well. This international orientation explains why the national park service seems to be about the only American institution, outside of scientific and medical circles of course, still promoting the metric system.

National Lands

Everyone knows of the nation's crown jewels—America's national parks. Few realize that America boasts a dozen more kinds of national lands, most of which allow, in fact, encourage, hiking.

Check out the web sites for these national lands and national pathways. You'll discover a lot of happy—and possibly not-so-well-known trails.

- **National Conservation Area** Similar to National Monument status; applies solely to BLM lands. Granted only by Congress. Individual site determines allowable recreational activities.
- **National Forest or Grassland** Land managed by the U.S. Department of Agriculture, and may allow a wide variety of activities including logging, mining, and oil and gas drilling, as well as trail activities, hunting, fishing, snowmobiling, and OHV use.
- **National Historic Trail (NHT)** Federally designated extended trails, which closely follow original routes of nationally significant travel (explorers, emigrants, traders, military, etc.). NHTs do not have to be continuous, can be less than 100 miles in length, and can include land and water segments. The Iditarod, the Lewis and Clark, the Mormon Pioneer, and the Oregon trails were the first to be designated as NHTs in 1978.
- **National Monument** Federal areas of unique ecological, geological, historic, prehistoric, cultural, or scientific interest. Traditionally used for historic structures or landmarks on government land; more recently used to grant national park-like status to tracts of western land. Designated by Congress or the president. Individual site determines allowable recreational activities.
- **National Park** Managed by the National Park Service primarily to protect resources and recreation opportunities. Some allow grazing, but do not allow hunting, mining, or other extractive uses.

State High Points

State	Peak	Height	Roundtrip Hiking Mileage
Alabama	Cheaha Mountain	2,407	0
Alaska	Mount McKinley	20,320	46
Arizona	Humphreys Peak	12,633	9
Arkansas	Mount Magazine (Signal Hill)	2,753	1
California	Mount Whitney	14,494	21.4
Colorado	Mount Elbert	14,433	9
Connecticut	Frissell-S. Slope	2,380	3.6
Delaware	Ebright Azimuth	448	0
Florida	Lakewood (Britton Hill)	345	0
Georgia	Brasstown Bald	4,784	1
Hawaii	Mauna Kea	13,796	0.4
Idaho	Borah Peak	12,662	6.8
Illinois	Charles Mound	1,235	0.4
Indiana	Hoosier Hill	1,257	0.1
Iowa	Hawkeye Point	1,670	0.1
Kansas	Mount Sunflower	4,039	0
Kentucky	Black Mountain	4,145	0.1
Louisiana	Driskill Mountain	535	1.8
Maine	Katahdin (Baxter Peak)	5,267	10.4
Maryland	Backbone Mountain	3360	2.2
Massachusetts	Greylock	3491	0.1
Michigan	Mount Arvon	1,979	2
Minnesota	Eagle Mountain	2,301	7
Mississippi	Woodall Mountain	806	0
Missouri	Taum Sauk	1,772	0.4

- **National Preserve** Often linked with a national park. Allows mineral and fuel extraction, hunting.
- **National Recreation Area** Federal areas that have outstanding combinations of outdoor recreation opportunities, aesthetic attractions, and proximity to potential users. They may also have cultural, historical, archaeological, pastoral, wilderness, scientific, wildlife, and other values contributing to public enjoyment. Designated by Congress. Individual location determines allowable recreational activities.
- **National Recreation Trail (NRT)** Existing trails that provide a variety of outdoor recreation uses in or reasonably accessible to urban areas (over 800) recognized by the federal government (Secretary of Interior or Secretary of Agriculture, not Congressional action) as contributing to the National Trails System.
- **National Resource Land** Managed for grazing and extraction by the Bureau of Land Management (BLM); often unnamed. Allows all recreational activities.

50 Peak Experiences

State	Peak	Height	Roundtrip Hiking Mileage
Montana	Granite Peak	12,799	22.2
Nebraska	Panorama Point	5,424	0
Nevada	Boundary Peak	13,143	7.4
New Hampshire	Mount Washington	6,288	0.1
New Jersey	High Point	1,803	0.2
New Mexico	Wheeler Peak	13,161	6.2
New York	Mount Marcy	5344	14.8
North Carolina	Mount Mitchell	6684	0.2
North Dakota	White Butte	3,506	2
Ohio	Campbell Hill	1,550	0
Oklahoma	Black Mesa	4,973	8.6
Oregon	Mount Hood	11,239	8
Pennsylvania	Mount Davis	3,213	0
Rhode Island	Jerimoth Hill	812	0.6
South Carolina	Sassafras Mountain	3,560	0.2
South Dakota	Harney Peak	7,242	5.8
Tennessee	Clingmans Dome	6,643	1
Texas	Guadalupe Peak	8,749	8.4
Utah	Kings Peak	13528	28.8
Vermont	Mount Mansfield	4393	2.8
Virginia	Mount Rogers	5,729	8.6
Washington	Mount Rainier	14,411	16
West Virginia	Spruce Knob	4,863	0.4
Wisconsin	Timms Hill	1,951	0.4
Wyoming	Gannett Peak	13,804	40.4

- **National Scenic Area** Area that contains outstanding scenic characteristics, recreational values, and geological, ecological, and cultural resources.
- **National Scenic Trail (NST)** Federally designated extended trails (over 100 miles in length), which provide for the maximum outdoor recreation potential and for the conservation and enjoyment of the significant scenic, historic, natural, or cultural qualities of the areas through which they pass. The Appalachian and the Pacific Crest trails were the first to be designated as National Scenic Trails in 1968.
- **National Seashore** Coastal equivalent of a national park. Some allow hunting. National Trails System: A network of trails (National Scenic, Historic, or Recreation) throughout the country authorized by the 1968 National Trails System Act.
- **National Wildlife Refuge** Preserves wildlife habitat. Allows hunting and fishing; some allow overnight camping.

Hiking the Holy Mountain

I AWAKE from a fitful sleep, dress, lace up my hiking boots and step into a gray dawn, into the same dim light that was inside St. Ann's.

From the dew-dampened courtyard of the monastery, I look toward the Holy Mountain—or, at least where the Holy Mountain should be, for it is not yet illuminated by the light of the new day. It might be visible if I was observing it from the other side of the peninsula. Just about now, the daystar should be beaming its first rays at the outposts of eastern Orthodoxy on the other side of Mt. Athos, then sending its light traveling from the coast to the summit of the mountain.

We'll be coming 'round the Holy Mountain from opposite the morning sun, from what is now the dark side of the mountain. Theoretically, this side and our trail will be the last to get light, and hold it the longest; in the event our return to St. Ann's is delayed, we'll be hiking with the last light of the day.

I don't want to set out until we can clearly see the trail, so I'll let Spiro sleep a bit longer before I rouse him. By my calculations, we should have plenty of daylight for the climb.

Bend at the waist. Reach slowly to the toes of my hiking boots. Hold for 20 seconds. My normal pre-hike ritual consists of three parts: stretching, visualizing the hike to come, and drinking coffee.

Such is the pleasure of my long-practiced ritual that for an instant, I imagine that I really smell coffee. Truly, the thin rations and lack of sleep during my week in the monastic kingdom of Mt. Athos have only been minor deprivation. But even a day without my friend Caffeine is unbearable.

As I push my palms against the courtyard wall and stretch my legs, I conjure the Holy Mountain as depicted on the map I purchased earlier in the week in a Karvyes souvenir store. So far, at least for traveling coastal trails to St. Anne's, the Austrian-made topographic map has proven to be reliable.

The ancient shopkeeper who sold me the Athos-Kartenskizze would not vouch for the map's accuracy.

"Is it a good map?" I inquire.

He shrugs, blows the dust off the remaining half-dozen or so maps in his inventory. "Depends on where you're going."

"I'm climbing the Holy Mountain."

"I don't know anyone who's climbed the Holy Mountain with this map."

"The roads . . . footpaths . . . it's a good map?"

"Most men who come here. They go to one monastery. They know where they're going. They don't need a map. Why do you need a map?"

The customer is always right. Have you ever heard the expression? "I need to find the way to the Holy Mountain."

He points out the south window of his shop. "The Holy Mountain is right there."

I must be losing something in translation, I think, as I place the map and two packages of Greek cookies on the counter. Seems to me anybody who hikes around without a map, without knowing where they are going, is a fool. Me, I want to study the terrain and know exactly where I'm going.

That's why I like maps. With a good map and my good sense of direction, I can find my way most anywhere.

According to the map, the first few miles of the trail from the monastery of St. Ann to the Holy Mountain are a mellow contour around the southwest slope of the mountain. Then it gets challenging: a very steep northward ascent. The contour lines on the map are in increments of 100 meters and the trail crosses a whole bunch of them in a very short distance.

Standing on one leg, I pull the other up toward my butt. I face east, watching the upper ramparts of the Holy Mountain emerge in faint silhouette.

"Good morning, Yannis. Would you like some coffee?"

I turn around to see the old monk, who beckons me inside the monastery's kitchen.

Coffee. Proof positive there is a God.

Make a Pilgrimage

For thousands of years, the notion of a pilgrimage—a purposeful journey to a sacred center—has beckoned the spiritually oriented walker. Today, hikers venture to spiritually-compelling places around the world, from New Mexico to Tibet, Israel to India.

Pilgrims journey to Ireland make a *tura*, or circuit of holy wells and gravesites of Celtic saints. Hikers trek to Mayan sites in Mexico and in Japan follow in the footsteps of the great seventeenth-century poet-pilgrim Matsuo Basho.

One well-defined modern pilgrimage is along the Camino de Santiago in Spain. Since medieval times, pilgrims have journeyed to the legendary shrine of St. James the Apostle at Santiago de Compostela, located on Spain's northern coast. Some seekers hoped that the Saint, known as a miracle-worker, would heal them while others believed in the transformational power of a challenging walk and constant prayer.

Departing pilgrims from all over Europe first received the blessing of their local priest, then assembled the traditional apparel: a wide-brimmed hat, "official" scallop shell pilgrimage badge, a backpack called a scrip, and a walking stick.

Many a writer has chronicled the Camino, beginning with the twelfth-century guidebook, *The Pilgrim's Guide.* Actress Shirley MacLaine wrote *The Camino: A Journey of the Spirit*, a book that recounts her walk and a whole lot more—including intimate encounters with her soul-mate Charlemagne and visits to the lost city of Atlantis. Many readers were completely baffled at MacLaine's New Age ventures far off the trail, but we can thank the peripatetic entertainer for putting the spotlight on the Camino and celebrating the value of a pilgrimage.

Certainly the Camino can be enjoyed simply as a terrific hike through lovely countryside, with fine meals and lodging, and close-up views of a remarkable array of architectural and cultural treasures. Ah, but The Way of St. James has a way of inspiring and illuminating today's traveler, and transforming a hike into a pilgrimage.

Traveling to defined Buddhist, Hindu, Islamic or Christian holy sites can indeed be a pilgrimage. However, it's the journey, not the destination, that makes a pilgrimage. A hike, solo or in the company of fellow seekers, offers a chance to reflect, an opportunity to gather spiritual wisdom. For the traveler intrigued by the notion of hiking in a beautiful place while simultaneously journeying inward, a pilgrimage is a special walk indeed.

Hike a National Wildlife Refuge

The National Wildlife Refuge System began in 1903 when President Theodore Roosevelt, one of our nation's most creative conservationists, came up with the then-novel notion of setting aside federal lands as wildlife habitat.

> *"Give me my Scallop shell of quiet.*
> *My staff of Faith to walk upon*
> *My Scrip of Joy, Immortal diet*
> *My bottle of Salvation:*
> *My Gown of Glory, hopes true gage,*
> *And thus I'll take my pilgrimage."*
> —SIR WALTER RALEIGH

Roosevelt was galvanized into action by the desperate plight of the birds on Florida's Pelican Island. Hunters were slaying the island's birds just for their ornate feathers, then popular in women's hats. Roosevelt declared Pelican Island to be a wildlife refuge on March 14, 1903.

America's National Wildlife Refuge System now encompasses more than 500 refuges and totals nearly 100 million acres. Administered by the U.S. Fish & Wildlife Service, these refuges protect creatures ranging from the whooping crane to the Arctic caribou and can be found in every state and nearly every major metropolitan area.

The best way to appreciate the nation's wildlife refuges is to actually get out and visit one. Refuges abound with opportunities for bird-watchers, hikers, anglers, nature photographers and yes, hunters (at some refuges) to get close-up views of wildlife.

During winter, visit wildlife refuges in the warmer regions of the nation. It's a great time to take a hike through a wildlife refuge when the temperature is down and the bird count is way up.

Hike a National Historic Trail

You need to drive a lot, hike a little and use your imagination often when you explore the country's National Historic Trails. Imagine breaking trail where no one had mapped or trekked before. Imagine leaving home and family behind and following a sketchy trail to what someone promised was the promised land.

National Historic Trails honor routes of national historic significance. The National Park Service program started designating these trails in 1968, about a decade after beginning the National Scenic Trails System.

While many people follow National Historic Trails by auto, numerous sections lend themselves to exploration by boating, cycling or hiking. Historic Trails travel through cities and wilderness, past bird sanctuaries and shopping malls. Two of my favorite historic trails are the Lewis and Clark and the Juan Bautista de Anza.

Most of the Lewis and Clark NHT, at 3,700 miles the second longest in the system, follows the Missouri and Columbia Rivers. It begins in Illinois and passes through portions of Missouri, Kansas, Iowa Nebraska, South Dakota, North Dakota, Montana, Idaho, Oregon and Washington. Phew!

At President Jefferson's request, those intrepid explorers Meriwether Lewis and William Clark and their Corps of Discovery explored the West—mapping the territory, recording the flora and fauna, meeting the indigenous peoples. Not surprising is how much the land has changed since Lewis and Clark headed west in 1804. What is surprising is how many places still resemble the wilderness that greeted the Corps of discovery 200 years ago.

I particularly enjoyed retracing the explorers' route through Oregon, along the Columbia Rive and over to the Oregon Coast.

Apparently, though, hiking the coast is easier now than it was when Captain Clark wrote: "Sea looked wild, breaking with great force against the scattering rocks and rugged points under which we were obliged to pass and, if we had unfortunately made one false step, we should inevitably have fallen into the sea and dashed against the rocks in an instant. . . ."

Still, Clark later warmed up to the scenery, when he reached a promontory (that would later be named in his honor), savored the view and proclaimed it "the grandest and most pleasing prospect which my eyes ever surveyed."

Juan Bautista de Anza got his marching orders from a completely different country than William Clark. Just about the same time American colonists began battling British soldiers at Bunker Hill, Concord and other East Coast locales, the Spanish sought to establish control over the Pacific Coast of what is today's United States. The Viceroy of New Spain assigned Captain De Anza to press Spain's claim to the New World.

The De Anza Trail was the route of the Juan Bautista de Anza Expedition of 1775-6, which brought 200 colonists from Mexico across the Colorado Desert and up the coast to found the city of San Francisco. Historically, the Anza Trail is much better documented than the Lewis and Clark or other trails that opened up the west. This is due to the meticulous diary-keeping of Anza and the expedition's chaplain, Father Font.

For the most part, the historic trail, today followed closely by paved highways, is an auto route with many interpretive displays along the way. Nevertheless, numerous hiking opportunities beckon the sojourner afoot along the trail in Mexico, Arizona and California.

National Historic Trails

- Lewis and Clark (1978)
- Mormon Pioneer (1978)
- Iditarod (1978)
- Oregon (1978)
- Overmountain Victory (1980)
- Nez Perce (Nee-Me-Poo)(1986)
- Trail of Tears (1987)
- Santa Fe (1987)
- Juan Bautista de Anza (1990)
- Pony Express (1992)
- California (1992)
- Selma to Montgomery (1996)
- El Camino Real de Tierra Adentro (2000)
- Ala Kahakai (2000)
- Old Spanish (2002)

Hike a Desert Park

Many travelers drive along America's coast or through the country's forests and mountains and feel inspired by the scenery. A drive through the desert, however, rarely provides similar inspiration. Many motorists consider the desert too flat, too barren, and too unaccommodating to inspire.

The desert demands a closer look. To fully appreciate the desert's beauty requires the visitor to slow down and take a hike: along a nature trail looping around a park campground, down a rocky canyon to a palm oasis, up a rugged mountain to a craggy peak. Without a doubt, the desert is most seductive—and challenging—when approached on foot.

But the desert, first in the hearts of the many who love it, was the last of the America's regions to be preserved. Early conservationists worked to preserve America's glorious mountains and forests first; next came the seashores and coastal ranges. And finally, came the desert.

The desert's recreation potential followed a similar pattern. First Americans took to the mountains, then to the coast, lastly to the desert. At the beginning of the twentieth century, resorts were built and recreation of all sorts took place in the country's alpine and coastal regions, but only a few hardy prospectors roamed the desert.

It wasn't until the 1920s and the development of (somewhat) dependable autos that Americans began discovering the desert. During that decade, there was a worldwide fascination with the desert, prompted in part by exploration of the ancient Egyptian pyramids and a fascination with Egyptology.

Horace Albright, a founding father of the National Park Service, was instrumental in the creation of Death Valley National Monument. In 1913, Albright interrupted his study of mining law at the University of California to take a job in Washington as confidential clerk to the Secretary of the Interior. He soon teamed with wealthy borax industry executive Stephen Mather to establish the National Park Service, serving as superintendent of Yellowstone National Park and as Mather's field representative. For two decades, Albright explored and evaluated dozens of potential parks and historical sites.

"Death Valley National Park was in many ways a tough sell," Horace Albright told me in a 1976 interview. After all, he explained, in the early 1930s, the general public—and most members of Congress—regarded the desert in general, and Death Valley in particular, as a trackless wasteland. And then President Herbert Hoover came from a mining background, and often tilted more toward industry than scenery.

Albright, who became National Park Service director in 1930, helped convince Hoover to sign an executive order to withdraw two million acres of the Death Valley region for inclusion in a national park or monument. Although Albright pushed for park status, Congress approved the designation of Death Valley National Monument in 1933. Not only did this legislation protect a vast and wondrous land, it helped to transform one of the earth's least hospitable spots into a popular tourist destination

Like a proud father with many children, Albright declined to name a favorite park, but he confessed that Death Valley had always occupied a special place in his heart. His upbringing in the nearby town of Bishop, his interest in mining, and his major role in the park's creation, all contributed to his love of the valley. When I asked him what was it about Death Valley that attracted him, he adjusted his hat, pulled on his string tie, and said suddenly: "The rocks. You can see almost the whole history of the earth in those rocks."

During the 1940s and 50s, the military became a major presence in the American desert. What the military viewed as worthless terrain was used for desert warfare training exercises, bombing and gunnery practice, and weapons testing. These military maneuvers and activities continue today.

Public perception of the desert completely changed over the years. Land that had previously been considered hideously devoid of life was now celebrated for its spare beauty; places that had once been feared for their harshness were now admired for their uniqueness.

Today many threats are massed at the boundaries of desert parks in California, Nevada, Arizona, Utah, and New Mexico. Millions of tourist dollars are spent in and around "gateway" towns located at desert park borders. No wonder area business owners and local politicos have begun to see that it is in their enlightened self interest to preserve the beauty and tranquility of these parks.

Even if certain Congress members and Chamber of Commerce members still cannot hear the silent symphony of the desert or appreciate the beauty of its composition, perhaps they will at least listen when money talks and cash registers ring. Our desert parks must be staunchly defended and legally protected so that politicos and developers, deaf to the desert's music and blind to its beauty, keep their hands off our public lands.

One of my favorite places to hike is Death Valley, the largest national park outside Alaska, which preserves more than 3.3 million acres of this Great Basin desert. One place to take in the enormity of the park is from the crest of the Black Mountains at Dante's View or Coffin Peak. A never-to-be-forgotten panorama unfolds. A vertical mile down lies Badwater, the lowest spot on the continent. Across the valley rises Telescope Peak and the snow-clad summits of the Panamints. Farther still, on the western horizon, loom the granite ramparts of the Sierra Nevada. North and south of Dante's View rise the Funeral Mountains. Fitting, eerie names for an otherworldly place.

Many of Death Valley's topographical features are associated with hellish images—Funeral Mountains, Furnace Creek, Dante's

View, Coffin Peak and Devil's Golf Course—but the national park can be a place of great serenity for the hiker.

Mountains stand naked, unadorned, the bitter waters of saline lakes evaporate into bizarre, razor-sharp crystal formations; jagged canyons jab deep into the earth. Oven-like heat, frigid cold and the driest air imaginable combine to make this one of the most forbidding spots in the world.

Badwater, the lowest point in the Western Hemisphere at 282 feet below sea level, is also one of the hottest places in the world, with regularly recorded summer temperatures of 120 degrees F.

Perhaps you'll want to begin your desert hiking adventures with trails in the Utah National Parks—Arches, Canyonlands, Capitol Reef, Bryce and Zion—or in the California national parklands, including Death Valley, Joshua Tree and Mojave National Preserve. But don't stop there! The Great American Desert includes millions of acres in the care of the U.S. Bureau of Land Management. Dozens of BLM locales are now managed as wilderness areas and offer breathtaking adventure way off the tourist track.

Hike a Coastal Trail

Take a coastal hike—around precious wetlands, through wind-bowed forests, along precipitous bluffs, across white sand beaches, around bays, across islands, to lighthouses…

The continent's mountain trails are far better known than its coastal trails—an oversight I work hard to correct. My pioneering of the California Coastal Trail has led to a fascination, perhaps even an obsession, with other coastal trails around North America. Here are eight great ones, my North American favorites, from East to West:

Cape Chignecto Coastal Trail I'm going out on a red-spruce limb to make a prediction: Once the good word gets out to European and American hikers, Nova Scotia's Cape Chignecto will become an international attraction, because hikers here find one of eastern Canada's most compelling lengths of shoreline.

Cape Chignecto beckons hikes with stands of red spruce and yellow birch. The trees stand at the edge of 600-foot cliffs looking down at tides that rise as much as 70 feet—the world's highest—in the Bay of Fundy. Peregrine falcons swoop overhead, and moose and white-tailed deer browse the lush vegetation of the bluff tops.

The 30-mile Cape Chignecto Coastal Trail is ideal for backpacking expeditions of at least three days. Half a dozen hike-in camps with enticing names such as Stoney Beach, Big Bald Rock Brooks and Seal Cove are half a day's walk apart along the trail. The path also has many day-hiking opportunities.

Acadia National Park New England's only national park, preserves the best of the coast forever. Cadillac Mountain towers 1,530 feet above the surf, making it the highest point on the East Coast.

Acadia's mountains are geographically positioned to be among the first in America to greet the rising sun. Somes Sound, said by the imaginative to cut Mt. Desert Island into the shape of a lobster claw, is the U.S. East Coast's only true fjord.

As an East Coast hiking destination, Acadia National Park is matchless. More than 120 miles of hiking trail ascend every hill, cross every dale. Connecting trails allow the energetic hiker, good map in hand, to reach the summits of several Acadia peaks in a day's walk. The park offers an entire summer's worth of sojourns: beach walks, harbor meanderings, pondside paths, interpreted nature trails, and steep summit ascents that require climbing ladders and iron rungs. Paths range in difficulty from easy walks in the woods to traverses across bare granite, the route marked with paint blazes and cairns.

New Hampshire Coastal Trail Dear hiker, if I proposed that you hike from Massachusetts to Maine, would you think me mad? And, if I suggested that you make this journey in one day, would you consider me madder still?

Crazy or not, the fact is this coast walk is do-able in a day. Between the lengthy coastlines of Massachusetts and Maine lies New Hampshire's 18-mile long coast, the shortest shoreline of any state that borders salt water. You could explore this coast by car in a half-hour or spend a week at one of Hampton Beach's oceanfront hotels, but I propose that you walk the coast in a single day.

You'll walk sandy beach, rocky shore, boardwalk, sidewalk, and along the shoulder of Route 1A as you journey past a half-dozen state parks and beaches. You certainly won't starve along the way. Eateries en route offer espresso, pizza, fried dough, lobster rolls—much more than the average stomach can handle.

Henry David Thoreau's Cape Cod It's as east as the East Coast gets. Cape Cod thrusts farther out into the Atlantic Ocean than any other part of America. "A man may stand there and put all America behind him," wrote Henry David Thoreau in his classic book, *Cape Cod*, published in 1865.

For the hiker, there is much to explore on what is often described as the bent elbow of Massachusetts. Cape Cod National Seashore has a diversity of terrain including cliffs, sand dunes, native pitch pine woodlands and a 40-mile stretch of shoreline know as "The Great Beach."

Thoreau-loving hikers sometimes retrace part of the great naturalist's classic hike up Cape Cod. The pilgrimage of choice is usually a 30-mile jaunt from Chatham to Provincetown. Carry a paperback copy of *Cape Cod* on this great American walk and enjoy a rhapsodic book as well as joyous beachcombing.

Santa Rosa Island Imagine a lovely island where you can hike into dramatic canyons, through quiet pine groves, and along pristine beaches. If you're thinking you need to travel through several time zones to find a rarely visited island with terrific hiking trails, think again. Because Santa Rosa Island in Channel Islands National Park, is just a short flight or modest boat ride away from the mainland.

Hikers can traverse an isle of unique flora and fauna—"America's Galapagos" with an extensive archeological record that includes "Arlington Woman," believed to be the oldest human remains ever found in North America.

Old ranch roads form the nucleus of great trail system. Currently, the National Park Service is designing a splendidly scenic 50-mile coastal trail that will circle Santa Rosa and will enable hikers to visit all the island's highlights and wonderful beaches.

Lost Coast Trail When it comes to coast hiking, it doesn't get any wilder than California's Lost Coast, where towering shoreline cliffs rise abruptly like volcanoes from the sea. California has a very long coastline, and millions of acres of wilderness, but it has only one wilderness coast.

Explore this remote region with the 50-mile long Lost Coast Trail, which crosses and connects Sinkyone Wilderness State Park and King Range National Conservation Area. The path alternates between deep forested canyons and prominent ridges and offers spectacular vistas up to 100 miles of coastline.

The sea is an overwhelming presence here, and provides a thunderous background for a walk along land's end. Other highlights include redwood groves and a 24-mile long wilderness beach. The sky is filled with gulls and pelicans, sea lions and seals gather in the coves below the trail, and a herd of Roosevelt elk roams the bluffs.

Olympic National Park's Coast Trail It's Washington's wettest and wildest shore, a 62-mile long strip practically unchanged since famed explorer Captain James Cook sailed by in 1778. Monumental sea stacks, dramatic capes and coves, rocks and reefs—the park's ocean shore is one to remember.

This land on the far northwestern part of the continental U.S. is pounded by rain; some 100 inches a year falls on these beaches in the shadow of mighty Mt. Olympus. Above the beach thrives a forest of Sitka spruce, red cedar and hemlock, towering above a forest floor that's a tangle of ferns, mosses, salal, sorrel and ocean spray. Elk, raccoons, black-tailed deer and black bear roam the coastal bluffs.

The hiking opportunities are many: weekend and week-long backpacking trips, half-day and all-day treks, easy beach walks and what might be some of the most difficult shoreline treks in America.

Vancouver Island's West Coast Trail It lures hikers from five continents. The dramatic coastal wilderness is one reason. The challenge of completing the trail is another.

The 47-mile long route between Port Renfrew and Bamfield is a mélange of forest trails, beach and a low-tide sidewalk of sandstone at water's edge. Bold headlands bookend large crescent beaches. Above the beaches are coastal slopes forested with Sitka spruce, western red cedar and western hemlock.

The Pacific Rim National Park map of the trail highlights evacuation sites. Difficulties facing hikers include mud and muck, high rivers, high tides, rogue waves, and fallen trees. More than 100 inches of rain a year falls on the trail. Even when it's not raining, expect everything—logs, rocks, sand and trail—to be wet.

Hike a Tropical Trail

What's more enticing to a hiker in mid-winter than the thought of trekking a tropical isle?

I believe in four-season hiking for all hikers, regardless of where they happen to live. Escape the snow and cruel winter, or just get away from it all, by taking a tropical trail. With some aggressive internet shopping or the help of a good travel agent, an island getaway can be surprisingly affordable—even downright cheap.

Many islands in the Caribbean and in the South Pacific offer what you expect—great beaches and fruity tropical concoctions; they also offer the unexpected in the form of some great hiking. Here's a half-dozen of my island favorites to get you started thinking about tropical trails.

Bermuda Railway Trail During the 1930s and 1940s, passengers on the Bermuda Railway were treated to breathtaking views of palmetto-fringed shores, picturesque hamlets and a profusion of subtropical plants and flowers. The train is long gone, but the Bermudan government in 1984 converted the rails to trails. The result is a 22-mile footpath that offers hikers an intimate look at the island.

The grade, as you might expect, is easy. Oleander and hibiscus hedges line the trail, which at times give hikers the feeling they're stepping down a garden path. Countless subtropical flowers perfume the salt air. The trail visits—or travels near—virtually every park and preserve on the island. You'll hike through small groves of native Bermuda cedar and fiddleneck woodland, as well as stands of allspice trees and Surinam cherry.

The islanders are extremely polite and helpful and particularly friendly to anyone exploring their island on foot. All of Bermuda—cities, sites and beaches—is within reach of the Railway Trail.

Virgin Islands National Park St. John has everything that a Caribbean island should have: white-sand beaches, quiet turquoise lagoons, mangrove swamps and tropical jungle. For the hiker with an eye for the exotic and thick skin against no-see-ums, it's paradise found.

On wetter parts of the island, the hiker finds a mixture of native and exotic species with intriguing local names such as clashie melashie, elephant tree, bellyache balsam, better man better and jumbie cutlash. This subtropical forest is an extremely diverse one, with 20 to 30 full-size species per acre.

Trails lead to some still-stately-but-overgrown rum trees, and to the ruins of sugar cane processing factories. Rangers can direct you to the national park's historic sites, petroglyphs and secluded beaches. You could spend a pleasant week exploring the park's land and undersea nature trails.

Hawaii Volcanoes National Park Your first impression of Hawaii Volcanoes National Park, when you see all the turnouts and parking lots placed near scenic attractions, is that it was engineered with the automobile in mind. Without a doubt, though, hikers get the best view of the park's lava-built scenery.

Hikers can trek 120 miles of park trail, ranging from the spectacular pathway up Mauna Loa to strolls through a lava tube. The national park is dominated by Kilauea Volcano, which steams, bubbles and generally frets. Hikers can explore the naked sandscape of the Ka'u Desert, passing over mobile sand dunes of ash and pumice.

A hike along the crater rim shows the profound difference between the windward and leeward sides of the volcano. The tradewinds bring copious rainfall, allowing a young rain forest to recapture a lava field. If lava fields, a desert and a rain forest aren't enough to explore, the national park also boasts a black-sand beach, the result of hot lava meeting the cold Pacific and exploding into fragments of basalt. The surf crushed the basalt into sand.

Kauai's Na Pali Coast Hawaiians call the island's north shore Na Pali. That means "The Cliffs," which happen to lunge 2,000 to 3,000 feet out of the frothing surf. It's a wilderness of jungled valley and crumbling cliffs, waterfalls and lost Hawaiian settlements, extending from Haena on the North Shore to Polihale State Park on the west side, and fanning back inland to the Alakai Swamp-Waimea Canyon area.

A magnificent 11-mile long trail leads atop the clifrs from road's end to the Kailalau Valley. Except for some restoration work decades ago, this is the original trail built and used by the ancient Hawaiians who inhabited the beaches and hanging valleys of the Na Pali coast.

Kalalau Valley, at trail's end, delivers a lush reward—a four-mile deep, fruit-filled valley, a tangle of hala, bananas, mangoes and monkeypod. It's supremely isolated; for 1,000 years, the only entry has been via the turbulent sea or this trail.

Fiji The flash of a sari on the riverbank, a mynah bird scolding from a treetop, a bullock chewing sugar cane, village children waving and calling "*Bula!*" as you pass. . . . These are some of the sights you'll see while hiking on Fiji's main island, Vitu Leveu.

A good place to begin discovering Fiji afoot is in Tholo-i-Suva Forest Park, a lovely mahogany forest near the capital city of Suva. Park trails lead to swimming holes and waterfalls. Mt. Victoria (islanders call it Tomanivi) is Fiji's highest summit at 4,341 feet. It's a four-mile climb to the top, on a trail seasonally decorated with red orchids. The great mountain divides the wet and dry sides of the island and you can readily discern dramatic differences between the flora from the summit. Singatoka River Trail offers a two- to three-day hike a from its headwaters high on Mt. Victoria to the sea.

Tahiti Exotic tropical forests, mysterious caves, waterfalls and ancient stone ruins, these are some of the delights of trekking Tahiti and Moorea, two islands in French Polynesia with terrific pathways. These islands feature jagged volcanic formations, deep valleys and abundant bird life. In 1835, Charles Darwin hiked through the Tahitian mountains, where his observations led to his Theory of Evolution.

Hibiscus abounds along the trails, as do such trees with edible fruit as mangoes, guavas, coconut and bananas. Tree trunks are often covered by moss and surrounded by wild orchids. The hiker often literally runs into the nonnative lantana, which forms a thick and nearly impenetrable shrubby barrier.

The main island of Tahiti has more than two dozen trails. Little Moorea, 11 miles long and seven miles wide, has half a dozen or so good hikes and is a great place to begin exploring Polynesian pathways.

Chapter 20   Trail Memories

THE NEXT BEST THING TO WALKING A TRAIL IS TALKING ABOUT IT. I love talking trail—whether it's recalling a marvelous hike or planning a new adventure. In this final chapter of our hike together, I share some of my tips for remembering your happy trails and finding new ones.

Photos are one of the best ways to preserve memories of your favorite hikes and to show your friends the pleasures of a particular trail so that they may be encouraged to follow in your footsteps. I've looked at thousands of photos of people hiking, and taken a whole lot of them myself, and let me tell you it's darn hard to make hiking look halfway as fun and intriguing as it really is.

The challenge of getting great hiking photos is due in part to the nature of an outdoor sport park bureaucrats term "passive recreation". Hiking per se, like walking, is not all that visually compelling.

(Of course plenty of things are way harder to photograph well than hiking—eating, for example. No one looks good eating.)

Preserving memories is one part of the hiking experience and looking forward to the next hike is another. Often the two go hand-in-hand. Hiking, like many of life's endeavors, is a process of examing where you've been to better determine where you're going.

> *"Today we must realize that nature is revealed in the simplest meadow, wood lot, marsh, stream, or tidepool, as well as in the remote grandeur of our parks and wilderness areas."*
> —ANSEL ADAMS

A PICTURE, as the saying goes, is worth 1,000 words. A photograph speaks at least that, if not more. Many a hiker can be found peering behind a lens, in hopes of capturing a tangible impression of a journey that will linger long in the mind. The photographic images you capture can become treasures that help describe to others the people, places, trails, details and emotions of your hiking adventure.

There's no better way to hold on to the great memories of a hike in a unique place than to photograph it well. Many hikers take along cameras: focus, point and shoot and hope for the best. But many of us are disappointed with the results of our efforts, realizing once we review the photos that we didn't quite capture the place on film in the way we experienced it.

By remembering a few tips and with a little practice, you can get some good hiking photos with a 35mm point-and-shoot camera. Even better is a more advanced, but nevertheless compact 35mm camera with a feature that lets you manually override the automatic exposure. (Each year the automatic exposures get better and better, but they still don't think as well as a hiker with a little outdoors photography experience.) Digital cameras are here to stay. Expect to see camera makers create more durable and weatherproof models.

Share your photos via mail or e-mail with your companions, with folks you met on the trail, or anyone else you think might enjoy a glimpse into your hike. The cost is negligible, the good will immeasurable. Good photos are always welcome for nature center publications, outings club newsletters, outdoors e-zines, small newspapers, and web sites. Your photos can help hikers plan a trip or in some cases aid preservation efforts on behalf of a particular park or pathway. You might find yourself a welcome guest speaker if you put your photos together with a narrative in a Power-Point presentation (or old-fashioned slide show).

Obviously studying photography as a hobby or art form will help you with your photos. Take a photography class at a local adult education center or community college. After you learn the basics, you might want to take a nature photography class or a seminar/field trip offered by a professional outdoors photographer.

Obviously studying photography as a hobby or art form will help you with your photos. Take a photography class at a local adult education center or community college. After you learn the basics, you might want to take a nature photography class or a seminar/field trip offered by a professional outdoors photographer.

Sharp focus, good composition, and proper lighting are important, but in addition there are several other important criteria that will help you tell the story of your hike and help communicate the experience. Below are some hike-specific photo tips to help produce the results you want: increasing the visual appeal of a hike and sharing the experience with your friends.

The best images tell the story of a hike in an up-close and personal way, convey in an instant the charm, beauty and distinctive pleasures of experiencing a particular place on foot. The best photos subtly evoke emotion and beckon the viewer to action.

Emotion	Desired Viewer Response
What a great idea it is to take a hike!	"I'd like to do that!"
What a great place that is!	"I want to go there!"
Those people are having fun!	" I could have fun too."
These people had a great hike.	"I'd like to do that hike."

Hiking Along Photographs of people hiking alone or in groups tend not to be too compelling unless there are other elements to add scale, drama, perspective, color, etc.

Smiling Groups The typical image of the smiling group standing in a nondescript location—while nice for a memento—is not terribly fascinating. Think instead of an animated couple chatting or holding hands, a few women admiring something, kids wandering off and doing something silly, a couple of guys chuckling, a small group interacting with locals, etc.

Large Groups vs. Small Ones Long lines of hikers are particularly uninteresting because they often look likes ants on the trail or you get the reaction: "I don't want to go there—it's too crowded." Depending on the setting, the magic number of hikers can range from four to eight. Look for a perspective, such as hikers on switchbacks, that use numbers to your advantage.

Go for interesting characters—not just everyone who's young and fit. Someone with creases, wearing an old hat, someone grizzled, charming, weatherworn, exotic, etc. Shoot to get this reaction from the viewer: "I would love to meet someone like that!"

Pre-hike and Post Hike Relaxing in a woodsy campground, sitting in porch swing at a graceful B&B, a quirky-looking innkeeper, a couple in a Jacuzzi with their hiking boots nearby . . . again, think of telling a story of the whole weekend hiking experience.

Local Culture Record not only the trail but the whole environment, including the nearby architecture and artifacts that reflect the spirit of a place: cottages, carts, vehicles, boats, tools, signs, etc. Capture a time gone by with farm implements, an old settlers cabin, an abandoned barn. Individuals wearing distinctive clothing, or obviously looking like they're of another place, even a different time, or who certainly don't look like your next door neighbors.

Perspective Shots Think of pulling the viewer into the photo—with narrow dirt roads, a fence line, a line of trees, a path leading into the woods, along a shoreline, a line of walkers shot from above (or below) These shots have great impact and emotional pull.

Color Think in terms of the vibrancy of a place. What are the distinctive colors and hues that enhance it? The cool greens and blues of Ireland. . . .The emerald greens of the Pacific Northwest rain forest, the hot golden sands of New Mexico, the vibrant flower fields of Provence. . . .Think not only of the color palette of a place but of the contrasting and complementary colors that will set it off.

Tips for Better Pics

- **Don't center your subject in the frame.** Allow the terrain, the trail and the surroundings to help tell the story.
- **In a flash.** For photography in the forest, overexpose by a stop or two and use a flash.
- **Don't fight the light—use it.** Silhouettes add an offbeat dimension to the usual buddies-on-the-trail shots. By all means, take good advantage of bad weather and shoot in rain and fog.
- **A sign to remember.** Include a sign in your coverage: a trail sign, wilderness, mileage. Signs are useful as little inserts in a publication or to help you remember a great day on the trail.
- **Details please.** One or two flowers are often more compelling than a long shot of a flower-dotted meadow.
- **Up-close and personal.** Get some emotion. Sure a winsome grin is nice, but how about showing some fatigue, grime, sweat, tears?
- **Make friends with Mr. Time Release.** Use your camera's delayed shutter release to good effect: Put yourself in the picture. I've strapped my camera to a tree with a shoelace, balanced it on rocks.
- **Don't be shy about asking someone to photograph you.** I know hikers who made it to the top of Whitney and didn't ask a fellow peak-bagger to take a photo. And I know another hiker, who went on a trip-of-a-lifetime walking vacation in Tuscany, and returned with fourteen rolls of photographs and not a single one of herself.

Remembering Your Hike

Logbooks, Journals, Sketchbooks

When you first tell the story, you'll recall the special moments of the trail: the lightning-split tree, burned but unbowed; the sword ferns that seemed to point the way to a babbling brook; that huge flat-topped boulder you dubbed "Lunch Rock"; the turkey vulture circling overhead that your friend joked has a taste for hikers.

In the first telling, you'll recall many details, later retellings some of the details. As the weeks and months and years pass, the details will fade. Record the facts of your hike in logbook form right away, then add the finer details soon thereafter.

A memorable day hike, like a memorable story, has a beginning, middle and an end. This built-in dramatic structure, this "epic" journey from trailhead to trail's end can help the novice wordsmith fashion a memorable narrative.

There are whole books written on how to keep a nature journal, but the most important lesson to remember is to do it! Write what you remember so you never forget.

Sketchbooks, too, are a wonderful way to record your impressions of a hike. Draw what you like or need to keep the scene fresh in your mind. You don't need fancy art supplies or leather-bound books, but if that's what you prefer, by all means take along quality tools of the trade. If you're in an area where it's permissible to pick flowers, grab a few and press them in your journal.

Appendix

Hiking Songs

Dale Evans, "The Queen of the West," and movie cowboy-singer Roy Rogers together recorded more than 400 songs, but it is "Happy Trails" that we best remember. Evans wrote the song in 1950 and for many years it served as the closing song for the couple's television series. The simple tune and catchy lyrics—"Happy Trails to you, until we meet again"—just stay with you.

Here are a few favorite tunes for the trail. Collect more for your repertoire and enjoy them with your friends.

I'm Happy When I'm Hiking
(English hiking song; original author unknown)

Tramp, tramp, tramp, tramp, tramp, tramp, tramp, tramp.
I'm happy when I'm hiking, pack upon my back.
I'm happy when I'm hiking, off the beaten track.
Out in the open country, that's the place for me
With a true Scouting friend to the journeys end,
Ten, twenty, thirty, forty, fifty miles a day.
Tramp, tramp, tramp ...

Over The River
(original author unknown, sung to: "Over the River")

Over the river, along the trail,
The hikers march along.
And as they go, they love to sing
Their favorite hiking song.

Over the river, along the trail,
They love to hike and sing.
They're filled with all the wonders
A nature hike can bring.

Along The Trail
(original author unknown, sung to: "Frère Jacques")

Let's go marching, let's go marching,
Along the trail, along the trail.
I love to march fast,
I love to march slow,
Along the trail, along the trail.

Additional verses: (substitute other actions for marching)

March and Sing
(original author unknown, sung to: "The Mulberry Bush")

Along the trail we march and sing,
March and sing, march and sing.
Along the trail we march and sing,
Along the trail today.

Additional verses:
We huff and puff; skipped and whistle; swing our arms

I Met A Bear Original Author Unknown
(Sung to: "Skip to My Lou")

I met a bear along the trail,
I met a bear along the trail,
I met a bear along the trail,
I better step aside.

Additional verses:
I met a skunk; squirrel; deer

The Scat Rap
(original author unknown)

CHORUS:
It starts with an "S," ends with a "T."
It comes out of you, and it comes out of me.
I know what you're thinking, it could be called that,
But be scientific and call it scat.

You're walking through the woods and your nose goes "ooh."
You know some animal's laid scat near you.
It may seem gross, well that's okay.
They don't have toilets to flush it away.

Now don't go screamin' and lose your lunch,
If you picked it apart you could learn a bunch about—scat

If you wanna find out what animals eat,
Take a good look at what they excrete.
Inside of their scat are all kinds of clues
Parts of food their bodies can't use, and that's—scat

If you park your car in woods or a field,
You might find scat on your windshield.
Some of it's purple and the rest of it's white:
You just got bombed by a bird in flight and that's scat.

It tells us what they eat and it tells us who they are.
That's what we know about scat so far
If you wanna find out what animals are around,
The place to start looking is the scat on the ground.

How-to Books

Throughout this book I've urged hikers to get more information, take classes and read books about certain specialized and important topics such as orienteering and first-aid. Certain aspects of hiking are covered much better than others in contemporary books. For example, there seems to be a veritable cottage industry in making how-to books about backpacking. Many backpacker manuals are quite thorough (some might find the 845-page, *The Complete Walker IV*, a little too comprehensive), particularly when it comes to detailing gear and setting up camp. Other hikers can't get enough on their favorite subject and devour how-to books like their favorite flavors of freeze-dried ice cream.

Other subjects have a shortage of books—or at least good ones—such as hiking with children.

Backpacking

Backpacker's Handbook by Chris Townshend. Ragged Mountain Press, 1996.

Backpacking Basics by Winnett & Findling. Wilderness Press, 4th edition, 1994.

The Complete Walker IV by Chip Rawlins and Colin Fletcher. Knopf, 2002.

Hiking and Backpacking by Karen Berger. Norton, 1995.

Children

Sharing Nature with Children by Joseph Cornell. Dawn Publications, 2001.

Compass

Be Expert with Map & Compass by Bjorn Kjellstrom. Hungry Minds, Inc., 1999.

Sierra Club Land Navigation Handbook by William S. Kals, Sierra Club, 1983.

First Aid

Backcountry First Aid and Extended Care by Buck Tilton. Globe Pequot, 4th edition, 2002.

Fixing Your Feet by John Vonhof. Wilderness Press, 3rd edition, 2004.

GPS

Outdoor Navigation with GPS by Stephen W. Hinch. Annadel Press, 1st edition, 2004.

Mountaineering

Mountaineering, The Freedom of the Hills, edited by Stephen M. Cox and Kris Fulgaas. The Mountainers Books, 7th edition, 2003.

Photography

Photography Outdoors: A Field Guide for Travel & Adventure Photographers by Mark Gardner and Art Wolfe. The Mountaineers Books.

Trail Running

Trail Running: From Novice to Master by Kristin Poulin, Stan Swartz, and Christian Flaxel, M.D. The Mountaineers Books, 2002.

Tracking

The Science and Art of Tracking by Tom Brown. Berkley Books, 1999.

Books That Inspire

Some of our favorite stories are accounts of great walks. And some of our favorite walks seem to inspire great stories.

Perhaps writers who travel and, especially, writers who walk have such great appeal to us because we imagine life itself to be a journey. When I travel, I enjoy visiting writers' homes and haunts and hiking through the landscapes that generated their literary passions.

In America, I've hiked John Muir's High Sierra and Henry David Thoreau's Cape Cod, and in England tramped James Herriot's Yorkshire and William Wordsworth's Lake District. I've been known to take guilty pleasure from a slick page-turner set in locales I like to hike.

Meditations of John Muir, Chris Highland, Editor. Wilderness Press, 2001.

Journey Home, A Walk Across England, by John Hillaby. Holt, Rinehart & Winston, 1984.

A Tramp Across the Continent by Charles F. Lummis. First published 1920. University of Nebraska Press, 1982.

A Walk in the Woods, Rediscovering America on the Appalachian Trail by Bill Bryson. Broadway Books, 1998.

Into A Desert Place, A 3000 Mile Walk Around the Coast of Baja, California, by Graham MacKintosh. W.W. Norton & Company Ltd, 1995.

A Walk Along Land's End, Discovering California's Living Coast, by John McKinney. HarperCollins, 1995.

The Man Who Walked Through Time by Colin Fletcher. First published Alfred A. Knopf, 1968. Vintage, Random House.

A Thousand Mile Walk to the Gulf by John Muir. Written 1867, first published 1916. Sierra Club Books.

Where the Waters Divide, A Walk Along America's Continental Divide, Karen Berger and Daniel R. Smith. Harmony Books, 1993.

The Art and History of Walking

The Art of Pilgrimage, The Seeker's Guide to Making Travel Sacred by Phil Couisineau. Conari Press, 1998.

Wanderlust, A History of Walking, by Rebecca Solnit. Viking, 2000.

Walking by Henry David Thoreau. Many editions of this classic essay, first published after the great naturalist's death.

The Walker's Literary Companion, edited by Roger Gilbert, Jeffrey Robison and Anne Wallace. Breakaway Books, 2000.

The Winding Trail, A selection of articles and essays for walkers and backpackers, edited by Roger Smith, Foreword by John Hillaby. Diadem Books Ltd, London, 1981.

Hiking by the Numbers

- In the year 2002, 73.3 million Americans went hiking. 25 percent of these hikers said they hike at least 30 times a year.
- The popularity of hiking has tripled in the last 20 years. Survey after survey show hiking is the most popular form of outdoor recreation among Americans.
- Walking for fitness is by far the favorite leisure time activity of Americans, with about 100 million walking for exercise.
- Utah and Idaho have the highest per capita rate of participation for hiking and backpacking, while California and Washington have the largest overall number of hikers and backpackers.
- Californians lead the way down the trail. Two recent surveys report that Californians say hiking is their number one outdoors sport.
- The U.S. Forest Service predicts steep increases in hiking, including an 80 percent increase in the Southern and Pacific Coast regions over the next 50 years.
- National parks, forests, refuges and other public lands cover about one in every three acres of the nation's surface area and attract some two billion visits annually.
- Walking vacations/hiking holidays are the fastest growing segment of the burgeoning active-vacation industry.
- Hiking boot sales grew by as much as 20 percent in some parts of the country in 2002.
- The Forest Service's trail system is larger than all the other trail systems in the U.S. combined, with more than 125,000 miles. More than 30 million visitor days are spent each year on national forest trails.
- The Bureau of Land Management's 270 million-acre domain includes 2,500 miles of National Historic Trails, 500 miles of National Scenic Trails, 350 miles of National Recreation Trails, plus another 6,000 miles of hiking trails.

Sources: American Recreation Coalition, American Hiking Society, Outdoor Industry Association, California State Parks, National Sporting Goods Association.

Long-Distance Trail Information

Appalachian National Scenic Trail
Appalachian Trail Conference
799 Washington Street
P.O. Box 807
Harpers Ferry, WV 25425
(304) 535-6331
www.appalachiantrail.org

California Coastal Trail
Coastwalk
7207 Bodega Ave.
Sebastopol, CA 95472
www.californiacoastaltrail.org

Continental Divide National Scenic Trail
Continental Divide Trail Alliance
P.O. Box 628
Pine, CO 80470
(888) 909-CDTA
www.cdtrail.org

Florida National Scenic Trail
Florida Trail Association
5415 SW 13th St.
Gainesville, FL 32608
(877) HIKE-FLA or (352) 378-8823
www.florida-trail.org

Ice Age National Scenic Trail
Ice Age Park & Trail Foundation
207 East Buffalo Street, Suite 515
Milwaukee, Wisconsin 53202
(414) 278-8518 or (800) 227-0046
www.iceagetrail.org

Long Trail
The Green Mountain Club
4711 Waterbury-Stowe Rd.
Waterbury Center, VT 05677
(802)244-7037
www.greenmountainclub.org

Natchez Trace National Scenic Trail
Natchez Trace Parkway
Rural Route 1, NT-143

Tupelo, MS 38801-9718
Phone: 601-680-4025 or 1-800-305-7417
North Country National Scenic Trail
North Country Trail Association
229 East Main Street
Lowell, Michigan 49331
(888) 454-NCTA (6282)
www.northcountrytrail.org

Oregon Coast Trail
Oregon State Parks & Recreation
1115 Commercial St. N.E.
Salem, Oregon 97310
(503) 378-6305.

Ozark Highlands Trail
Ozark Highlands Trail Association
Box 1074
Fayetteville, Arkansas 72702
(501) 442-2799

Pacific Crest National Scenic Trail
Pacific Crest Trail Association
5325 Elkhorn Blvd., # 256
Sacramento, CA 95842
(888) 728-7245
www.pcta.org

Potomac National Scenic Trail
Potomac Trail Council
P.O. Box 3738
Frederick, MD 21705
(888) 223-4093
www.potomactrail.org

Cyber Trails

All About Hiking

American Hiking Society
www.americanhiking.org

American Trails
www.americantrails.org

Conservation

Sierra Club
www.sierraclub.org

Leave No Trace
www.lnt.org

Gear

Altrec
www.altrec.com

REI
www.rei.com

Fogdog.com outdoor products
www.fogdog.com

Information

GORP—Great Outdoor Recreation Page
www.gorp.com

www.thetrailmaster.com

Government

National Park Service
www.nps.gov

U.S. Forest Service
www.fs.fed.us

www.recreation.gov

Bureau of Land Management
www.blm.gov

Maps

Trails Illustrated Maps

www.trailsillustrated.com

MapLink
www.maplink.com

Maps.com
www.maps.com

Tom Harrison Maps
www.tomharrisonmaps.com

Trail Descriptions
www.trails.com

Walking

The Walking Connecton
www.walkingconnection.com

American Volksport Association
www.ava.org

Hiking Humor

How to Cross a River

One day three men were hiking along and came upon a wide, raging river. They needed to get to the other side, but it looked impossible to ford, and they had no idea of how to do it.

The first man prayed: "Please God, give me the strength to cross this river."

Poof! God gave him big strong arms and legs and he was able to swim across the river—though it took him two hours to do it.

Seeing this, the second man prayed: "Please God, give me the strength and ability to cross this river."

Poof! God gave him a rowboat and he was able to row across the river—though it took him three hours to do it.

The third man had observed how this had worked out for his two hiking buddies, so he also prayed, saying, "Please God, give me the strength, ability and intelligence to cross this river."

Poof! God turned him into a woman. He looked at the trail map, and in a minute walked across the bridge.

If You See Bigfoot . . .

Once there was a group of hikers traveling through the deep woods in the Pacific Northwest. The group leader gave the hikers a very stern warning: "If, by chance you see Bigfoot, run. But whatever you do, don't touch Bigfoot!"

That night, after the group had set up camp, one hiker was in his tent, when Bigfoot appeared. The huge creature stood in the doorway of the tent. The hiker was so scared, he ran screaming out of the tent, but on his way, he touched Bigfoot. Bigfoot ran after him. The guy ran as fast as he could through the dark forest, Bigfoot was in hot pursuit.

He made it back to the trailhead, jumped in his car and sped home. A few days later, Bigfoot showed up at his back door. Panicked, the guy starts running as fast as he can, Bigfoot right behind. Finally, exhausted, he trips and falls. Bigfoot catches up to him, plants his huge feet right next him.

Shaking, the guy gets to his feet and shouts, "What do you want?!"

Bigfoot reaches out to him and says, "Tag, you're it."

Hiking in Bear Country

A guy's going on a hiking vacation into the remote mountains out west. Before heading into the wilderness, he stops at a small town general store to get some supplies.

After picking out provisions, he approaches the crusty old guy behind the counter.

"I'm going hiking up in the mountains, and was wondering—do you have any bears around here?"

"Yup," replies the storeowner.

"What kind?" asks the hiker.

"Well, we got black bears and we got grizzlies," he replies.

"I see," says the hiker. "Do you have any of those bear bells?"

"Say what?"

"You know," explains the hiker, "those little tinkle-bells that hikers wear in bear country to warn the bears that they are coming, so the bears aren't surprised and attack them."

"Oh, yeah. Back there," he says, pointing to a dusty shelf on the other side of the store.

The hiker selects some bells and returns to the counter to pay for them. "Another thing," the hiker inquires, "how can I tell when I'm hiking in bear country anyway?"

"By the scat," the old fellow replies, ringing up the hiker's purchases.

"Well, uh, how can I tell if it's grizzly country or black bear country?" the hiker asks.

"By the scat," the storeowner replies.

"Well, what's the difference?" asks the hiker. "I mean, what's difference between grizzly scat and black bear scat?"

"The stuff that's in it."

Frustrated, the hiker persists, "Okay, so what's in grizzly bear scat that isn't in black bear scat?" he asks, an impatient tone in his voice.

"Bear bells," replies the old man as he hands the hiker his purchases.

Complaints to the U.S. Forest Service

How well do you know your fellow hikers? How smart do you think they are, anyway? These are actual complaints to the Forest Service from trail users.

- "Escalators would help on steep uphill sections."
- "Instead of a permit system or regulations, the Forest Service needs to reduce worldwide population growth to limit the number of visitors to wilderness."
- "Trails need to be wider so people can walk while holding hands."
- "Ban walking sticks in wilderness. Hikers that use walking sticks are more likely to chase animals."
- "All the mile markers are missing this year."
- "Trails need to be reconstructed. Please avoid building trails that go uphill."
- "Too many bugs and leeches and spiders and spider webs. Please spray the wilderness to rid the area of these pests."
- "Please pave the trails so they can be plowed of snow in the winter."
- "Chairlifts need to be in some places so that we can get to wonderful views without having to hike to them."
- "The coyotes made too much noise last night and kept me awake. Please eradicate these annoying animals."
- "Reflectors need to be placed on trees every 50 feet so people can hike at night with flashlights."
- "Need more signs to keep area pristine."
- "A McDonald's would be nice at the trailhead."
- "Too many rocks in the mountains."
- "The places where trails do not exist are not well marked."

Oh, Canada! Complaints and Questions

Staff at Canada's Banff National Park compiled a list of the "All Time Most Dim Questions" asked by park visitors. Read 'em and groan.

- How do the elk know they're supposed to cross at the "Elk Crossing" signs?
- Are the bears with collars tame?
- I saw an animal on the way to Banff today—could you tell me what it was?
- Where can I buy a raccoon hat?
- Are there birds in Canada?
- What's the best way to see Canada in one day?
- Where can I get my husband really, REALLY, lost?
- Is that 2 kilometers by foot or by car?

Life Lessons from the Trail

- A pebble in a hiking boot always migrates to the point of maximum irritation.
- The return distance to the trailhead where you parked your car remains constant as twilight approaches.
- The sun sets two-and-a-half times faster than normal when you're hurrying back to the trailhead.
- The mosquito population at any given location is inversely proportional to the effectiveness of your repellent.
- Waterproof rainwear isn't. (However, it is 100% effective at containing sweat).
- The width of backpack straps decreases with the distance hiked. To compensate, the weight of the backpack increases.
- Average temperature increases with the amount of extra clothing you're carrying in your day pack.
- Given a chance, matches will find a way to get wet.
- The weight in a backpack can never remain uniformly distributed.
- When reading the instructions for a water filter, "hour" should be substituted for "minute" when reading the average quarts filtered per minute.
- The little toothpick in your new Swiss Army knife will disappear the first time you take it on a hike.

Walking Vacations and Hiking Holidays

With some companies, you saunter from inn to inn while a van transports your luggage and a walk manager makes lunch reservations. With others, you spend several nights in one place and hike from there.

Hiking holidays range from serious treks in exotic locations to easy walking down country lanes. As a first step to researching the hiking holiday that's right for you, check out the following companies:

- Above the Clouds Trekking
www.aboveclouds.com
- Active Journeys
www.activejourneys.com
- Backroads
www.backroads.com
- British Coastal Trails
www.bctwalk.com
- Butterfield & Robinson
www.butterfield.com
- Country Walkers
www.countrywalkers.com
- Country Inns Along the Trail
www.inntoinn.com
- Himalayan Treasures & Travel
www.himalayantrekking.com
- Journeys International
www.journeys-intl.com
- Knapsack Tours
www.knapsacktours.com
- Mountain Travel-Sobek
www.mtsobek.com
- New England Hiking Holidays
www.nehikingholidays.com
- REI Adventures
www.reiadventures.com
- Sierra Club
www.sierraclub.com
- Volunteer Vacations
www.americanhiking.org
- The Wayfarers
www.thewayfarers.com

Index

American Hiking Society

Founded in 1976, American Hiking Society is the only national non-profit membership organization dedicated to establishing, protecting, and maintaining America's foot trails. American Hiking's mission, as the national voice for hikers, is to work in partnership with the outdoor community to promote and protect foot trails and the hiking experience.

American Hiking members are committed to beautiful places to hike, strong outdoor ethics, and the belief that the preservation of hiking trails and their surrounding environments is an important and worthwhile legacy to leave the next generation.

Visit the American Hiking website to locate a hiking trail near you, find a local hiking club, or learn more about National Trails Day and Volunteer Vacations.

For more information or to join American Hiking Society, please contact:

American Hiking Society
1422 Fenwick Lane
Silver Spring, MD 20910
voice: 800-972-8608
fax: 301-565-6714
e-mail: info@AmericanHiking.org
web: www.AmericanHiking.org

JOHN MCKINNEY is the author of a dozen books about walking, hiking, and nature, and has described more than 10,000 miles of trail in his narratives, essays, and guidebooks. His books include *Great Walks of the Pacific Northwest* and *A Walk Along Land's End,* a lyrical account of his 1,600-mile hike along the California coast to pioneer the new California Coastal trail. For eighteen years he wrote a weekly hiking column for the *Los Angeles Times* and now writes articles and commentaries about hiking for national publications, promotes hiking and conservation on radio and television, and serves as a consultant to a hiking holidays company. He lives with his family in Santa Barbara, California.

**For more of John McKinney's
tips, tours, trails, and tales visit:
www.TheTrailmaster.com**